Library of
Davidson College

Joyce's Use of Colors
Finnegans Wake and
the Earlier Works

Studies in Modern Literature, No. 75

A. Walton Litz, General Series Editor
Professor of English
Princeton University

Richard J. Finneran
Consulting Editor
Professor of English
Newcomb College, Tulane University

Daniel Mark Fogel
Consulting Editor
Professor of English
Louisiana State University
Editor, The Henry James Review

Other Titles in This Series

No. 5	*Studies in Joyce*	Nathan Halper
No. 15	*The Sources and Structure of James Joyce's "Oxen"*	Robert Janusko
No. 38	*Joyce's Visible Art: The Work of Joyce and the Visual Arts, 1904–1922*	Archie K. Loss
No. 56	*The Museum World of Henry James*	Adeline Tintner
No. 64	*Poets, Poems, Movements*	Thomas Parkinson
No. 76	*Yeats: An Annual of Critical and Textual Studies, Volume V, 1987*	Richard J. Finneran, ed.

Joyce's Use of Colors
Finnegans Wake and the Earlier Works

by
J. Colm O'Sullivan

Ann Arbor / London

Copyright © 1987, 1985
John Colm O'Sullivan
All rights reserved

Produced and distributed by
UMI Research Press
an imprint of
University Microfilms, Inc.
Ann Arbor, Michigan 48106

Library of Congress Cataloging in Publication Data

O'Sullivan, J. Colm (John Colm), 1935-
Joyce's use of colors.

(Studies in modern literature ; no. 75)
Revision of the author's thesis (Ph.D.),
University of Western Ontario, 1985.
  Bibliography: p.
  Includes index.
  1. Joyce, James, 1882-1941—Criticism and
interpretation. 2. Colors in literature. I. Title.
II. Series.
PR6019.O9Z775   1987   823'.912   87-13741
ISBN 0-8357-1816-6 (alk. paper)

In memory of my sister Claire

Contents

Acknowledgments   *ix*

1 Shall I Wear a Red Yes: Colors in the Earlier Works   *1*

2 The Grianblachk Sun of Gan Greyne Eireann: Native vs. Invader   *47*

3 A Chameleon at Last: Colors of the Male   *79*

4 Whiteyoumightcallimbs: Colors of the Temptress   *119*

5 From Their Roseaced Glows to Their Violast Lustres:
   The Colors of the *Wake*   *165*

Notes   *179*

Bibliography   *191*

Index   *203*

Acknowledgments

With gratitude and affection I wish to record the patience and tolerance of my family and friends, especially Helen, John and Ruth, on those many occasions over the past decade when I Waked them into Yawndom. My sincere thanks are also due to Dr. Michael Groden and Dr. Ninian Mellamphy, both of the University of Western Ontario's English Department, for their professional guidance and their personal support.

Material from *Dubliners* by James Joyce, copyright 1916 by B.W. Huebsch, Inc., definitive text copyright 1967 by the Estate of James Joyce, is reprinted with permission of Viking Penguin, Inc., Jonathan Cape, Ltd., and the Society of Authors, as representatives of the Executors of the James Joyce Estate. Material from *A Portrait of the Artist as a Young Man* by James Joyce, copyright 1916 by B.W. Huebsch, Inc., definitive text copyright 1964 by the Estate of James Joyce, is reprinted with permission of Viking Penguin, Inc., Jonathan Cape, Ltd., and the Society of Authors, as representatives of the Executors of the James Joyce Estate. Material from *Ulysses* by James Joyce, copyright 1914, 1918 by Margaret Caroline Anderson, renewed 1942, 1946 by Nora Joyce, renewed 1961 by George Joyce and Lucia Joyce, copyright 1984 by the Trustees of the Estate of James Joyce, is reprinted with permission of Random House, Inc., The Bodley Head, Ltd., Garland Publishing, Inc., and the Society of Authors, as representatives of the Executors of the James Joyce Estate. Material from *Finnegans Wake* by James Joyce, copyright 1939 by James Joyce, renewed 1967 by George Joyce and Lucia Joyce, is reprinted with permission of Viking Press, Inc., and the Society of Authors, as representatives of the Executors of the James Joyce Estate. Material from *The Letters of James Joyce,* Vol. I, ed. Stuart Gilbert, copyright 1956, 1957 by Viking Press, Inc., is reprinted with permission of Viking Penguin, Inc., and the Society of Authors. Material from *James Joyce in Padua,* ed., trans. and intro. Louis Berrone, is reprinted with permission of the Society of Authors. Material from *The Collected Poems* of W.B. Yeats, copyright 1912 by Macmillan Publishing Co., renewed 1940 by Bertha Georgie Yeats, is reprinted with permission of Macmillan Publishing Co., New York, and A.P. Watt, Ltd., on behalf of Michael B. Yeats and Macmillan London, Ltd.

1

Shall I Wear a Red Yes: Colors in the Earlier Works

Readers of Joyce are inclined to notice that certain color patterns in his works are important. Few serious readers of *A Portrait of the Artist as a Young Man* will have forgotten the colors of Dante's brushes.[1] The sirens' "gold by bronze" in *Ulysses* and the rainbows in *Finnegans Wake* insist on calling themselves to the reader's attention.[2] Yet little critical attention has been paid to such color patterns in Joyce's works. Opinions such as this one of Clive Hart generally go unchallenged:

> The colour structure of Books I and III [of *Finnegans Wake*], if it really exists, is like that of *Ulysses*, of very minor importance. Joyce was, in fact, never a great colourist and even in *Finnegans Wake*, his most kaleidoscopic book, colours tend to be fixed and artificial, as on a tapestry. In *A Portrait* (190), Stephen is made to disclaim any interest in the subject of verbal colour.[3]

The passage in *A Portrait* to which Hart refers runs:

> The phrase and the day and the scene harmonised in a chord. Words. Was it their colours? He allowed them to glow and fade, hue after hue: sunrise gold, the russet and green of apple orchards, azure of waves, the greyfringed fleece of clouds. No, it was not their colours: it was the the poise and balance of the period itself. Did he then love the rhythmic rise and fall of words better than their associations of legend and colour? Or was it that, being as weak of sight as he was shy of mind, he drew less pleasure from the reflection of the glowing sensible world through the prism of a language many-coloured and richly storied than from the contemplation of an inner world of individual emotions, mirrored perfectly in a lucid supple periodic prose?

Much of Hart's statement is in the realm of free-standing opinion and therefore not easily disproved (are colors on a tapestry necessarily "fixed and artificial"?). The degree of metaphor in Hart's use of the word "colour" is quite uncertain; the same can be said of Stephen's use of the word in the passage

Hart refers to. In any event Stephen's comments scarcely constitute a rejection, on the part of his creator, of "verbal colour."

Joyce is known to have paid an almost superstitious attention to certain details of color in his everyday life, as for instance in his persistence in the matter of the publication of *Ulysses*—the cover of "the Blue Book of Eccles" must match exactly the blue of the Greek flag. And there was also his confiding to Miss Weaver that in order to ward off "the complete eclipse of my seeing faculties," he is dressing himself in green, grey and black, "the three colours of successive stages of cecity as the Germans divide them."[4] *Finnegans Wake*, is, in the literal sense, a very colorful book, having an average of more than five color references per page, by my count.[5] Concentrations of color and striking patterns of color association occur at high points of the text. It is my contention that Joyce's use of colors is a significant feature of his work and a promising point of entry for a study of *Finnegans Wake*.

The questions I propose to raise regarding colors in the *Wake* are of this sort: How are the color references distributed throughout the work? At what points are there concentrations of color references? What are the recurring color associations and their contexts? Which colors attach to the various events and characters? Which colors predominate? Which color patterns appear to have structural and symbolic significance? What light do the answers to such questions cast on the larger meanings of the work?

I shall begin by examining the ways in which Joyce uses colors in the major works preceding *Finnegans Wake*, namely *Dubliners*, *A Portrait of the Artist as a Young Man*, and *Ulysses*.[6] For purposes of my discussion of these three works I shall divide the ways in which authors use colors in fiction into three major categories: first, naturalistically, i.e., simple description with a minimum of symbolic overtone, e.g., the priest's "black snuff-box" in "The Sisters" in *Dubliners*, p. 12; second, traditionally, with conventional associations, e.g., "black sinners" in Mr. Casey's speech at the Christmas dinner in *A Portrait*, p. 32; and third, symbolically and structurally, where the writer deliberately constructs about a color reference or a cluster of such references patterns of association that relate to the themes or larger meanings of the work, e.g., in *Ulysses*, the black panther dreamed of by Haines or Boylan's tan shoes.[7] Obviously the categories overlap. For *Finnegans Wake* they simply will not work. But my discussion of the colors in the earlier works will focus on the third, symbolic category of color use since it is my premise that Joyce deliberately uses colors in this way in all of his major works.

Dubliners is a collection of stories depicting failure. The failure is fundamentally a moral one, a refusal to accept moral responsibility and the courage and independence of thought and imagination that go with it. Robert Scholes captures the idea of this failure accurately, I believe, when he writes:

> Joyce felt... that it was precisely their religious orthodoxy, combined with other sorts of "belatedness," that made the Irish so conscienceless. They had turned over the moral responsibility for their lives to their confessors and religious leaders. Thus their ability to react sensitively to moral problems, to make ethical discriminations—to use their consciences—had atrophied.[8]

In *Dubliners* Joyce details this moral failure in a variety of characters and situations, points out its consequences and makes a powerful condemnation of it. Again and again the characters treat delicate matters of human motivations and relationships with ready-made, conventionally sanctioned stock responses. Mrs. Mooney is far from being the only one of whom it might be said, "She dealt with moral problems as a cleaver deals with meat" (p. 63)— she just happens to do so with the almost indifferent ferocity of the jungle predator. The results of such behavior are the confounding of truth, the isolation and eventual brutalization of the individual, and a great deal of suffering. There is much psychic pain in evidence in *Dubliners*. The sufferers are very much aware of the aggravation of psychic pain by economic deprivation and insecurity but seem very unaware of its deeper roots. Some of them endure as Eveline does, "passive, like a helpless animal" (p. 41). Farrington and Mrs. Sinico seek the numbing effects of alcohol. Corley and Mrs. Mooney turn to cynical exploitation of their fellow man. Little Chandler and Farrington are driven to a tortured abuse of those near to them. Others appeal to their religion and their church for emotional succor. The sorry procession of clerics which parades through the pages of *Dubliners* demonstrates the emptiness of that hope.

The events of the stories present the protagonists with opportunities for self-knowledge and self-realization but in almost every case they choose to cling to the lie they know rather than to risk the hazards of striking out for intellectual and imaginative freedom. In "Clay," Maria chooses a denial of her own real feelings for the sake of an appearance of order and peace. In "A Painful Case," Mr. Duffy rejects the messy vulnerability of human contact in favor of a living death of isolation. In "The Boarding House," Mrs. Mooney condemns her daughter to a repetition of her own empty life. The boy narrator of each of the first three stories does have the possibility for change and escape although it is only a possibility. At this point in his maturation the inconsistencies between the realities which force themselves on his attention and the grand schemes for living he has been given by his society and his church drive him not towards questioning those authorities but towards self-recrimination. Only in the case of Gabriel Conroy at the end of the final story of the collection is the reader left with the distinct possibility that there may be an escape from the old lies and a realization of self. And this possibility is surrounded with ambiguities.

4 Colors in the Earlier Works

A work concerned with such themes could hardly be expected to display many patterns of bright and vibrant colors. Indeed, *Dubliners* exhibits the lowest incidence of color references of Joyce's major works, an average of fewer than two and a half words per full page of text by my count, and somber colors predominate.[9] Obviously, sheer numbers of color words provide far too crude a yardstick by which to measure the "colorfulness" of a work or passage in a work. The intensity of one color reference or even of an implied color reference may have more impact on the reader than two or three explicit color words. What are clearly important are clusters of color words, concentrations of colors, and recurring patterns of color association.

The earliest concentration of colors in *Dubliners* appears on pages 11–12 and is part of the description of the paralyzed priest in "The Sisters." The dominant colors here are almost unrelievedly somber and they set the color tone of the book. Prominent among them are the black, green and grey later identified by Joyce as the colors of blindness. Blindness *is* a kind of paralysis, of the sight. *Dubliners* has an unusually high incidence of greys, twenty-eight explicit references by my count, which puts grey numerically ahead of all other colors except white, black, red and brown. The greys are fairly scattered through the text—only "Araby," "Eveline" and "Counterparts" are without greys. The first three occurrences of grey all refer to the paralytic priest's face in "The Sisters." In the first two instances (p. 11) he is alive but paralyzed and doomed. In the third (p. 14) he is dead. Of the last four occurrences of grey in *Dubliners* three refer to Aunt Julia (pp. 176, 179) in the story named "The Dead." Gabriel thinks that Aunt Julia may soon die and imagines her wake (p. 222). The very last grey appears in the second to last paragraph of the book as Gabriel lies beside his sleeping wife and contemplates life and death: "His own identity was fading out into a grey impalpable world: the solid world itself which these dead had one time reared and lived in was dissolving and dwindling (p. 223)." Despite the presence in *Dubliners* of some neutral and even cheerful greys, it is fair to say that grey here is primarily the color of death, and of paralysis which is a kind of living death. This is a rare example of Joyce's using a traditional color system, since in our culture grey has traditionally been associated with depression, inertia, dullness, ashes, death.

"The Dead" is by far the most colorful story in *Dubliners*. It contains a real oddity in the recurrence of Mr. Browne's name no fewer than forty-five times. In addition the word "brown" in its own right occurs eight times and the name of the poet Browning three times. In view of Joyce's use of Giordano Bruno of Nola and the Dublin booksellers Browne and Nolan in *Finnegans Wake* to illustrate the opposite but not quite separated natures of the twins, or, more accurately, the contradictory qualities of the Shaun-Shem composite man, the extraordinary emphasis given Mr. Browne's name in "The Dead" is of especial interest for me.

Mr. Browne is a great many things Gabriel Conroy is not and has chosen not to be. He is brash, vulgar, thick-skinned, loud and convivial in company, does not appear to suffer self-doubt, and he lives for the minute. At the party in the story he is odd man out in that he is a Protestant and has neither blood connection nor musical connection with the family. Yet he can relax and joke with Freddy Malins and call him by a pet name he has invented, Teddy. He, the outsider, is in the thick of things, while Gabriel, the insider, is alone, unsure and ill at ease. Gabriel, to be sure, does not think these things though he does speak slightingly of "that Browne" to Gretta (p. 217). Not only is Mr. Browne's name everywhere in "The Dead" but this ubiquity is attributed to Browne himself: "—Browne is everywhere, said Aunt Kate, lowering her voice" (p. 206). The same kind of ubiquity marks the clash of self and other, of Browne and Nolan, in *Finnegans Wake*. And the ambivalent feelings Gabriel exhibits about the Browning quotation are also typical of the twins' relations in the *Wake*.

In his article "Colour and Light in 'The Dead,'" Thomas F. Smith presents the interesting thesis that the characters divide into dark or colorful doers and pale, timid nondoers. Among the former he lists Gretta, Michael Furey, Bartell D'Arcy, Aunt Kate and Mr. Browne, and among the latter, Lily, Aunt Julia, Freddy Malins and Gabriel. He goes on to suggest the point of the contrast:

> Joyce... wants us to think of "pale" and "dark" complementing each other rather than being antagonistic. He is subtly preparing us, I submit, for the coming together of all colors, all light, all values in the whiteness of the snow at the story's end. That most of the story beforehand shows the pale Gabriel and his world impinged upon by the dark and the colorful should prepare us for a resolution of the two realms of value... [10]

I find Smith's discussion instructive for my consideration of Bruno's role in *Finnegans Wake*, but I cannot agree with all of his conclusions. Two points, especially, need to be established here. Firstly, there is as much opposition as there is complement in the relationships illuminated by the patterns of color. I hope to show that concentrations of colors in "The Dead" and throughout *Dubliners* mark points of tension and inner conflict, particularly the tension associated with frustrated sexual desire. Secondly, Smith falls into the trap of seeking resolution and conclusion at the end of Joyce's book in "the coming together of all colors, all light, all values in the whiteness of the snow at the story's end." None of Joyce's major works reaches a conclusion or ends in a resolution of all the conflicts that have gone before. Instead, each ends at a point of tentative and momentary stasis, poised for the renewal of ongoing life and struggle. The final paragraphs of "The Dead" do not emphasize the whiteness of the snow; they actively deemphasize it. The final section of the story has seven color words, six of which occur in the last two paragraphs. Certainly, Gabriel has reached a point of equanimity, temporary equanimity, as he recognizes his own failure and contemplates the inevitability of death. He thinks that: "his own identity [is] fading out into a grey impalpable world" (p. 223). In the final paragraph he watches the snow, "the flakes, silver and dark, falling obliquely against the lamplight" (p. 223). He thinks of the snow "falling on every part of the dark central plain, on the treeless hills, falling softly upon the Bog of Allen and farther westward, softly falling into the dark mutinous Shannon waves" (pp. 223-24). The color words here are "grey," "silver," "dark," "dark," "Allen" (Irish, "white"), and again "dark." The word "white" does not appear; neither does "black." But two words do carry some sense of white, "silver" and "Allen," as well as the word "snow" itself. The repeated "dark" carries some sense of black. Grey does appear, and what it and the combination of the other color words present is a sense of grey, of the grey of paralysis and death in the opening story of the collection and in the title and closing paragraphs of the final story.

There are of course bright, lively colors in *Dubliners* too, and some concentrations of such colors. One way in which they work is by emphasizing the surrounding darkness, by making the gloom more visible. Often they consist of flashes of sunlight or the green of growing things momentarily illuminating the squalid urban scene and accentuating its harshness. Some examples are: "the tawny gold of a great bank of clouds" in "The Sisters" (p. 14); the mall "gay with little light green leaves" in "An Encounter" (pp. 21-22); the "bright brick houses, with shining roofs" (p. 36) and Frank's "face of bronze" (pp. 38-39) in "Eveline"; the "gaily coloured crowd" in "Two Gallants" (p. 49); and the "shower of kindly golden dust" (p. 71) and the "pale blue summer blouse" (p. 82) in "A Little Cloud."

In "The Dead," before we come to the strongly colored scenes of Gabriel's vision of his wife, there are two color concentrations of note. The first of these occurs as Mary Jane plays the piano and Gabriel studies the picture of the princes in the tower and thinks of the waistcoat "his mother had worked for him as a birthday present" (p. 186). This leads to thoughts of his mother and of her snobbish attitude towards Gretta. The colors are inharmonious and jarring: "red, blue and brown wools"; "purple tabinet... lined with brown satin and having round mulberry buttons" (p. 186). Gabriel's thoughts are disturbed. It is the second incident of the evening to stir his unease, to rouse uncertainty in his mind of himself, his place in his society and the conflicting demands that society makes upon him.

The second of the color concentrations occurs in the description of the food prepared for the feast (pp. 196-97). The colors are bright and cheerful and the description is given without apparent irony, indeed with an almost

Dickensian heartiness which, however, has for the reader the effect of emphasizing Gabriel's unease and alienation. Thomas F. Smith, in the article from which I have already quoted, captures the effect of this scene succinctly and convincingly:

> This cluster of color references reinforces a basic theme—the difference between Gabriel and the elements of life around him. While he is "pale," all these colors are associated with the feast.... On the surface... Gabriel is accepted—he belongs—but we have seen many indications of his alienation from things Irish.[11]

But Gabriel's "alienation from things Irish" is also part of what rescues him from the sense of hopeless inevitability that surrounds most of the protagonists in the collection of stories. However one interprets the symbolic ambiguities of snow and death and of Gabriel's imaginative relationship with them at the end of the story, it is difficult to avoid the conclusion that Gabriel does grow in self-knowledge and that he has achieved some degree of self-realization in his feeling of unity with "all the living and the dead."

One important way in which the bright colors function in *Dubliners* has considerable significance for my study of the *Wake* since it adumbrates some specific color uses in the later work. I have in mind the association of bright colors with woman as the object of sexual desire, especially frustrated desire. In "Two Gallants" the girl with whom Corley has the assignation is given a cluster of eleven color references (pp. 54–55). Black, white, blue and red are the colors of her clothes and features, the black being her jacket and accessories and the red being her cheeks and the flowers at her bosom. The blue and white are her dress and hat and receive primacy of mention. They are the colors of the Virgin, observed in the statue on the banks of the Tolka by Stephen in *A Portrait*, associated with Gerty MacDowell and contemplated by Bloom in *Ulysses*, and associated with Issy in *Finnegans Wake*. It should be noted that the servant girl in "Two Gallants" is seen not through Corley's eyes but through Lenehan's, for whom she is clearly the object of frustrated lust.

In "Counterparts," a small but striking concentration of colors attaches to the actress who is the conscious object of Farrington's admiring gaze in Mulligan's pub (p. 95). She wears "an immense scarf of peacock-blue muslin," "bright yellow gloves reaching to the elbow" and has "large dark brown eyes." For Farrington she epitomizes the romantic, exotic possibilities so utterly out of reach of his squalid life.

Then there are the clusters of colors surrounding Gretta Conroy in "The Dead," in those scenes in which her husband Gabriel looks at her with curiosity, tenderness and desire. As she stands above him on the stairs listening to Bartell D'Arcy sing "The Lass of Aughrim," he observes her, himself unnoticed:

> He could not see her face but he could see the terracotta and salmonpink panels of her skirt which the shadow made appear black and white.... There was grace and mystery in her attitude as if she were a symbol of something. He asked himself what is a woman standing on the stairs in the shadow, listening to distant music, a symbol of. If he were a painter he would paint her in that attitude. Her blue felt hat would show off the bronze of her hair against the darkness and the dark panels of her skirt would show off the light ones. *Distant Music* he would call the picture if he were a painter. (pp. 209–10)

Though Gabriel is struck with this vision of his wife, his response at this point is stilted and self-conscious. He wonders what she is "a symbol of." The little games and lies and subterfuges of the personality to protect itself from the truth are very much in evidence here. What Gabriel will find if he looks at Gretta with open eyes is not a symbol of some vaguely evocative late Victorian painting, but a mirror of the harsh truth of himself and Gretta and their relationship. But, as Eliot tells us, man cannot bear very much reality. Gabriel is not ready yet. The road to Dublin is not the road to Damascus. Joyce's heroes proceed, if they proceed at all, not by apocalypse but by small epiphanies. A little later in the story under discussion we are told that

> Gabriel watched his wife who did not join in the conversation. She was standing right under the dusty fanlight and the flame of the gas lit up the rich bronze of her hair.... Gabriel saw that there was colour on her cheeks and that her eyes were shining. A sudden tide of joy went leaping out of his heart. (pp. 211–12)

The colors Gabriel observes in Gretta's clothes and person mark the tensions of his struggle for perception. The joy he feels is real enough but it is composed of tenderness and romance and want and lust. In essence it is founded on a sentimental self-indulgence deriving from an inability or a refusal, as yet, to face the truth of their selves and their relationship. It is not until Gretta's revelation of the basis of her sadness, Michael Furey and his death, that Gabriel can bear to perceive and face the reality of their lives, and attain that calm plateau of feeling with which the story ends. At that point the colors are few and muted.

My final observations on *Dubliners* concern the color white. White is the most commonly mentioned color in *Dubliners*, as it is in most works of fiction. In *Dubliners*, white seems in most of its appearances to function as a normal feature of realistic description. But we find that there is a pattern: white occurs frequently in connection with woman in her sexual aspect and with women's garments. Only a few whites are associated with Gretta Conroy in "The Dead" but the pattern is clearly in evidence in many of the other stories. We have already seen that there are whites in the colors of the young woman in "Two Gallants." The "old josser" in "An Encounter" talks lovingly of a "nice young girl" and "her nice white hands and her beautiful soft hair" (p. 26). The narrator in "Araby," describing the girl who is the object of his longing, writes: "The light from the lamp opposite our door caught the white curve of her neck," and "caught the white border of a petticoat, just visible as she stood at ease" (p. 32). In "The Boarding House," Polly's "white instep shone in the opening of her furry slippers" (p. 67), and "the white pillows" remind her of their lovemaking (p. 68). This pattern is, I believe, clear though faint in *Dubliners* but it will be prominent in the other works.

Except for some of those woman-associated whites, white in *Dubliners* is at best neutral but more often quite negative. There is the dead priest's white hair in "The Sisters." At the end of the story that bears her name we have that striking image of Eveline: "She set her white face to him, passive, like a helpless animal" (p. 41). Other examples of negative whites are Lenehan's tennis shoes in "Two Gallants" (pp. 50, 56), the whites associated with Polly's father, "that shabby stooped little drunkard," in "The Boarding House" (p. 61), Little Chandler's childish white hands and teeth in "A Little Cloud" (pp. 70, 79), the whites of Mr. Duffy's lonely room in "A Painful Case" (p. 107) and the "white vacant face" of Mr. Fitzpatrick in "A Mother" (p. 139). The traditional symbolic connotations of the color white in our culture have been innocence, purity, peace, faith, timelessness, revelation, transfiguration and transcendence. Obviously Joyce's whites in *Dubliners* have little truck with any of those notions. Indeed, in *Dubliners* the traditional associations of the common colors generally appear to have been scrupulously avoided. Grey is the exception.

These whites, which I have been discussing, effectively exemplify Joyce's use of colors in *Dubliners* and the way in which that use fits neatly within Joyce's chief techniques in creating that work, what A. Walton Litz has described as "that combination of scrupulous detailed realism and complex symbolism which is the hallmark of Joyce's achievement in the major stories of *Dubliners* and in *A Portrait of the Artist*."[12] As we meet these whites in contexts where they may appear normal features of realistic description we may, as readers, initially attribute to them some of the traditional associations such as innocence, spirituality and the like. But the unpleasant or ambiguous nature of so many of the images in which the whites occur gradually builds patterns of negative association in the reader's mind, patterns which undercut the traditional symbolism and point to a fundamental rottenness in the society being portrayed. Thus white, in association with the young women in "An Encounter" and "Araby" and "The Boarding House," cumulatively suggests not purity or innocence but secret desires, shame, guilt and sexual entrapment. The attribution of the Virgin's blue and white to the "slavey" in "Two Gallants" constitutes a mockery of the pretensions and sexual mores of turn-of-the-century Dublin.

Colors in the Earlier Works

The infrequent clusters of bright colors that we find in *Dubliners* do little to relieve the general gloom of the collection of stories. Most frequently they mark a disturbing excitement of thought on the part of a protagonist, such as a peak of insecurity and sexual frustration, and serve to accentuate the alienation or misery or surrounding squalor. Only towards the end of "The Dead" do the bright colors and the whites as well lose their consistently negative tones and partake in the ambiguity which marks the ending of the final story.

One aspect of the final story in *Dubliners* which makes it different from the other stories in the collection is the difficult position in which it places the reader. Up until the last eight pages or so of "The Dead" the reader can feel reasonably comfortable within what he feels to be the familiar position legislated by the conventional contract authors have traditionally made with their readers. The ambiguities of the ending of "The Dead" undermine that contract to some degree and undermine also in the reader's retrospection the assurance he has felt in reading the preceding stories. This mild intellectual discomfort becomes more pronounced for the reader of *A Portrait of the Artist as a Young Man*. It is not merely a question of being kept in doubt—that is a normal experience for the reader within the terms of the traditional contract. The problem for the reader of *A Portrait* centers on uncertainty as to the author's relationship with his hero, on the suspicion that the distance between author and protagonist varies unpredictably, and on a consequent feeling that the reader's subjective response contributes to the cumulative meaning of the work to a degree that is far removed from the conditions of the traditional reader-author contract.

Ambiguity is a key feature of *A Portrait of the Artist* and it arises primarily from the double vision of, on the one hand, the perceptions of the youthful Stephen as he undergoes the experiences being described and, on the other, the perspective of the mature authorial persona who is recalling these events and experiences years later. It is the relationship of these two viewpoints that causes the reader trouble—the narrative itself pretends that the second figure and his viewpoint do not exist, that we are at all times eavesdropping on the younger Stephen, even though the narrative technique casts him in the third person and, generally, in the past tense. The necessary existence of this mature narrator, who never gives himself away and yet selects and edits for the reader every word and phrase concerning the young Stephen, upsets some readers and makes others downright belligerent, and leads to such questions as: "How seriously are we to take the villanelle?"

In his discussion of narrative technique in *A Portrait* Breon Mitchell writes: "Stephen's thoughts are given in the third person, past tense, but they still retain the flavor of his actual speech." Mitchell then points out that "the continual presence of the author, recalling the development from a point outside the process itself, is implicit in the technique."[13] A crucial phrase here as far as the reader's difficulties are concerned is "from a point outside the process itself." The reader, I believe, has an uneasy sense of the author, "from a point outside the process itself," manipulating the materials in his story and his reader's responses without adherence to any contractual rules the reader can rely on. The fact that most readers of *A Portrait* have some familiarity with Joyce's other major works and are likely to have perused the extant fragment of *Stephen Hero* merely adds to their sense of outside interference.

We have to accept, I believe, the presence in *A Portrait of the Artist* of both sympathy and irony on the part of the author towards his protagonist. The "villanelle" is indeed the kind of poem we might expect a neophyte poet, full of *fin de siècle* influence, to write. I have no doubt that Joyce looked with irony at the product, with irony and some sympathy at the process of composition, and with a great deal of sympathy at the larger process of maturation of which the composing of the villanelle is an important landmark. The apparent disappearance of the narrator and the change to diary format in the last five pages of the novel allow us a look at close hand at the unfinished nature of Stephen's emotional growth. But we should be well aware already, from his "spiritualization" of the earthy components of the bird-girl epiphany and the composition of the villanelle, that Stephen still has much further growth ahead of him before he realizes the truth of his own emotions. That makes his struggles through adolescence no less noble, his pain no less real and his courage no less admirable.

We can expect, then, that the color patterns of *A Portrait* will partake of the ambiguities at the core of the novel, and that is indeed what we find when we look at the occurrences of black/dark.

Although the color patterns in *A Portrait of the Artist as a Young Man* are not quite as somber as those in *Dubliners*, nevertheless black/dark is the single most frequently occurring color in *A Portrait*.[14] Most of the blacks are quite naturalistically used, as in Davin's "black sweater" (p. 250), Cranly's "black hair" (p. 232), Uncle Charles's "black twist" (p. 60) and "thumbblackened prayerbook" (p. 62). But dark occurs more than twice as often as black and its use is much more complex. From the point of view of color, dark is a tricky word to deal with, since it is not a true color word such as mauve or even rusty, and its color content can vary somewhat, I believe, from one context or one user to another. Thus when Stephen speaks of "a dark corner of the chapel" (p. 74) the word, it seems to me, has less color connotation than when he recalls "the dark turfcoloured water of the bath in Clongowes" (p. 174) or notes Temple's "darky gipsy eyes" (p. 229). Because of the subjectivity inherent in such shifts of color and because the word dark always carries some color connotation, I have chosen in this study to ignore such variations and to treat dark as having considerable color impact in all its appearances.

When Stephen is sick in Clongowes the key word in his thoughts is dark; the words dark and darkly occur fourteen times in the space of three pages. Dark suggests to Stephen's mind on the one hand the warm security of peasant cottages and on the other a vague fear of the unknown:

> It would be lovely to sleep for one night in that cottage before the fire of smoking turf, in the dark lit by the fire, in the warm dark, breathing the smell of the peasants, air and rain and turf and corduroy. But, O, the road there between the trees was dark! You would be lost in the dark. It made him afraid to think of how it was. (p. 18)

Most instances of dark in these pages have to do with the chapel, the halls and the entrance hall of the college. Further on in section 1 the darks are for waves and the land on which they break (p. 27), "the dark cabinet" in the infirmary (p. 22), the "silent sacristy" (p. 40) with its "wooden presses" (p. 40), and the low, narrow corridor leading to the rector's room (pp. 54, 55). Another image which occurs on the Clongowes pages and with very similar associations eventually coalesces in Stephen's memory with the dark halls. This is the "turfcoloured" or dark brown, water: "He remembered with a vague fear the warm turfcoloured bogwater" (p. 22). The connection of the two images has already been established in the passage I quoted above, in which "dark," "rain," "warm" and "turf" are juxtaposed. Later on at the Christmas dinner, "he remembered the evening in the infirmary in Clongowes, the dark waters" (p. 35), and at the beginning of section 5 we find Stephen sitting in the kitchen at home, "staring into the dark pool of the jar. The yellow dripping had been scooped out like a boghole and the pool under it brought back to his memory the dark turfcoloured water of the bath in Clongowes" (p. 174).

For the young Stephen, the environs of Clongowes constitute the West, the rural peasant Ireland rejected by Gabriel Conroy in "The Dead." It is the source, the primitive real Ireland on which Dublin city is the civilized superstructure. The images he associates with Clongowes are strongly suggestive of the womb—dark, rain, dark water, warm, halls, corridors, cabinets, presses. The foetus is the artist or the artistic faculty which Stephen calls the soul: "—The soul is born, he said vaguely, first in those moments I told you of. It has a slow and dark birth, more mysterious than the birth of the body" (p. 203). Both Hugh Kenner and Richard Ellmann have pointed to the presence of the birth process in *A Portrait*. Kenner identifies "the vaginal imagery of gates, secret places, and darkness" in a later episode (the Mercedes fantasy, p. 65),[15] while Ellmann writes:

> For *A Portrait of the Artist as a Young Man* is in fact the gestation of a soul, and in the metaphor Joyce found his new principle of order. The book begins with Stephen's father and, just before the ending, it depicts the hero's severance from his mother. From the start the soul is surrounded by liquids.... The atmosphere of biological struggle is necessarily dark and melancholy until the light of life is glimpsed.[16]

A number of darks in *A Portrait* refer to people's eyes. Mr. Casey, under emotional stress at the Christmas dinner, has a "dark fierce face" and "dark eyes... never fierce" (p. 35). At the Belvedere play Stephen recalls that Emma's "dark eyes had invited and unnerved him" (p. 82). The rector as he speaks to the boys at Belvedere to prepare them for the retreat has "dark stern eyes" with "dark fire" (p. 108). Stephen, suffering under the weight of guilt at the retreat, looks "out of darkened eyes" (p. 111). Early in section 5, Stephen connects Cranly with an imagined "guilty priest" with "dark womanish eyes" and adds: "Through this image he had a glimpse of a strange dark cavern of speculation but at once turned away from it, feeling that it was not yet the hour to enter it" (p. 178). Temple and Cranly are each said, more than once, to have dark eyes (pp. 197, 229, 245). What all of these instances of "dark eyes" have in common is that each marks a point at which Stephen is in doubt, in difficulty of understanding. In the process of his soul's birth these are challenges and mysteries and invitations to embrace a cause or choose a loyalty which in every case he rejects. They mark false paths to life, paths to the wrong loyalties and the wrong kind of light. They lead to the nets of which Stephen speaks: "When the soul of a man is born in this country there are nets flung at it to hold it back from flight. You talk to me of nationality, language, religion. I shall try to fly by those nets" (p. 203).

In the retreat sermon, dark and darkness are epithets given to hell in the traditional fashion. But it also seems that a descent into the darkness of sexual sin is a descent into hell that Stephen must undergo if his soul is to be born. Dark is associated with the utterance of his secret sexual fantasies which he finds in the word "Foetus" carved into the desk in University College, Cork, both in "the darkening lands" the Cork train speeds by (p. 87) and "the dark stained wood" into which the word has been cut (p. 89). Dark occurs again in his "memory of dark orgiastic riot" (p. 99). As he is about to embark on his first liaison with a prostitute, he tells us that "he wanted to sin with another of his kind, to force another being to sin with him and to exult with her in sin. He felt some dark presence moving irresistibly upon him from the darkness" (pp. 99–100). As he embraces the prostitute two powerful images we are given are "the dark pressure of her softly parting lips," "and between them... an unknown and timid pressure, darker than the swoon of sin, softer than sound or odour" (p. 101). These darks are gathered to a point in the strange autoerotic fantasy of Emma that is part of the artistic release that creates the villanelle:

> A sense of her innocence moved him almost to pity her, an innocence he had never understood till he had come to the knowledge of it through sin, an innocence which she too had not understood while she was innocent or before the strange humiliation of her nature had first come upon her. Then first her soul had begun to live as his soul had when he had first sinned: and a tender compassion filled his heart as he remembered her frail pallor and her eyes, humbled and saddened by the dark shame of womanhood. (pp. 222-23)

A few lines later, almost at the point of artistic birth, if we can designate the composition of the villanelle as such a point, the erotic content of the imaginings intensifies and "her eyes, dark and with a look of languor, were opening to his eyes." On the one hand we have here the medieval monkish notion of woman as temptress, as succuba, with a seductive appearance barely masking the most horrid bestiality; the tension between woman seen as Virgin and woman seen as Whore. On the other hand, the repetition of the birth imagery, "dark," "opening," "nakedness," "warm, odorous and lavishlimbed," "enfolded him like water with a liquid life," makes it clear that the waking of the woman to the consciousness of her sexuality and the man's desire, the man's awareness of this, the birth of the soul and the writing of the villanelle are one.

This idea is carried a step further when woman is entangled with bat and bird. William York Tindall traces this set of connections:

> Woman is not only rose but bird and sometimes bat.... Bats are anticipated by images of blinding.... When they appear at last, bats gather up these anticipatory associations with woman, custom and country. Davin's peasant woman at her door along the lonely road seems to Stephen "a type of her race and of his own, a batlike soul waking to consciousness of itself in darkness and secrecy and loneliness...." Like the images of bird and flower, the bat is ambivalent, not only bad but good.[17]

It is worth noting that *dorcha*, the Irish word for dark, also means "blind" and occurs with that meaning in *Finnegans Wake*. The link between Clongowes, rural Ireland, water, unknowing, birth, sin, bat, bird and woman is dark/blind. All awaking to consciousness, whether trivial or profound, venal or apocalyptic, is for Stephen subsumed under the birth of his own artistic faculty. After the creation of the villanelle Stephen stands on the steps of the National Library and watches the flight of the birds, "their dark darting quivering bodies flying clearly against the sky," "a dark flash, a swerve," "the dark frail quivering bodies wheeling and fluttering and swerving," "flying darkly against the fading air" (pp. 224–25).

> A sense of fear of the unknown moved in the heart of his weariness, a fear of symbols and portents, of the hawklike man whose name he bore soaring out of his captivity on osier woven wings, of Thoth, the god of writers, writing with a reed upon a tablet and bearing on his narrow ibis head the cusped moon. (p. 225)

The patterns of association of dark in *A Portrait of the Artist* are so pervasive as to characterize the forces Stephen must deal with to attain personal maturity and artistic freedom. Neither good nor bad in itself, this darkness marks a wide range of phenomena that impinges corporeally and imaginatively on Stephen and that he must try to come to grips with: the seemingly safe predictability of peasant life; the comforting darkness of the womblike halls of Clongowes Wood; the eyes of those who make demands on him; woman; the wheeling birds against the evening sky and the freedom they symbolize. The enticement of the unknown for Stephen and his own unsureness are captured in this "dark" as they are in the *ignotas* of the book's motto.

While dark and black do not have particularly bad or negative connotations as they are used in *A Portrait*, lack of color or fading or paling of color have such connotations. The word "nocoloured" occurs three times in the book, all in the same very negative context, the eyes of the cruel and unjust prefect of studies who "pandies" Stephen in Clongowes (pp. 50, 52, 55). Not only does Father Dolan refuse Stephen a hearing, humiliate him and cause him physical anguish, he also robs him of his identity: "He heard the voice of the prefect of studies asking him twice what his name was. Why could he not remember the name when he was told the first time?" (p. 55). What Stephen begins to learn is that the system in spite of its fine ideals can be unjust and at the mercy of its ministers, and that virtue is no protection. Because of his successful appeal to a higher authority within the system, his vindication in the eyes of his peers and in his own eyes is a vindication of the system. Thus the resolution Stephen attains at the end of section 1 is in ironic contrast to his resolution at the end of section 5 when he has learned the Blakean lesson that the only way to avoid entrapment by the system is to make his own, namely in Stephen's case, by silence, exile and cunning.

The word "colourless" also appears three times in *A Portrait*. Two of these occurrences appear on the same page (238) as Stephen contemplates the Maple Hotel in Kildare Street: "The name of the hotel, a colourless polished wood, and its colourless quiet front stung him like a glance of polite disdain" (pp. 237–38). What Stephen is facing is the impossibility of life for him in Ireland. The hotel symbolizes for him "the sleek lives of the patricians of Ireland housed in calm." The arrogant, lumpish aristocracy are armed in privilege and ignorance against the transforming mission of the artist. It is interesting that Stephen should once again cast that mission in terms that are heavily sexual: "How could he hit their conscience or how cast his shadow over the imaginations of their daughters, before their squires begat upon them, that they might breed a race less ignoble than their own?" (p. 238).

The third instance of colourless refers to the sky at which Stephen gazes as the director at Belvedere speaks to him of his possible vocation to the priesthood (p. 157). Indeed as the authority of the Church impinges on Stephen's life, its colors are pallid and faded, a muted repetition of Father Dolan's "nocolour." Father Arnall's face is "pale" as he begins the sermon at the retreat (p. 108). So are the eyes of the dean of studies as he lights the fire in the physics theater (p. 185), and on the following page they are "pale loveless eyes." This paleness extends to some of Stephen's fellow students, especially as they appear to Stephen to be making demands upon him that he must reject.

Heron has "a pale dandyish face" (p. 75) and a "shock of pale hair" (p. 76) and "closeset prominent eyes which [are] light and inexpressive" (p. 76). MacAlister, the student with "the sharp Ulster voice" and the mark accountant's attitude to learning, has "tangled twinecolored hair" and a "wheypale face" (p. 193). O'Donovan has "a pallid bloated face" that "expressed benevolent malice" (p. 210). Even Cranly has on occasion "a priestlike face, priestlike in its pallor ... priestlike in the lips that were long and bloodless and faintly smiling" (p. 178). But the Church and its priesthood are at the center of this paleness, the essence of which is inhumanity: "the inhuman voice that had called him to the pale service of the altar" (p. 169). The central section of the book, dealing with the retreat and Stephen's repentance, has a very low incidence of color words. The sermon is a rhetorical tour de force aimed at arousing fear and guilt in the listeners. It is in a sense the Church-sponsored "art form" the function and effect of which are purely kinetic. Its artificiality and Church sponsorship are evident in its dearth of color. Even the light in the chapel is "dull scarlet" and "wan" (p. 116). The colors associated with Stephen's repentance are "pale" and "white" (pp. 145–46). When Stephen fantasizes himself as Jesuit, there is a very revealing color concentration:

> The Reverend Stephen Dedalus, S.J.
> His name in that new life leaped into characters before his eyes and to it there followed a mental sensation of an undefined face or colour of a face. The colour faded and became strong like a changing glow of pallid brick red. Was it the raw reddish glow he had so often seen on wintry mornings on the shaven gills of the priests? The face was eyeless and sourfavored and devout, shot with pink tinges of suffocated anger. (p. 161)

The colors and the image are repellent. Here is the perfect parody of the white and rose and ardent of the making of the villanelle. Instead of a joyful sexuality and the drive to artistic creation, the passion which fuels the colors here is "suffocated anger."

Grey is a prominent color in *A Portrait*, as indeed it was in *Dubliners*.[18] But whereas grey in *Dubliners* was associated with paralysis and death, its use in *A Portrait* is more complex and much more ambiguous. In the Clongowes section and in the earlier parts of the book generally, grey is warm, pleasant, supportive: the grey light (pp. 8, 22, 26); "his belted grey suit" (p. 9); "the soft grey sky" and "the soft grey air" (pp. 41, 45, 59). Some of the later greys echo the warm early greys, as in "the grey sheet of water" (p. 167) and "the grey warm air" (pp. 168, 170). But other greys are hostile and repellent. Father Dolan's face is said to be "whitegrey" (pp. 50, 52), and he has a "baldy whitegrey head" (p. 50). In Stephen's vision of hell there are "bristling greygreen weeds" and "Goatish creatures with human faces, hornybrowed, lightly bearded and grey as indiarubber," and we are told that "a rictus of cruel malignity lit up greyly their old bony faces" (p. 137).

In addition, a large number of seemingly neutrally used greys are scattered through the book: the "loose grey clothes" of the imagined Cork student (p. 90); the "long grey beard" of the confessor (p. 142); "the grey light" and "the grey dull day" as Stephen attends the university lecture (p. 191). But other greys, and a few of those I have just cited, tend to pick up echoes of the "good" and "bad" greys I have described above, and to be biased by those echoes. Thus "the grey curtain of the morning" that Stephen sees in connection with Cranly's "priestlike face, priestlike in its pallor" (p. 178) echoes Father Dolan's priestly greys, while the "small grey handball" Cranly takes from his pocket (p. 196) echoes the indiarubber grey of Stephen's vision of hell. The greys of the dean of studies and the bursar at the university also echo the greys of Father Dolan. On the other hand, in the scene following the composition of the villanelle, the greys Stephen associates with Emma (p. 228) are generally warm, affectionate and reminiscent of the Clongowes greys—but with a hint of shame, incest, menace.

The progression of grey and its association through *A Portrait* reflects Stephen's maturing sense of discrimination. The early greys are warm and good and comforting; then some of them, shockingly, are found to be hostile and bad. Finally, greys are ambivalent, capable of being good or bad, or good and bad. Two striking images involving ambivalent grey occur in the book. The first occurs after the bird-girl incident: "Evening had fallen. A rim of the young moon cleft the pale waste of sky like the rim of a silver hoop embedded in grey sand" (p. 173). Greyness is the dullness of the mass of humanity which the sickle of the artist's creation must disturb and arouse and ennoble. If this is to happen, then the potential for ennoblement must exist in the greyness; otherwise, the artist's function is meaningless. Here is the second ambivalent image:

> The grey block of Trinity on his left, set heavily in the city's ignorance like a great dull stone set in a cumbrous ring, pulled his mind downward; and while he was striving this way and that to free his feet from the fetters of the reformed conscience he came upon the droll statue of the national poet of Ireland. (p. 180)

The turning in upon themselves of the parts of this image is worthy of *Finnegans Wake*. The jewel which should light the ring in which it sits is itself "dull" and "grey." And yet the grey also suggests grey matter, the brain and the mind striving for knowledge and truth. But the freedom of knowledge promised by the reformed faith merely fetters Stephen while the other Ireland symbolized by the statue of Thomas Moore provides him with no satisfactory alternative. To avoid these nets he must flee and create his own system.

The most important color word in *A Portrait* is "rose," and it is even more important in both *Ulysses* and the *Wake*. In the popular mind and in literary tradition roses are most often red, sometimes white. In Stephen's imagination they can be green. And rose itself suggests rose color, roughly a reddish pink, which associates quite naturally with blushing or flushing. Finally, the most popular traditional significations of rose are beauty, love, sacrifice, woman and female genitalia. When rose occurs in *A Portrait*, most of these traditional associations are at least dimly present even if the author, for the most part, merely counts on their echoes' reverberating in the reader's mind. In *A Portrait*, rose is placed at the center of a net of associations that permeate the book.

Rose occurs with green in the opening lines of *A Portrait*: "*O, the wild rose blossoms / On the little green place.*" Two lines further on the rose and the green are pulled together in "*O, the green wothe botheth*" (p. 7). This adumbrates the clash of red and green at the Christmas dinner as does also Stephen's recollection in Clongowes of the "wild rose" and "green place" and of the impossibility, at least in Ireland, of reconciliation between the two: "But you could not have a green rose. But perhaps somewhere in the world you could" (p. 12). The Christmas dinner scene is again foreshadowed in Stephen's anticipation of Christmas at home with the red and green of fire and holly and ivy (p. 20), and, once more, in the realization of these images on Christmas Day. Primarily, red and green are Britain and Ireland and the strife between them, red being British imperialism and its intransigence in the face of the green, or the nationalist or Home Rule fervor of which the late Parnell is the personification. The source of the acrimony at the Christmas dinner is the Church's throwing of its weight against Parnell. The result is a bitter clash of ideals and loyalties that frightens and puzzles the young Stephen with the conflicting demands they make upon him: "He wondered which was right, to be for the green or for the maroon" (p. 16). These demands he will see later as nets flung in the way of his artistic development.

The sentence just quoted above is particularly interesting in that in Stephen's recollection the clash of red and green has become the clash of maroon and green. As well as rose and green, maroon and green also appear on the opening page of the text. "The brush with the maroon velvet back was for Michael Davitt and the brush with the green velvet back was for Parnell" (p. 7). After Stephen's musings on green and maroon in Clongowes, maroon never agains appears in *A Portrait*. Maroon is of course a dark red, but any identification of Davitt's maroon with British imperial red is, on the face of it, ludicrous. Davitt, though a close ally of Parnell's, was also allied to that faction which believed that the pike and the gun constituted the only realistic method by which Ireland might wrest justice from Britain. Davitt had been a Fenian and his tactics in the Land League were close to being the extralegal dimension of Parnell's parliamentary struggle. Nor was Davitt a favorite of the Irish Church's leaders. Ironically, it was the fall of Parnell that brought about in Ireland the final discreditation of parliamentary tactics and of the Church's authority in political life and opened the way once more for men of Davitt's stamp, the men of force who were to prevail in 1916 and 1922. At this point in his maturation Stephen can only conceive of one clash of ideals at a time—he conflates the red-green polarity with the maroon-green distinction, and this suggests further irony. The Church in Ireland could forgive violence but it would never forgive love.

But the red rose and green place of the opening page of *A Portrait* have other connotations that lead in other directions. Since "the green place" suggests Ireland and the natural world of fields and growing things, the reader tends to identify the red rose with artifice and art, with the creations of the imagination and the intellect. In the latter sphere you can have a green rose, like Oscar Wilde's green carnation. Later in the novel Stephen thinks as he crosses the Green: "Stephen's, that is my green" (p. 249). In fact, one block of city parkland is enough countryside for the urban Stephen, as it was for his creator. After the Christmas dinner scene, green fades away in the book while the rose continues to gain in importance. It becomes, in William York Tindall's blunt phrase, "Stephen's image of woman and creativity."[19] Indeed, artistic creation on the one hand and woman as sexual object and stimulus on the other are inextricably entangled in *A Portrait*. They seem, much of the time, to be identical in Stephen's consciousness. In addition, both are associated not only with the red rose and the white rose but with rich and varied concentrations of color. And, as was the case in *Dubliners*, white has a special affinity with woman in her sexual aspect.

White rose and red rose first occur in *A Portrait* in the classroom in Clongowes, where Stephen leads the York, or white rose, team (p. 12). His thoughts at this point of roses and the colors of the placecards constitute the single most intense concentration of color words in the book.[20] The importance of this episode, I believe, is that it is the first occasion on which Stephen perceives the possibility of another kind of clash or competition which will not act as a threat or a net and at which he can excel. This is the academic competition, and by extension the challenge of artisitic creation, seen in Stephen's thoughts in the emphasis placed on the beauty of the colors. Stephen's oncoming sickness gives his thoughts at this point a kind of delirious prescience.

Stephen's thoughts of woman are marked by color, especially white. His first thoughts of Eileen that the reader is made privy to occur at the Christmas dinner when he connects her with the ivory and gold of the Litany of the Blessed Virgin. Eileen is Protestant, "and the protestants used to make fun of the litany of the Blessed Virgin. *Tower of Ivory*, they used to say, *House of Gold!* How could a woman be a tower of ivory or a house of gold?" (p. 35). The answer, which the youthful Stephen is unable to see, is: in the literary imagination. In Stephen's thoughts Eileen's hands, "long and white and thin and cold and soft," are the ivory (p. 36). Back at Clongowes, Simon Moonan's varicolored sweets bring his thoughts once more to Eileen and her "long thin cool white hands.... like ivory; only soft" (p. 42). And Stephen connects

Eileen's hair with the gold of the Litany: "Her fair hair had streamed out behind her like gold in the sun. *Tower of Ivory House of Gold*" (p. 43). The imagined Mercedes is also associated in Stephen's mind with white and roses when he envisages her "small white house and the garden of rosebushes" (p. 99). Then in his temporary conversion to a life of piety and devotion to the Virgin, it is she who is given these associations: "His prayers ascended to heaven from his purified heart like perfume streaming upwards from a heart of white rose" (p. 145). But the Virgin, like Eileen and Mercedes, turns out to be merely another precursor of the bird-girl on the beach.

The epiphany of the bird-girl comprises the last eight pages of section 4 (pp. 167–73) and is the richest color passage in the novel. The color references are not scattered evenly through these pages but are gathered into seven clusters. The first of these occurs as Stephen crosses the bridge to the Bull Wall and passes the "squad of christian brothers" with their "uncouth faces...stained yellow or red or livid by the sea..." (p. 165). The bridge, according to William York Tindall, "marks his passage from old custom to freedom and the waters of life." Tindall goes on: "What reveals Stephen's character is the contempt with which he regards those who are intellectually and socially inferior to the Jesuits. The episode, therefore, includes both his escape from one tyranny and his submission to another, the greater tyranny of pride."[21] Certainly there is a rejection on Stephen's part of conventional Christian humility and charity, of "humble and contrite hearts" (p. 166). The colors involved in this rejection, "stained yellow or red or livid," do not have pleasant or positive associations in *A Portrait:* the "thick yellow scum" on the water by the quays (p. 66), the "red" of anger, and the "livid" palm of his hand after Father Dolan's caning (pp. 50–51).[22] He turns away towards the very different hues which comprise the second cluster:

> He drew forth a phrase from his treasure and spoke it softly to himself.
> —A day of dappled seaborne clouds.
> The phrase and the day and the scene harmonised in a chord. Words. Was it their colours? He allowed them to glow and fade, hue and hue: sunrise gold, the russet and green of apple orchards, azure of waves, the greyfringed fleece of clouds. No, it was not their colours: it was the poise and balance of the period itself. Did he then love the rhythmic rise and fall of words better than their associations of legend and colour? Or was it that, being as weak of sight as he was shy of mind, he drew less pleasure from the reflection of the glowing sensible world through the prism of a language manycoloured and richly storied than from the contemplation of an inner world of individual emotions mirrored perfectly in a lucid supple periodic prose? (pp. 166–67)

Stephen obviously relishes the color he relegates to a secondary place. It is part of "his treasure." The duality he sets up is something of a straw man— the precious posturing of the young artist testing possibilities. Despite the superficial clarity of the paragraph it is in fact quite obscure. It is extremely difficult to determine with any precision the position of the word "color" as used here on a scale from literal to metaphoric. The question he is pondering is given to us only in a kind of shorthand version of his stream of thought and there is missing one vital element of the question: "Was it their colors?" —Was *what* their colors? In fact the pattern of colors here is of that attractive, almost hypnotic kind, which for the young artist is a part of the artistic or creative moment as in the vision of the bird-girl or the composition of the villanelle.

The third color cluster is part of the description of his friends' bodies stripped for swimming. The repellent colors emphasize his difference from them: "Their bodies, corpsewhite or suffused with a pallid golden light or rawly tanned by the suns [sic], gleamed with the wet of the sea" (p. 168). The fourth cluster consists of three occurrences of "radiant" and characterizes "an ecstasy of flight," a great deliverance of his spirit from "the dull gross voice of the world of duties and despair," a deliverance his mind sees as identical with "the hawklike man flying sunward above the sea" (p. 169). Echoes of this ecstasy and its color appear throughout the following page in scattered color words, "flame," "aflame," "glimmer," "gleamed," and "lightclad gayclad" (p. 170)

What we see in the four clusters of colors to this point is Stephen's consciousness swinging from one side to the other of a polarity which it creates: on the one hand there are the bad, ugly, repellent colors of "the dull gross world," and on the other the good, beautiful, transcendental colors of the "ecstasy of flight." The bird-girl epiphany itself, the fifth cluster, reflects this dichotomy by first presenting the colors of the sea water and seaweed and air ("emerald," "black," "russet," "olive," "dark," "grey" and "faded") and then the colors of the girl (pp. 170–71).

The passage has been much discussed. Frank O'Connor considered it "insufferably self-conscious, as though Walter Pater had taken to business and commercialised his style for the use of schools and colleges...."[23] Harry Levin is hardly less severe:

> Stephen dips self-consciously into his word-hoard.... We are given a paragraph of word-painting which is not easy to visualize.... This is incantation, and not description. Joyce is thinking in rhythms rather than metaphors.... Specification of the bird appeals to the sense of touch rather than to the sense of sight. What is said about the hair and face is intended to produce an effect without presenting a picture.[24]

If we set aside for the moment the questions begged by Levin when he substitutes "Joyce" for "Stephen" in the above passage, we can, I believe, accept his charge as accurate. What I find most interesting about Levin's point is how neatly it fits with Stephen's earlier musing on words and their colors. But the colors here are very much in evidence and they gather together the color strands that have been prominent throughout the novel: the Virgin's white and blue, and the ivory of the Litany; the sexual white of thighs and intimate garments; the green rose of art in the "emerald trail of seaweed ... upon the flesh"; the red rose in the "faint flame [that] trembled on her cheek" (and in Stephen's cheek); and the birth of the soul in the "darkplumaged dove" (p. 171). Since this is the artistic equivalent of a religious vision, in which not only the girl but Stephen is transfigured, realism of description has little place in it.

The sixth cluster of colors describes Stephen's feelings of ecstasy as a result of the vision and they obviously look forward to the great moment of the composition of the villanelle. The color words are "full crimson," "palest rose," "soft flushes," and "flush" (p. 172). The seventh and last cluster involves the moon Stephen sees after he has slept, "like the rim of a silver hoop embedded in grey sand" (p. 173). As I have suggested earlier, this image seems to me to indicate Stephen's newborn vision of the artistic integrity to which he is now committed while the pale sky and grey sand signify the life-choices he has rejected and those parts of life that the artist's genius can enlighten.

But there is a further peak to be reached both in the growth of the artist within the confines of this novel and in the progress of colors that accompanies that growth. This is the composition of the villanelle (pp. 217–24). The concentration of color which accompanies the composition of the villanelle is dominated by rose, ardent, and scarlet. These are directly identified with the woman to whom the villanelle is addressed. Essentially, the woman is the source of the poet's inspiration, his muse in fact, and in Stephen's imagination she is both the Virgin and all the women who have attracted his desire. Here is Robert Scholes's elucidation of that paradox:

> He turns, finally, from thoughts of the girl to a vision of the temptress of his villanelle, a personification of a feminine ideal.... Stephen's spiritual copulation with her is a symbolic equivalent for that moment of inspiration when "... the word was made flesh...." The physical copulation of the human animal and the spiritual copulation of the artist ... are valid and complementary manifestations of the same human impulse towards creation.[25]

Whatever difficulties may arise from this sexual-aesthetic identification, the colors of the composition episode are straightforward enough. The redness of the rose is intensified to scarlet and ardent, and this burning red is the color of sexual and artistic consummation and of bloody birth. It is impossible to believe that Joyce is treating the young artist without irony when we find the climax of self-arousal and self-indulgence maintained by "the great overblown scarlet flowers of the tattered wallpaper" in whose "scarlet glow" Stephen "tried to warm his perishing joy" (pp. 221–22). These are shabby roses indeed. I have mentioned earlier the connection of white with frustrated sexual desire. Throughout the composition scene Emma and her white are in the background, providing a muted counterpoint to the triumphant reds, reminding us of the women Stephen has longed for, has failed to win and has now turned his back on in favor of commitment to the pure muse of his art.

The piling up of reds for effect in the villanelle scene is, I believe, the moment of "the birth of the soul"; nothing like it occurs in Joyce's writings after this point.

The color patterns of *A Portrait of the Artist as a Young Man* are most closely associated with the ambiguities present in the novel, especially with the confusion and misunderstandings of the protagonist. Only a lack of color is unequivocally negative and sterile and it attaches notably to the Church and its demands upon Stephen. The special affinity of white with woman as temptress is prominent here as it was in *Dubliners*. The use of white in this way in *A Portrait* is complicated by the introduction of rose and the resulting tensions and harmonies of white rose and red rose which reach a climax in the composition of the villanelle and underscore the sexuality which underlies that process, a sexuality that Stephen attempts to sublimate. The color concentrations of *A Portrait* most frequently attend the efforts of the maturing Stephen to discriminate between the conflicting demands his society and his nature place upon him. Dark and darkness characterize the puzzling mystery of those demands. For such processes of discrimination colors and their perception provide a particularly appropriate analogue: even minute shades of difference between colors are easily apprehended by the eye; colors can shift and shade into each other almost instantly; colors readily combine to form soothing harmony or clashing disharmony or a pleasing contrast or a new color altogether. Their apprehension is as subjective and mutable as the emotions of the adolescent.

The Stephen whom we meet on the gun platform of the Martello tower in "Telemachus" is much changed from, if not much older than, the Stephen we left at the end of *A Portrait of the Artist*. In the diary entries which close the *Portrait* Stephen was poised for flight into a larger life. The horizons were unbounded. Now we find that his first flight was abortive and he is back in the mean pub life of Dublin tangled in the very nets he had determined to fly by. His artistic genius is confined to the shrunken channels to which Dublin society reduces all talent within it—fanciful theories and drunken speeches expounded to idle, shiftless drinking cronies. The most noticeable change we perceive in Stephen's behavior is a morose and defensive taciturnity sporadically relieved by alcoholic outbursts. As Patrick White points out: "Although his intellect is that of the earlier Stephen, his will is not. The Stephen of *Ulysses* has lost his verve, his optimism. He no longer exults in his power to create."[26]

Of the *Ulysses* Stephen Hugh Kenner writes: "He has not changed fathers after all; and, no longer sustained by the myth of sonship to the fabulous artificer, he is becoming another improvident Dublin character. People notice his resemblance to his father."[27] Kenner adds: "Stephen in *Ulysses* is no longer in search of a father, as he was in *A Portrait*. He is obsessed with a dead mother, and as for fathers, living or mythic, elected or adoptive, his present instinct is to get clear of them."[28] Stephen is the only character in *Ulysses* who still has some choices-of-becoming left, whose future self is not predetermined but can be affected by his own volitional acts. The fate of all the others is sealed within the narrow confines their society will tolerate. Obviously Bloom spends much of June 16 mulling over choices of his own, especially the choice of how to deal with Molly's adultery. But it is a qualitatively different choice from those facing Stephen. Bloom's choice is not one of becoming but of finding out within himself what he has become and then choosing to act according to that truth or to take refuge in lies. In his thoughts in "Sirens" we overhear him passing that test superbly if not with equanimity. Through the hallucinatory catharsis of "Circe" he attains the equanimity as well.

Stephen has not much time or room for choices left. He must act decisively and soon if he is not to drown in Dublin as he perceives his father to have drowned and his siblings to be drowning. It is not surprising that the figure of Hamlet and images of drowning are so much on his mind this day. Little occurs in the events of *Ulysses* to give us much realistic hope that Stephen will escape drowning and will realize his creative potential. His decision not to return to the tower and his surrendering of the key to Mulligan may constitute a small beginning but not much more. Only our extratextual knowledge of James Joyce's career and achievements leads us to suppose a like future for Stephen. Joyce is up to his old tricks with his readers.

Bloom provides us, and to a much less degree he provides Stephen, with the model of a man who can escape his society's vices and yet continue to live within that society. But the price he has to pay is high. Though friendly and magnanimous and prosperous he is treated with malice and ridicule. He is an uncomfortable reminder to those about him of their own despair and the threadbare lies by which they live. Bloom's successful revolt against the impoverished moral order of his society is most graphically demonstrated in his sexuality, in his rejection of the mechanical sexual roles into which the society forces its members. Joseph Allen Boone describes the destructiveness of this "rigid polarization of male-female roles" in Joyce's Dublin:

> Just as the majority of Joyce's male characters are obsessed by shows of power, force, virility, and sheer brawn, the women believe themselves to be passive, receptive and intuitive creatures who complement their "feminine" virtue with a forgiving indulgence of "masculine" bravado.
>
> One consequence of such sex-role differentiation is that, especially for the men, life becomes a fight bordering on savagery. This sense of intense competition, based on force, appals the mild-mannered Bloom.[29]

Bloom's forgetting of his front-door key and Stephen's surrendering of the tower key to Mulligan have at least this symbolic significance in common that both men are disavowing the roles Dublin society prescribes for them. In

Bloom's case this letting go of possessiveness marks his coming to terms with the truth of the masculine role that is natural and proper to him, even as it includes acceptance of the fact of his cuckoldry. The conflicts that matter in *Ulysses* are those going on within the minds of Bloom and Stephen, conflicts that are literally worked out in the fantasies of "Circe." Calm acceptance reigns in both men's minds in "Eumaeus" and "Ithaca" and only the reader has to journey with Molly through "Penelope."

But then neither Bloom nor Stephen but the reader is the real hero of *Ulysses*. *Ulysses* is not so much about the writing of *Ulysses*, "the tale of the telling" as Brook Thomas calls it,[30] as it is about the reading of *Ulysses*. As Richard Kain points out, "It is we, the readers, not Stephen or Bloom, who reach the point of artistic detachment, sympathy, and understanding."[31] And it is we, not Stephen or Bloom, who are aware of the Homeric parallels, of the book in which the characters play their parts, of James Joyce and his other writings. We have an access to the workings of the fictional world of *Ulysses* denied to those who live in it. The structure that finally matters in *Ulysses* is the complex of associative patterns the attentive reader builds in his mind as he reads and rereads the text, bringing to bear on every fragment of it words, phrases and incidents from earlier and later parts of the work and from outside the work. As the reader's quest takes him backwards and forwards through the streets and pubs of Joyce's Dublin, his Ithaca remains for ever just over the horizon. He journeys to write the book of himself as he reads "the Blue Book of Eccles."

We have for *Ulysses* colors designated by the author for some of the episodes and contained in the two schemas he issued before he had completed the final, published form of the book. In his *"Ulysses" on the Liffey* Richard Ellmann reproduces and compares the two schemas.[32] Here are the colors given in the schemas:

EPISODE	LINATI	GILBERT-GORMAN
1. Telemachus	gold, white	gold-white
2. Nestor	chestnut	brown
3. Proteus	blue	green
4. Calypso	orange	orange
5. Lotus Eaters	brown	—
6. Hades	black, white	black, white
7. Aeolus	red	red
8. Lestrygonians	blood color	—
9. Scylla and Charybdis	—	—
10. Wandering Rocks	rainbow	—
11. Sirens	coral	—
12. Cyclops	green	green
13. Nausicaa	grey	grey, blue
14. Oxen of the Sun	white	white

15. Circe	violet	—
16. Eumaeus	—	—
17. Ithaca	starry milky	starry milky
18. Penelope	starry milky then new dawn	starry milky then new dawn

But when we examine the text of each of these episodes we find that neither schema gives a good fit, although the later or Gorman-Gilbert schema is less imperfect than the Linati. "Telemachus" is supposed to be white and gold but contains in fact only three gold references.[33] But white/pale/fair does indeed constitute the dominant color of the episode. The color given for "Nestor" is brown (or chestnut in the Linati schema) but the episode contains not a single incidence of brown or chestnut. "Proteus" is supposed to be blue and green, and although both colors are prominent in the episode they are less so than yellow or white. "Calypso" is supposed to be orange but not one of the seventeen occurrences of the word orange in *Ulysses* is to be found in "Calypso." The designated brown is not important in "Lotus Eaters." Black and white are conspicuous in "Hades" as they should be according to the schemas, but the appearances of grey, though slightly less numerous than the other two, are much more striking. Red does dominate "Aeolus," as it is supposed to, but in a rather mechanical fashion. Blood color, rainbow, coral and violet, designated by the Linati schema for "Lestrygonians," "Wandering Rocks," "Sirens" and "Circe" respectively, are either not in evidence or of no apparent importance in those episodes. Green is noticeable in "Cyclops" though black, white and red are each numerically stronger. Grey is of minimal importance in "Nausicaa" but the Madonna's blue is clearly Gerty's color. White in "Oxen of the Sun" is no more prominent and, as far as I can see, no more important than black, red, green or yellow. Of course sheer numbers are not everything, but no matter how I play around with the color references in these episodes I can find little help in the schemas for tracing patterns of color significance; the schemas simply do not stand up. I might add that Elliott Coleman in his article "Heliotropical Noughttime" has worked out a set of liturgical patterns of colors for "Telemachus," "Proteus," "Aeolus," "Nausicaa" and "Oxen of the Sun," but since he depends on Gilbert's schema rather than an examination of the colors that actually appear in the episodes his results are not really convincing.[34]

Ulysses has proportionately more color references than *Dubliners* but slightly fewer than *A Portrait*. In *Ulysses* the occurrences of white/fair/pale are about equal in number to those of black/dark but bright vibrant shades are more numerous and more striking than in *A Portrait*. In that sense *Ulysses* is not as dark or gloomy a book as either *A Portrait* or *Dubliners*. Much of the color of *Ulysses* is scattered through the book in a seemingly naturalistic way but as in *A Portrait* there are frequent concentrations of colors at dramatic points of the novel. Furthermore, to a far greater degree than in *A Portrait*, certain scenes and certain characters in *Ulysses* have almost their own color signatures. Thus tan shoes are a signature for Boylan and we find an extraordinary concentration of gold and bronze in "Sirens." Of the fifty occurrences of bronze in *Ulysses*, forty-one appear in "Sirens" while, of the remaining nine, six are in "Circe."

As they ponder various subjects at various times throughout the day both Stephen and Bloom display a high consciousness of colors. Bloom has a high awareness of the colors of the phenomena about him and blends these into his speculations with the colors he remembers from other happenings in his life. Stephen, on the other hand, tends to incorporate colors he happens to notice into abstract patterns of thought in which colors carry considerable symbolic significance. Only once does Stephen in *Ulysses* display a distinct and literal color aversion, when in "Telemachus" he refuses Mulligan's gift of trousers because they have a grey-striped pattern (1.120). I presume that the "etiquette" referred to by Mulligan as the cause of Stephen's refusal is the custom of wearing black for mourning, for the death of Stephen's mother in this case. Undoubtedly, the color involved is of far less importance to Stephen than the symbolic ritual of which it is a part.

By far the most colorful episode of *Ulysses*, in the sense that it contains proportionately more explicit color words than any other episode, is "Proteus." As he "is walking into eternity along Sandymount strand" (3.18-19) Stephen ticks off most of the concerns that haunt his thoughts on this sixteenth of June, relates them to each other and to the phenomena he apprehends as he walks, and ponders them: sight and space and visual art, time and eternity, his ruined father, Paris and exile, sea and shore and history and the tyranny of the past, man and woman, mother and sea and drowning, escape. Through the rapidly shifting thought fragments of the episode the sea, beside which Stephen walks and of which Proteus is a god, again and again asserts its presence.

The first color word Stephen applies to the sea in his thoughts is "snotgreen" (3.3) which harks back to Mulligan's remarks in the opening scene of "Telemachus": "A new art color for our Irish poets: snotgreen.... Isn't the sea what Algy calls it: a great sweet mother? The snotgreen sea. The scrotumtightening sea" (1.73-78). Green-sea-mother-castration: these images lead Stephen's thought inexorably to his mother's recent death.

> Across the threadbare cuffedge he saw the sea hailed as a great sweet mother by the wellfed voice beside him. The ring of bay and skyline held a dull green mass of liquid. A bowl of white china had stood beside her deathbed holding the green sluggish bile which she had torn up from her rotting liver by fits of loud groaning vomiting. (1.106-10)

This is the most distressing image that haunts Stephen's consciousness throughout June 16 and its primary trigger is the color green. Mulligan's mention of "Irish poets" above reminds us that green is also the color of Stephen's other mother, Ireland, whose importunities he must also flee if he is not to be drowned or unmanned or thwarted from his destiny. A little further on in "Telemachus" the white of the bowl at his mother's deathbed reechoes in connection with the green sea: "Inshore and farther out the mirror of water whitened.... White breast of the dim sea.... Wavewhite wedded words shimmering on the dim tide.... shadowing the bay in deeper green. It lay beneath him, a bowl of bitter waters" (1.243-49).

On two other occasions on June 16 the green-white-mother-drowning image breaks painfully through the defenses of Stephen's consciousness. The squalid state of the family's fortunes strikes him keenly when he sees his sister Dilly buying the French book on Bedford Row: "She is drowning. Agenbite. Save her. Agenbite. All against us. She will drown me with her, eyes and hair. Lank coils of seaweed hair around me, my heart, my soul. Saltgreen death" (10.875-77). To avoid drowning and to fulfil his artistic destiny he must perpetrate a second act of murderous betrayal, this time on his remaining family. And in "Circe" the ghost of Stephen's mother appears to his inflamed imagination, in "*a torn bridal veil, her face worn and noseless, green with gravemould*" (15.4158-159). Her hand becomes "*a green crab*" which sticks its claws in Stephen's heart. It is now that Stephen finally rejects her demands: "*Non Serviam!*" His blow to the chandelier is his exorcism of the demands of mother and church and country and a symbolic act of commitment to "the intellectual imagination."

Another event in "Proteus" suggests a further dimension of the sea-mother-drowning-green-white complex of images. This is Stephen's imagining a drowned man surfacing in the bay: "Full fathom five thy father lies.... A corpse rising saltwhite from the undertow.... A quiver of minnows, fat of a spongy titbit, flash through the slits of his buttoned trouserfly.... he breathes upward the stench of his green grave..." (3.470-81).

As Suzette Henke has pointed out, the quotation from *The Tempest* symbolically identifies the drowned man with Stephen's father, Simon Dedalus:

> Simon has been emasculated by maternal Ireland, by Mother Church, and by his dead wife Mary.... The man "found drowned" has merged with the "great sweet mother," forfeiting his masculinity. His genitals are "a spongy titbit" for a quiver of minnows, and he himself is an object to be devoured by fishes.[35]

The father has become for Stephen an example of the drowning that Stephen must avoid. The image of the drowned man has occurred to Stephen earlier in the novel with "saltwhite" and with an adjacent green (1.676, 681) but his thoughts at that point have not yet sorted out the hard relations of the various images. That sorting out is precisely the task and the achievement to which

Stephen devotes June 16, 1904, and colors are frequently markers of the distinctions he makes as he goes, as indeed they also were in *A Portrait of the Artist as a Young Man.*

Bloom's attention to colors focuses primarily on the passing phenomena that catch his eye, but he too on occasion ponders colors in a more formal and abstract fashion. Near the end of "Nausicaa," as he sees the Bailey lighthouse begin to shine, his mind wanders idly: "Some light still. Red rays are longest. Roygbiv Vance taught us: red, orange, yellow, green, blue, indigo, violet" (13.1075-76). And then the stream of his thought continues to slip idly over the surfaces of other objects, other notions. A little later he again thinks idly of patterns of light and dark and color as he notices the bats flying in the dusk and remembers the colors of various cats in the past (13.1131-38). In "Ithaca," one of the questions on which Bloom meditates has to do with the constellations, and their "various colors significant of various degress of vitality" is the first feature to be considered (17.1104). But on none of these occasions does the initial cluster of ideas lead to extended abstract speculation. Such is simply not Bloom's kind of thinking. Bloom's concerns are the realities of the world about him as they impinge on people's lives and the driving forces of human nature as he observes it. In these contexts he has a great deal to say about colors, but in a concrete and associational way. But one of the more interesting and curious features of Joyce's method in *Ulysses* (and one which looks forward to the *Wake*) is the way in which thoughts from one character's mind can echo in another's, even without the opportunity for normal communication. An example of this, involving the green-white images I have been discussing with reference to Stephen, occurs in "Hades." As Bloom contemplates the moldering corpses under the Glasnevin soil he thinks: "Saltwhite crumbling mush of corpse: smell, taste like raw white turnips" (6.993-94). "Saltwhite" is the exact epithet that Stephen uses in "Proteus" and it is a sufficiently uncommon term to be most unlikely to crop up at random in the thoughts of two such different people, and therefore argues some deliberate manipulation on the part of the author. A little earlier in Bloom's thoughts on the dead the color green also appears: "Turning green and pink decomposing" (6.777).

Beyond the sea-drowning-mother cluster of images, the colors green and white stretch off in their separate directions, into other nests of association and meaning. Green is used in Joyce's major works only to a limited degree and generally in a negative way; scarcely ever does Joyce use the nature-growth-spring associations which are the strongest traditional associations of green. We have already seen the most prominent cluster of green associations in *Ulysses,* namely the imagery of mother-sea-drowning-corpse. That most colorful figure, Molly Bloom, is given scarcely any greens. The green of Ireland and Irish nationalism is used extensively but almost always negatively. The undermining of national green begins in the opening scene of the novel with Mulligan's mockery: "—The bard's noserag! A new art color for our Irish poets: snotgreen. You can almost taste it, can't you?" (1.73-74). Kevin Egan, that sad figure in Stephen's memory of a nationalist Irish exile in Paris, has the vicious green of the absinthe with which he is poisoning himself, "green fairy" and "the green fairy's fang thrusting between his lips" (3.216-26). A pompous clichéd headline in "Aeolus," "ERIN, GREEN GEM OF THE SILVER SEA" (7.236), undermines sentimental nationalist pretensions and is echoed in the parody of Irish newspaper prose: "*bosky grove and undulating plain and luscious pastureland of vernal green, steeped in the transcendent translucent glow of our mild mysterious Irish twilight*" (7.322-24). This kind of diminution continues through various parts of the novel; in Stephen's thought, "Gaptoothed Kathleen, her four beautiful green fields, the stranger in her house" in "Scylla and Charybdis" (9.36-37); in the "gigantism" of "Cyclops"; in the drunken bluster of "Oxen in the Sun"; and in the colorful parodies of public rituals in "Circe."

It is probably Joyce's rejection of vainglorious, jingoistic Irish nationalism that is the basic reason for his apparent dislike of green. None of the *Ulysses* characters with whom we are likely to feel much sympathy are given many greens. On the other hand the sadistic, sex-changed Bello in "Circe" is given some greens and, according to Bloom, Mulligan is the one who has come up with the "scheme of color containing the gradation of green" (17.1316). Gerty MacDowell has many greens, most of them having to do with her clothes, which are so important to her, and the fireworks display which climaxes with Gerty's more intimate display.

Most of the other greens in *Ulysses* are used more or less neutrally and naturalistically but a few merit mention. Bloom uses green twice in "Lestrygonians" in connection with food and eating. The first instance is his vision of the lunch eaters in the Burton restaurant: "Stink gripped his trembling breath: pungent meatjuice, slop of greens. See the animals feed" (8.650-52). The second instance is different only in that Bloom is contemplating his own lunch, "with relish of disgust": "Mr. Bloom ate his strips of sandwich, fresh clean bread, with relish of disgust pungent mustard, the feety savor of green cheese" (8.818-19). Neither instance does much to raise the otherwise low status of green in *Ulysses*. Another unusual occurrence of green is the dress of the Jew's daughter in the song Stephen sings to Bloom in "Ithaca" and of Bloom's reception of which we are told: "With mixed feelings. Unsmiling, he heard and saw with wonder a jew's daughter, all dressed in green" (17.830-931). Finally, there is one facet of the greens associated with Gerty MacDowell which though barely present in *Ulysses* will be quite important in *Finnegans Wake*. A comment of Bloom's after Gerty has left the beach captures what I have in mind: "Like to be that rock she sat on. O sweet little, you don't know how nice you looked. I begin to like them at that age. Green apples" (13.1084–86). "Green apples" in the *Wake* are the young girls desired by the older man and they always carry a hint of incestuous longings. In "Nausicaa" there is no overt evidence of the incest theme—except that such a May-December liaison is always open to such an interpretation. It is interesting that the same color, green, marks Stephen's tortured complex of thoughts of his dead mother, a complex that clearly has the potential of being analyzed in terms of its oedipal and incestuous roots.

White is the most important single color in *Ulysses* and its most significant set of associations is one I have already noted in *Dubliners* and *A Portrait of the Artist,* namely white/woman/sexuality.[36] The association is Bloom's especially but it occurs also in the thoughts of the other principal characters and in the observations of the narrators. It first appears in "Calypso," as Bloom stands in Dlugacz's butcher shop and thinks "a young white heifer" (4.158–59). Ostensibly the heifer is one of the cattle in the picture of the model farm at Kinnereth. In fact, what is really engaging Bloom's attention is the "nextdoor girl" who stands in front of him at Dlugacz's counter, and whose "vigorous hips" and "skirt swinging" as she beat the carpet in the garden have evoked his prurient interest. He wants to hurry with his business in the butcher's so that he may walk home "behind her moving hams" in voyeuristic bliss.

In "Lotus Eaters," as Bloom talks to M'Coy on the street, he watches a society lady about to climb up on an outside car: "Watch! Watch! Silk flash rich stockings white. Watch!" (5.130). This is merely the anticipation. A few seconds later he curses the tramcar driver who blocks his view. Clearly the white here is not merely a flash of woman's leg encased in white stockings but signifies the full voyeuristic ritual of a revelation of hidden sexual secrets. A little later when Bloom tears up and throws away Martha's titillating letter, he sees it as "a white flutter" (5.302). In the chemist's shop he orders the lotion for Molly and thinks: "It certainly did make her skin so delicate white like wax" (5.492). And this white goes beyond the purely visual for Bloom. In "Lestrygonians" he wonders about the sensations the blind young man would experience in touching a woman: "His hands on her hair for instance. Say it was black, for instance. Good. We call it black. Then passing over her white skin. Different feel perhaps. Feeling of white" (8.1129–31). And in "Wandering Rocks," as Bloom looks through a titillating book he thinks: "Flesh yielded amply amid rumpled clothes: whites of eyes swooning up" (10.619–20). Finally, while Ben Dollard sings "The Croppy Boy" in the bar of the Ormond Hotel, Bloom studies the barmaid Lydia Douce and muses: "Play on her. Lip blow. Body of white woman, a flute alive" (11.1088–89).

That Bloom's association of white with woman goes beyond any white-skin cliches and involves glimpses of women's underwear becomes clear when we examine other whites that cross his mind. In "Lestrygonians" he remembers a night when they returned home after a concert and he watched Molly undress: "Could see her in the bedroom from the hearth unclamping the busk of her stays: white" (8.196–97). In "Ithaca" he recalls "concupiscence caused by Nelly Bouverist's revelations of white articles of non-intellectual, non-political, non-topical underclothing while she (Nelly Bouverist) was in the articles..." (17.438–40). The white is a woman's panties, or drawers or knickers as they would have been called in 1904. To be more exact, Bloom's "white" is the voyeur's glimpse of skin and adjacent pants and the hidden secrets which the pants conceal but which by their innocent whiteness they suggest and whose mysterious essence they partake of. At the turn of the century such undergarments would almost always be white, at least if they had any pretensions to elegance, so that such a surreptitious glimpse of hidden treasures would have constituted the epitome of the casual visual stimulus for the voyeur. For Bloom, at this point of his complex inner strife about sex, voyeurism is both his most potent sexual stimulus and the most persistent accompaniment of his sexual release.

In "Nausicaa" Bloom reveals some of the sources of his interest in female undergarments: "*Lingerie* does it. Felt for the curves inside her *deshabille*. Excites them also when they're. I'm all clean come and dirty me.... Put them all on to take them all off.... Nuns with whitewashed faces, cool coifs..." (13.796–812). The whiteness of the panties signifies coolness, cleanliness, inviolability to the voyeur but that very whiteness suggests its opposite and constitutes an invitation to defilement. When in "Circe" Bloom is accused of having assaulted Mary Driscoll there is more than a hint of irony in his defensive statement, "I treated you white" (15.876), and in J.J. O'Molloy's character reference: "I regard him as the whitest man I know" (15.980).

The full degree of fetishism implicit in Bloom's interest in white and undergarments is made clear in the uninhibited fantasies of "Circe." In the following observation the speaker is Bello but the fantasy is assuredly Bloom's: "The scanty, darlingly short skirt, riding up at the knee to show a peep of white pantalette, is a potent weapon and transparent stockings, emeraldgartered, with the long straight seam trailing up beyond the knee, appeal to the better instincts of the *blase* man about town" (15.3115–19). Note that the focus of attention is shifting here from the woman's body to the garments themselves and that they constitute not an invitation but a "weapon." A little later Bloom shows interest in a chairseat still retaining the imprint of a woman's bottom:

> It overpowers me. The warm impress of her warm form. Even to sit where a woman has sat, especially with divaricated thighs, as though to grant the last favors, most especially with previously well uplifted white sateen coatpans. So womanly, full. It fills me full. (15.3424–27)

Again here the ambivalence in the sexual role in intercourse (the male speaker, not the woman, is filled) shifts the focus to the attendant circumstances of thighs and coattails and white. One other instance, this one from "Nausicaa," merits citation in this connection. It occurs at the end of the episode as Bloom reflects lovingly on his "encounter" with Gerty:

> O sweety all your little girlwhite up I saw dirty bracegirdle made me do love sticky we two naughty Grace darling she him half past the bed met him pike hoses frillies for Raoul de perfume your wife black hair heave under embon *senorita* young eyes Mulvey plump bubs me breadvan Winkle red slippers she rusty sleep wander years of dreams return tail end Agendath swoony lovey showed me her next year in drawers return next in her next her next. (13.1279–85)

Bloom draws together some of the sexual touchstones of his day, beginning with the cleanliness/inviolability/virginity/white underwear of Gerty's display, moving to the defilement/dirtying of his masturbation, for which Gerty is seen not only as accomplice but as instigator ("made me"), and then moving, via the actress Anne Bracegirdle and the heroine Grace Darling, to the center of his sexual universe, Molly.

It might be expected that Stephen's thoughts of sex would be distinctly different from those displayed by Bloom and the other characters in *Ulysses*, not only because of his much more sophisticated mind, but also because on this day Stephen's thoughts are morose. His images of women and many more remote topics are clouded by the shadow of his dead mother, a shadow he is trying to exorcise. Furthermore the author is far more guarded in the access he allows us to Stephen's mind than he is with Bloom or Molly or Gerty. Nevertheless there is evidence of the woman/white/sexuality linkage in Stephen's train of thought too. In "Proteus" he thinks of Eve: "Belly without blemish, bulging big, a buckler of taut vellum, no, whiteheaped corn" (3.42–43). The source of this image in the Song of Solomon, 7:2, reads: "Thy belly is like a heap of wheat, set about with lilies." The "white" of "whiteheaped" is Stephen's addition. His musings on the gypsy woman he sees on Sandymount strand include "A she fiend's whiteness under her rancid rags" (3.378–79), and the song he quotes in the same context begins "White thy fambles, red thy gan." In "Scylla and Charybdis" he posits Anne Hathaway's adultery and specifies the act thus: "Afar, in a reek of lust and squalour, hands are laid on whiteness" (9.654). Stephen's white/sexuality associations are far less numerous than Bloom's and they lack the white/lingerie and white/voyeurism associations so prominent in Bloom's thoughts, but it is interesting that he juxtaposes white/sexuality with dirt, squalor, defilement, in two of the examples I have quoted.

Molly Bloom's thoughts display a white/sexuality/woman's body pattern of associations too. In Molly's consciousness, the body, of course, is her own. As she sits on the chamber pot she recollects her coupling with Boylan: "I bet he never saw a better pair of thighs than that look how white they are the smoothest place is right there between this bit here how soft like a peach easy God I wouldnt mind being a man and get up on a lovely woman..." (18.1144-47). A little later, thinking again of her assignation with Boylan, she says: "I suppose its because they were so plump and tempting in my short petticoat he couldnt resist they excite myself sometimes its well for men all the amount of pleasure they get off a womans body were so round and white for them always I wished I was one myself for a change..." (18.1378-81). Clearly, Molly, like Bloom, sees female sexual appeal in terms of white skin and she finds such notions arousing: "they excite myself sometimes." For obvious reasons, namely the unlikelihood of a woman's owning a fetish for women's undergarments, Molly does not evince that lingerie aspect of Bloom's white/sexuality set of associations, but she does display some interesting white/sex associations of her own. Her memories of her assignation with her first love, Mulvey, include: "I had that white blouse on open in the front to encourage him as much as I could without too openly" (18.787-89), and "its the roundness there I was leaning over him with my white ricestraw hat" (18.797-98). And of her preparations for that same assignation she says: "I remember shall I wear a white rose" (18.768). In her fantasy of Stephen's visiting her she repeats the same sentence: "shall I wear a white rose" (18.1553-54).

In her romanticizing of her own appearance Gerty MacDowell also makes much of the white/woman/sexuality association: "The waxen pallor of her face was almost spiritual in its ivorylike purity.... Her hands were of finely veined alabaster with tapering fingers and as white as lemonjuice and queen of ointments could make them..." (13.87-90), and "when they were alone and he stole an arm round her waist she went white to the very lips" (13.201-3). Compared with the earthiness of Molly's whites, Gerty's have a cloying squeamish prurience that the reader finds far more offensive: "a soft clinging white" (13.338), arms "that were white and soft" (13.341), "the whitest of teeth" (13.527), "the whiterose scent" (13.639-40), "her alabaster pouncet box" (13.640), "little white hands stretched out" (13.669-70). At the climax of her exhibition for Bloom she leans back and "he could see her other things too, nainsook knickers... white and she let him and she saw that he saw" (13.724-26). "She would fain have cried to him chokingly, held out her snowy slender arms to him to come, to feel his lips laid on her white brow..."(13.733-35).

The white/sexuality set of associations is not confined to the minds of the principal characters nor is it entirely confined to woman's body and undergarments. The narrator of "Wandering Rocks" tells us, probably through the eyes of Corny Kelleher, that "a generous white arm from a window in Eccles Street flung forth a coin" to the one-legged sailor (10.222-23). This is Molly preparing for her assignation with Boylan. A little later the same sight is given from another, unidentified, viewpoint: "A plump bare generous arm shone, was seen, held forth from a white petticoatbodice and taut shiftstraps" (10.251-52). The male as sexual object does have some whites as well. For Gerty male arousal is "whitehot passion" (13.691). When Molly fantasizes fellating the male statue Bloom has given her, she thinks: "His lovely young cock there so simple I wouldnt mind taking him in my mouth if nobody was looking as if it was asking you to suck it so clean and white..." (18.1352-54). This is an interesting echo of Bloom's white/clean/dirty attitude. In "Sirens" we see Lydia Douce listening pensively to the singing of "The Croppy Boy" and stroking the beer lever in an obviously masturbatory fashion: "Fro, to: to, fro: over the polished knob... her thumb and finger... slid so smoothly, slowly down, a cool firm white enamel baton protruding through their sliding ring" (11.1113-17).

There are of course lots of comparatively neutral whites scattered through the pages of *Ulysses* but in many cases an otherwise neutral white picks up for the reader connotations from the pervasive white/sexuality set of associations. Thus when Bloom thinks of "nuns with whitewashed faces" (13.811-12) the reader's response is influenced by the white/clean/sexual/ defilement pattern which is also a product of Bloom's mind. Likewise our responses are affected to "*Senorita Blanca*" (15.216) and the nymph in "Circe," "*eyeless, in nun's white habit*" (15.3434), and to Stephen's phrase in "Telemachus," "White breast of the dim sea" (1.244-45). Any whites used by Gerty MacDowell are immediately suspect, especially as they piously apply to religious figures, as when her thoughts turn to Canon O'Hanlon conducting the benediction in Sandymount Church: "His hands were just like white wax and if ever she became a Dominican nun in their white habit perhaps he might come to the convent..." (13.451-52).

One other use of white in *Ulysses* deserves comment: it occurs as a term of opprobrium, but always an opprobrium of doubtful validity. In "Circe," Private Carr's noble testament of loyalty to his officer is: "God fuck old Bennett! He's a whitearsed bugger" (15.4796-97). And in "Cyclops" the ever angry citizen condemns "the Whitelivered Saxons" (12.1367-68). But the most frequent butt of white-associated insults is Bloom. In "Aeolus," where Bloom is the target of so much contempt, MacHugh and Lenehan enjoy Bloom as a figure of fun: "Both smiled over the crossblind at the file of capering newsboys in Mr. Bloom's wake, the last zigzagging white in the breeze a mocking kite, a tail of white bowknots" (7.444-46). In "Cyclops" the citizen calls him "that whiteeyed kaffir" (12.1552). In "Circe" Alexander J. Dowie accuses Bloom: "This vile hypocrite, bronzed with infamy, is the white bull mentioned in the Apocalypse. A worshipper of the Scarlet Woman, intrigue is the very breath of his nostrils" (15.1757-59). (By the way, there is no white bull mentioned in the Apocalypse.) When Molly thinks of the time when she thought there were burglars downstairs, she remembers Bloom "as white as a sheet frightened out of his wits making as much noise as he possibly could for the burglars benefit..." (18.1001-1003). Even at one point in "Circe" where the controlling consciousness is more Bloom's than it is anybody else's, Bloom is envisaged in a stage note in a ridiculous and derogatory white: "*Bloom in a torn frockcoat stained with whitewash. Dinged silk hat sideways on his head, a strip of sticking plaster across his nose, talks inaudibly*" (15.935-37).

At first glance these insults to Bloom may not appear to have much in common, other than the presence of white, but a closer examination reveals a distinct pattern and a definite relationship to the white/woman complex of associations. In full, the statement made by the citizen reads: "—Is it that whiteeyed kaffir? says the citizen, that never backed a horse in anger in his life" (12.1552-53). The ground of the insult is a lack of anger and a lack of careless spontaneity. Bloom upsets and aggravates the citizen not only by his foreignness but by his temperance, his self-containment, his unobtrusiveness, his quiet unassertive dignity, all of which imply a challenge to the jingoistic verbal violence that passes for the mark of manhood in the Dublin pubs. What Bloom lacks is the mindless aggressive masculinity that today might be termed macho. Cowardice and meanness of spirit are the pub-crawler's interpretation of such a difference. Bloom as white bull and his subservience to the robust red of the Scarlet Woman in Dowie's accusation reflect the same charge of a lack of manliness. Presumably his preference for intrigue suggests a fear of attacking directly. Ironically, this diminution of Bloom on the part of Dublin's men relates him more readily to the hero of the *Odyssey* than any praise they could give him: after all, the wily Odysseus was known to have saved himself behind women's skirts when a display of "manliness" would have been fatal. The virtues we find in Bloom are precisely those conventionally thought of as feminine, sensitivity, sympathy, gentleness, patience, benevolence towards his fellowman and an abhorrence of violence. Molly shows appreciation of this "new womanly man" and her comment on his cowardice contains unconscious ambiguity: "for the burglars benefit."

In refusing to strive for the masculine image acceptable to the denizens of the pubs, Bloom frees his finer feelings from repression and from the universal Dublin paralysis, and the women he comes in contact with sense this. Not only are women sexual objects for Bloom—and they most assuredly are—but he is the only character in *Ulysses* who really appreciates women and tries to understand them. Woman for Bloom is a white mystery, the center of desire and comfort and life, puzzling and ultimately unknowable:

> *Gazelles are leaping, feeding on the mountains. Near are lakes. Round their shores file shadows black of cedargroves. Aroma rises, a strong hairgrowth of resin. It burns, the orient, a sky of sapphire, cleft by the bronze flight of eagles. Under it lies the womancity, nude, white, still, cool, in luxury. A fountain murmurs among damask roses. Mammoth roses murmur of scarlet winegrapes. A wine of shame, lust, blood exudes, strangely murmuring.* (15.1324-30).

A number of color concentrations occur in Stephen's thought in addition to those already examined. In "Proteus" an isolated cluster of colors, in which a rich golden yellow predominates, marks his memories of his short stay in Paris (3.192-264). In "Proteus" too a concentration of colors accompanies his sequence of thought that begins with the picture of the Viking longboats beaching on Sandymount strand and is shifted by the appearance of the dog (which Stephen fears) to historical conflicts, pretenders and usurpers, and courage. Lurking behind the sequence of thought is the figure of Buck Mulligan. The line, "When Malachi wore the Collar of Gold" from the song "Let Erin Remember" brings Mulligan's given name, and the color most often associated with him, into Stephen's stream of thought (3.300-20). In "Telemachus" Stephen had pictured Mulligan as having "even white teeth glistening here and there with gold points. Chrysostomos" (1.25-26). "White" (1.76) and "pale" (1.132) and "fair" (1.186) are associated by Stephen with Mulligan in "Telemachus." White and gold are the colors of the papal flag and they are the colors in *Finnegans Wake* of Shaun, the self-proclaimed champion of churchly authority, public morality and paternalistic tyranny. Mulligan, though in private a mocker and a cynic, is well on his way to gaining the world's approval as a successful professional and public figure. Like Shaun in the *Wake* he is the fairhaired boy and the golden wonder of the ignorant populace. Mulligan is at Oxford and it is interesting that his whites/pales extend to his English friends—the "pale" Haines (1.573) and the other "Palefaces" (1.166). England itself is also white, in its ancient name of Albion, and, in the abuses poured on England by the "patriots" in Barney Kiernan's, white figures prominently as in the citizen's "whitelivered Saxons" (12.1368) and Lenehan's "*Perfide Albion!*" (12.1209). In the scene to which I referred earlier, that of Stephen's thoughts involving Mulligan in "Proteus," "a primrose doublet" crosses Stephen's mind. This is another version of the primrose, or golden yellow, waistcoat which is Mulligan's trademark.[37]

The most important focal points of color in *Ulysses* are Molly and Bloom and the "Sirens" episode. Before examining those, however, I must give some attention to four less important aspects of color in *Ulysses*, the color grey and the colors of the characters Gerty MacDowell, Blazes Boylan and Zoe Higgins. Grey is a color that occurs with high frequency in *Ulysses*,[38] and although there are many seemingly neutral and naturalistically used greys scattered through the novel, the pattern created by two large concentrations of grey affects the reader's responses to all the greys he meets.

The first of these concentrations is in "Hades" and, like the grey in *Dubliners* but not in *A Portrait*, its chief association is with death. John O'Connell, the "Charon" of Glasnevin cemetery, is given three greys (6.744-46). Bloom's thoughts in "Hades" have a number of seemingly unconnected and accidental greys such as the statue of Sir John Gray (6.258), Mr. Power's hair (6.242) and his own grey suit (6.830). He thinks of Paddy Dignam's face, grey in death, transformed from its alcoholic red (6.243), an image that recurs in "Circe" when the beagle appears to Bloom with "the grey scorbutic face of Paddy Dignam" (15.1204-05). But the most striking and dominating grey in "Hades" is that of the grandfather rat Bloom sees (6.973-76). Bloom remembers the image in "Aeolus": "and that old grey rat tearing to get in" (7.83), and again in "Circe" (15.1256-57). The image could have a certain ambiguity in that it represents life at its fiercest growing violently out of death. But for Bloom, and for the reader, it is a powerful and entirely negative image both of death as destroyer of the living flesh, and savage life representing the kind of violence that Bloom rejects throughout the day in whatever form he meets it.

The "Hades" greys are, however, less ugly than those of "Calypso." These occur in a cluster in Bloom's thought and the passage needs to be quoted for the full impact of the greys to be felt:

> A cloud began to cover the sun slowly, wholly. Grey. Far.
> No, not like that. A barren land, bare waste. Vulcanic lake, the dead sea: no fish, weedless, sunk deep in the earth. No wind could lift those waves, grey metal, poisonous foggy waters. Brimstone they called it raining down: the cities of the plain: Sodom, Gomorrah, Edom. All dead names. A dead sea in a dead land, grey and old. Old now. It bore the oldest, the first race. A bent hag crossed from Cassidy's clutching a naggin bottle by the neck. The oldest people. Wandered far away over all the earth, captivity to captivity, multiplying, dying, being born everywhere. It lay there now. Now it could bear no more. Dead: an old woman's: the grey sunken cunt of the world.
> Desolation.
> Grey horror seared his flesh. (4.218-30).

The rarity in Bloom's thoughts of an obscene word gives the obscenity here a horrifying impact. And the identification of barrenness, greyness and aging with death chills the reader's blood as it does Bloom's. It echoes in other seemingly innocuous greys in the novel: the appearance to Stephen in "Circe" of his dead mother "*in leper grey*" (15.4157-58); Stephen's appearance just before he smashes the chandelier, "*his features drawn grey and old*" (15.4223); the "twisted grey garter looped round a stocking: rumpled, shiny sole" which Bloom observes in the bedroom in "Calypso" (4.322-23); the evening hours as girls in grey imagined by Bloom in "Calypso" (4.534-36) and "Circe" (15.4075-78); the greys associated with Mrs. Keogh, the brothel cook in "Circe" (15.2923-24); and even Gerty's sentimental greys in "Nausicaa" (13.199, 211).

After Molly Bloom, the most colorful characters in *Ulysses* are Blazes Boylan, Gerty MacDowell and Zoe Higgins. That the latter two are in a sense surrogates for Molly and that Boylan is as it were a creation of Molly's fantasy for the satisfaction of her strongest sexual desires, which her husband can no longer fulfil, are, I believe, the chief reasons for their colorfulness.

Boylan is a phallus in bunting, a technicolored package of male aggressive sexuality. Marilyn French describes him as one "who lives by sensation rather than emotion."[39] Our apprehension of Boylan is gained almost entirely through Bloom's fleeting thoughts repressed as soon as they emerge and Molly's erotic musings. As a result all we remember of him is a blaze of colors and a rampant erection. He does not exist as a human being, but like a pornographic centerfold he is a set of garishly colored genitalia with a person only vaguely and distantly attached. Every appearance Boylan makes is indicated by a flash of one of his colorful garments. Bloom's first glimpse of Boylan on June 16 occurs during Dignam's funeral when Mr. Dedalus salutes someone from the carriage window: "From the door of the Red Bank the white disk of a straw hat flashed reply..." (6.198-99). Of the eight occurrences in *Ulysses* of the word "tan" six refer to Boylan's new shoes. His indigo suit is mentioned twice—Molly remembers it as blue (18.420). His blue socks, or at least his socks adorned with blue clocks and his blue-ribboned hat are frequently our only evidence of his presence. In "Wandering Rocks" Boylan practically offers himself to the viceregal party as a sexual sacrifice in gift-wrapping:

> By the provost's wall came jauntily Blazes Boylan, stepping in tan shoes and socks with skyblue clocks to the refrain of *My girl's a Yorkshire girl*. Blazes Boylan presented to the leaders' skyblue frontlets and high action a skyblue tie, a wide-brimmed straw hat at a rakish angle and a suit of indigo serge. His hands in his jacket pockets forgot to salute but he offered to the three ladies the bold admiration of his eyes and the red flower between his lips. (10.1240-46)

Seen as a dandy by his fellow *Dubliners*, Boylan, with his tan shoes, blue socks and tie, indigo suit, white hat with a blue ribbon, red flower and presumably red hair, is in fact a garish monument to bad color sense and bad taste. If we feel sympathy for some of the Dubliners who are pressed down by grinding poverty, here is our shining example of the kind of transformation that a little ill-gotten money can bring about. Here he is in the Ormond Hotel bar provoking Lydia Douce's garter-snapping: "Boylan, eyed, eyed. Tossed to fat lips his chalice, drank off his chalice tiny, sucking the last fat violet syrupy drops" (11.419-20).

Boylan's color is red, the red of engorged genitalia, sometimes set in contrast with white or pale or blond, as in Bloom's first glimpse of his white hat at the Red Bank restaurant. Oysters traditionally are an aphrodisiac and a symbol of male potency. The association of Red Bank oysters with the man who will cuckold him, the "worst man in Dublin" (6.202), echoes in Bloom's mind throughout the day. One of Molly's recollections of her coupling with Boylan runs:

> He must have come 3 or 4 times with that tremendous big red brute of a thing he has I thought the vein or whatever the dickens they call it was going to burst ... like iron or some kind of a thick crowbar standing all the time he must have eaten oysters I think a few dozen.... (18.143-49)

Presumably, Boylan got his nickname "Blazes" from the color of his hair, and in "Circe" one of Bello's taunts to Bloom is an image of Boylan tupping Molly with "a shock of red hair he has sticking out of him behind like a furzebush!" (15.3141-42). In "Circe" too there is a suggestion of Boylan and cuckoldry in Virag's comment, "Redbank oysters will shortly be upon us" (15.2437-38), and the comment provokes Bloom to thoughts of the promiscuity of woman. And yet it is the phallic-aggressive, unfeeling maleness symbolized by the Redbank oysters that helps Bloom, I believe, to come to terms with the fact of Boylan. It is interesting that another version of the unfeeling masculine violence rejected by Bloom is epitomized in this action in "Cyclops": "The citizen said nothing only cleared the spit out of his gullet and, gob, he spat a Red bank oyster out of him right in the corner" (12.1432-33).

The *locus classicus* of Boylan's red/sexuality counterpointed with white, or in this case, blond, is the scene in Thornton's shop where Boylan buys the fruit for Molly (10.299-336). The blond shopgirl is identified with the ripe and juicy fruit she packs. Like any well-favored woman Boylan encounters she becomes the immediate object of his ogling. As she bends over the "fat pears and blushing peaches" Boylan stares in her blouse at the fat pears and blushing peaches of her bosom, as he holds the red carnation he has appropriated, "the stalk of the red flower between his smiling teeth." The red Boylan phallus stalks the blond, ripe woman. The carnation has lost its fragile beauty and become a weapon of assault, "some kind of thick crowbar" in Molly's words.

"Nausicaa" is a splash of colors, reaching a concentration at the fireworks display—and Bloom's orgasm. Almost all the colors other than those of the fireworks have to do with the complexion and clothes that Gerty is so absorbed in: the brown of her hair, the whiteness of her skin and the colors of the ribbons for her underwear. A great deal of flushing and blushing and crimsoning goes on, due not surprisingly to Gerty's nicety and also to the heightened emotions: "Her woman's instinct told her that she had raised the devil in him and at the thought a burning scarlet swept from throat to brow till the lovely color of her face became a glorious rose" (13.517-20). The sexual connotations of "red" and "rose" in other parts of the novel underscore the real import of Gerty's reds, the sexual arousal which she cloaks from herself in a fog of romantic-conventional clichés.

Gerty's dominant colors are blue and white, the colors of the Virgin. We already know Bloom's notion of woman's white garments, that they are an invitation to defilement, and his interpretation of the Virgin's blue and white matches this. Here he is musing in "Sirens": "Bluerobed, white under, come to me. God they believe she is: or goddess . . . . That brings those rakes of fellows in: her white" (11.151-55). I have already examined Gerty's white in my discussion of white/woman/sexuality. Her blues are not as blatantly sexual but they are all involved with her narcissistic preoccupation with her clothes and her complexion—we may recall that the only other pattern of blues we have encountered is Boylan's. Gerty is the eternal coquettish virgin, in vulgar terms, the "cockteaser."

Zoe Higgins may appear to be a relatively minor figure in "Circe" but the strong pattern of color concentrations associated with her suggests that she is of considerable importance. She is first introduced thus: "*Zoe Higgins, a young whore in a sapphire slip, closed with three bronze buckles, a slim black velvet fillet round her throat*" (15.1279-80). Her eyes are tawny, her lips smeared with rosewater and she has "*little goldstopped teeth*" (15.1318-39). It is in contemplation of Zoe's dress and body that Bloom imagines the exotic "gazelle" scene with its "*womancity, nude, white, still, cool, in luxury*" (15.1324-30). Zoe draws together a great many colors from other personages and scenes in the novel. She is the only woman to whom both Bloom and Stephen relate. Stephen dances with her ever faster and faster as he reaches the point of release from his ghosts, the smashing of the chandelier. She almost coaxes Bloom into having normal sexual intercourse with her. Her name, in Greek, means "life."

Zoe is in strong contrast to the nymph, "*eyeless in nun's white habit*" (15.3434) who prates of her virtue and innocence but from whom when "*her plaster cast*" cracks "*a cloud of stench*" escapes (15.3469-70). What draws Bloom to Zoe is "*the odour of her armpits, the vice of her painted eyes, the rustle of her slip in whose sinuous folds lurks the lion reek of all the male brutes that have possessed her*" (15.2015-17). In his relationship with Zoe, Bloom is facing the fact of Molly's infidelity and exploring the distinction between outward and conventional morality (the nymph) and deeper truth. Zoe has an almost symbiotic relationship with light, color and music. Twice she turns up the gas jet, banishing darkness (15.2063-64; 2281-82). The light and color dwell on her body: as she turns in the sapphire slip, "*Blue fluid again flows over her flesh*" (15.2301). She shows "*the brown tufts of her armpits*" and the flesh of her thighs "*appears under the sapphire a nixie's green*" (15.2290, 2291-92). The chocolate she offers Bloom prompts him to a confused (or merely confusing) reverie on woman and color (15.2736-40). It is

Zoe who starts the pianola to music and "*Gold, pink and violet lights*" to which the colorful morning and evening hours appear and dance and the furious climactic dance of Zoe and Stephen is carried out (15.4016). Richly associated with light and color and life, Zoe triggers Stephen's blow to the chandelier, the symbolic act by which he exorcises the paralyzing, life-denying demands of his mother's ghost.

The most obvious manipulation of colors in *Ulysses* for most readers is the play with bronze and gold in "Sirens." By my count, of the ninety-five occurrences of gold (and its variants such as golden, goldskinned) in the novel, thirty-nine refer to Mina Kennedy, while of the fifty occurrences of bronze, forty-four refer to the other barmaid, Lydia Douce. The reiteration of bronze and gold has one set of effects that relate primarily to sound and the musical aspect of the episode. Not only are we continually reminded of the instruments that make up the brass section of the orchestra but, as well, the metallic ringing of gold and bronze echoes in our ears with other metallic/musical patterns such as the jingling of Boylan's sidecar (and Molly's bed), the "ringing steel" of "the viceregal hoofs," and the "peal after peal" of laughter and bells. But there is another kind of effect more closely connected with the color connotation of gold and bronze, namely the part they play in the narrator's attitude towards the barmaids and in the reader's ability to distance himself from that narrator. Marilyn French is, I believe, accurate in the main in her analysis of the "Sirens" narrator's derision of the barmaids:

> the narrator's lyrical language satirizes all the characters... a lyrical style that utilizes word play and many verse techniques such as repetition, alliteration, onomatopoeia, inverted word order (anastrophe), anthimeria, and synechdoche and metonymy. It works in a number of ways. By playing with language, it diminishes the importance of what is described. By playing with what is described it mocks it.[40]

Although Bloom thinks "bronze" and "gold" a few times during the singing, he does not use them in a derisive way—that belongs entirely to the usage of the narrator. Colors with classical and heraldic dignity of their own, bronze and gold become derisive of the barmaids through the kinds of techniques indicated by Marilyn French. By synechdoche the barmaids are reduced to the color of their hair and become nonpersons: "Bronze by gold heard the hoofirons..." (11.1); "Shrill, with deep laughter, after, gold after bronze, they urged each each to peal after peal..." (11.174-75): "Gold by bronze heard iron steel" (11.549-50); "gold by the beerpull, bronze by maraschino..." (11.516-17); "Bronze gazed far sideways" (11.1046). By combining bronze and gold into playful and fatuous neologisms the girls are made to appear mere sexy favors among the bar's appurtenances: "peepofgold" (11.10); "Bronzelydia by Minagold" (11.48), "bronze gigglegold" (11.159), "goldbronze voices" (11.158), "girlgold" (11.246);

"Shebronze" (11.365). The continual repetition of the two words and their wordplay forms part of the set of signals that eventually alert the reader to the malevolence of the narrator. Again, Marilyn French has caught this incisively:

> The narrator's position is so extreme that the reader is forced to rebel against it. By word play and artifice, the narrator diminishes what can be called static emotions—those that do not move outward toward an object, as sex and aggression, but must be kept contained, emotions like sorrow, loneliness, self-pity, fruitless yearning, and general undirected sensuality. The narrator implies that these feelings are ludicrous..., that their objects are meretricious.[41]

The rose which Lydia Douce wears is also used by the narrator to ridicule her and the men who watch her lecherously during the singing. The chief tactic here is the play between the two meanings of "rose," the flower and the past tense of rise. As Lydia listens to the song the men watch the rise and fall of rose and bosom: "A jumping rose on satiny breast of satin, rose of Castile" (11.8); "Bronzedouce, communing with her rose that sank and rose, sought Blaze's Boylan's flower and eyes" (11.398-99). Bloom's thoughts mirror initially the play on rose-rose made by the narrator but where the narrator displays a viciousness of contempt, Bloom displays compassion. This is the low point of Bloom's day. Suzette Henke explains:

> At no other point in his odyssey does Bloom suffer such anguish. Molly's adultery is imminent.... Once again Bloom confronts the whirlpool. Frustrated and helpless, he clutches at sentimental reminiscence only to recognize its futility.... Once again Bloom "snaps back" from sentimental reverie to the phenomenal world present at hand. He escapes the siren temptations of grief, vengeance and despair.[42]

For Bloom, as for the reader, Lydia Douce's "rose" has resonations unknown to the narrator. Lenehan's punning riddle on "Rose of Castile" must, because of its womanly, operatic and Spanish connections, bring Molly to Bloom's mind. Lydia and her rose are woman and as partakers in the universal human pain, must be sympathized with—and forgiven:

> Poor Mrs Purefoy. Hope she's over. Because their wombs.
> A liquid of womb of woman eyeball gazed under a fence of lashes, calmly, hearing.... At each slow satiny heaving bosom's wave (her heaving embon) red rose rose slowly sank red rose. Heartbeats: her breath: breath that is life.... And all the tiny tiny fernfoils trembled of maidenhair. (11.1102-1108)

The connection made initially by Mina Kennedy, but also by Bloom with the song "The Last Rose of Summer" (11.1178), points to Bloom as the last of his line. Where the singing group of men indulges in sentimentality, Bloom indulges in forgiveness, of himself, of Molly, of the race. He then turns briskly to what Suzette Henke calls (above) "the phenomenal world present at hand."

The strongest patterns of color association we find in reading *Ulysses* are those surrounding woman and most of the information comes from Bloom's thoughts. On two occasions he speculates directly on the relationship of colors to women. In "Circe" he thinks: "Confused light confuses memory. Red influences lupus. Colors affect women's characters, any they have. This black makes me sad.... Influence taste too, mauve" (15.2737-40). Obviously Bloom's feeling for color goes far beyond superficial appearance and his thoughts on color here and on other occasions tend to become multisensory in their associations and finally synaesthetic. Also worthy of note here is his quick identification with the woman's feelings. Color plays a part in his working out of the proper mixture of masculine and feminine traits appropriate to his nature and true feelings. In "Nausicaa" after Gerty has left the beach a whiff of her lingering perfume starts him on a typical sequence of quasi-scientific speculations linking women, smell and color. Of woman-smell he thinks:

> It's like a fine fine veil or web they have all over the skin, fine like what do you call it gossamer and they're always spinning it out of them, fine as anything like rainbow colours without knowing it. Clings to everything she takes off. Vamp of her stockings. Warm shoe. Stays. Drawers: little kick, taking them off. (13.1019-23)

Bloom's synaesthetic tendency with colors is evident again here. The central feature of his thoughts on colors is the image of woman in her sexual aspect. And for Bloom, woman is first and last Molly.

Molly Bloom is a very colorful character in the literal sense, and this is largely due to her own and her husband's preoccupation with Molly's clothes and appearance and the fact that they both fasten on the color aspect of things. She seems to love almost all colors—but she has no greens, pinks, purples, bronzes, or silvers, and very few blues—among the women of *Ulysses* the Virgin's color is appropriated by Gerty and Milly, and to a lesser extent by Zoe.

From Bloom's and Molly's thoughts, and some narrational observations as well, we are consciously aware of color details of Molly's person and clothes and surroundings not only on June 16, 1904, but of those occasions in her life which comprise her most important memories. We know that she wore grey garters on June 15 and that part of her dress for her assignation with Boylan consists of her new violet garters, black stockings and "an accordian underskirt of blue silk moirette" (17.2096). We know that she may shortly receive from Bloom a gift of "violet silk petticoats" (11.190). We know that she has "*large dark eyes and raven hair*" (15.301-302) and that she prides herself on and takes great care of her white skin, and that she thinks of her anus as "my brown part" (18.276, 1522). We know that Molly would like to have "a peachblossom dressing jacket" and "red slippers" (18.1494-97), and that she is likely to get the slippers from Bloom as a gift in the near future since she wears them in his fantasies (13.1240-41; 14.509). We know that she wore yellow at her first meeting with Bloom (11.725-26); when in "Circe" Bloom thinks he is reliving that encounter he realizes his mistake when he recognizes that the colors are wrong—they are Milly's, not Molly's. In "Ithaca" we are told the color of almost every object in the Bloom household. And in "Ithaca" too color plays a part in that marvellous description of Bloom's salute to Molly as he enters the connubial bed: "He kissed the plump mellow yellow smellow melons of her rump, on each plump melonous hemisphere, in their mellow yellow furrow, with obscure prolonged provocative melonsmellonous osculation" (17.2241-43).

From the variegated colors of "Penelope" these stand out: white and red and the association of both with rose. As we have already seen, Molly thinks of woman's sexual attractiveness in terms of white. In "Penelope" she envisages woman's body and clothing as a white rose offered to love. "He was looking at me I had that white blouse on open in the front to encourage him" (18.787-88). The white rose of woman unfolds its petals to the man's admiration and desire. As she fantasizes seducing Stephen she thinks: "Shall I wear a white rose" (18.1553-54) and imagines her home for the occasion: "Id love to have the whole place swimming in roses" (18.1557-58). The rose becomes red at the climax of her monologue: "I was a Flower of the mountain yes when I put the rose in my hair like the Andalusian girls used or shall I wear a red yes" (18.1602-1603). Her vision of the consummation of love mingles red roses and white and constitutes an acceptance and affirmation and celebration of human life in all its complexity and richness and pain. In this she draws together many strands of red and white and rose from the earlier episodes of *Ulysses* and from *A Portrait of the Artist* as well: the academic competition in which Stephen excelled at Clongowes; the small white house and rosegarden he associates with Mercedes; the "white rose" of his devotion to the Virgin after the Belvedere retreat; the "faint flame" on the cheek of the girl in the tide and the "palest rose" of Stephen's feelings after that encounter; the "rose" and "ardent" climax of the composition of the villanelle; and in *Ulysses*: the reds and whites of Boylan's encounter with the girl in Thornton's shop; Gerty's alabaster whites and telltale blushes; the roses in "Sirens"; and in "Circe" Bloom's "womancity, nude, white," with "damask roses."

Once could argue from evidence in the examples I have quoted in my discussion of colors in *A Portrait of the Artist* and *Ulysses* that there is a counterpoint of sexual reds and whites in Joyce's works, that, for instance, red is the aggressive, violating male and white the unsullied virgin, or that white is sexual attractiveness and red sexual consummation. That such patterns exist is undeniable but to conclude that Joyce portrays any aspect of life as a nicely balanced antithesis would be wrong. The sexual reds and whites mingle as often as they counterpoint and even a white rose carries within it a hint of "rose color" or red. And *Ulysses* contains images of red and white which neither balance nor merge and which fail to fit into the sexual or any other large pattern of colors. Hely's "sandwich-men" constitute a good example. They are white-smocked and white-hatted; they wear red sashes and the letters on their hats are red. Rather like the four old men and their donkey in *Finnegans Wake*, Hely's men traipse in their depressingly futile way in and out of the pages of *Ulysses*.[43] They seem like the red and white corpuscles of Dublin's tired lifeblood flowing sluggishly through the streets' veins. Instead of portraying life in crisp, categorical, black-and-white polarities Joyce in *Ulysses* portrays it through red and white pairings in which the antithetical and complementary relations of the colors are not readily identifiable or quantifiable.

The color patterns I have traced in *Dubliners*, *A Portrait of the Artist as a Young Man* and *Ulysses* are, in my judgment, of obvious importance in contributing to the meanings of those works. The patterns of color are most prominently in evidence in connection with the inner struggles of the protagonists and their mingling and clashing constitute a measure of the difficulty of clearly perceiving the terms of those struggles, a difficulty experienced by both the protagonist in question and the reader of the work. This functioning of color patterns is especially significant in the protagonists' ambivalent response to woman, the ambivalence that epitomizes the conflicts within the male psyche. It would be surprising indeed if in that book of dream, *Finnegans Wake*, similar functioning of color patterns did not attend the agonies of the dreamer fearing and wanting to face the repressed conflicts emerging from his unconscious.

2

The Grianblachk Sun of Gan Greyne Eireann: Native vs. Invader

Since even seasoned Wakeans may have difficulty in recalling the contents of a particular chapter or section of the work given merely the number of the book and chapter in question (e.g. I, 1) I shall identify chapters referred to through the remainder of this study by both numbers and some readily recognized event or piece of content from the chapter in question. Thus I shall identify I, 1 as the "Museyroom" or "Mutt and Jute" or "Prankquean" chapter and II, 3 as the "First Pub Scene" or "Norwegian Captain" or "Butt and Taff" or "Russian general" chapter.

The necessity for my making the above arrangements points to the most striking characteristic of *Finnegans Wake*, its obscurity, even after four and a half decades of reading and criticism. The roots of that obscurity and of the resulting confusion and frustration can be traced in Joyce's methods, I believe, all the way back to the ambiguities of the ending of "The Dead." The gradual shift in Joyce's methods and strategies are described in Michael Groden's *Ulysses in Progress* and are ascribed by Groden to the changes in Joyce's artistic goals: "His artistic goals changed to such an extent that a book that in some aspects began as a sequel to *A Portrait of the Artist as a Young Man* ended as a prelude to *Finnegans Wake*."[1] Groden details the effects of this change in the process of composition of *Ulysses* and shows that it resulted in a book with "many provocative dualisms."[2] Paraphrasing Arnold Goldman's argument, and quoting some of his terminology, Groden writes:

> The human drama of the opening episodes is gradually replaced by a "drama of the alternatives," the various methods of presentation; thus the roles of realism and symbolism, the problematic relationship of *Ulysses* to the *Odyssey*, and the book's ending all partake of a "radical ambiguity" that Joyce built into the book and that itself, rather than any one of the alternatives, constitutes the book's ultimate meaning. "We do not wish to strike through the mask to discover which of the alternatives is right, we wish to enjoy the drama of the alternatives."[3]

In Groden's view many critics have been unable or unwilling to face the "radical ambiguity" that Goldman glories in. As a result: "A prominent critical approach to the problem of *Ulysses*' dual tendencies has been to subordinate one aspect to the other."[4] He cites Stuart Gilbert and S. L. Goldberg as exemplars of the polar positions: "For Gilbert, Joyce only began to write *Ulysses* in 1919, but for Goldberg he should have stopped (with few exceptions) after 1918."[5]

When we turn to *Finnegans Wake* it would seem on the face of it that the tendency to polarity and exclusivity Groden finds in Ulyssean criticism could not occur. Since, stylistically, *Finnegans Wake* starts well beyond the point at which "Circe" leaves off, the Goldbergians simply have no "novel" to write about. Instead of a "radical ambiguity," here is a multitudinous conglomeration of simultaneous meanings that cannot be ignored. And this is to a degree the case. Some early champions of *Ulysses* had only puzzled frowns or dismissive expletives for the *Wake*. On the other hand the writers of the essays in *Our Exagmination Round his Factification for Incamination of Work in Progress* embraced with missionary fervor the puzzling, revolutionary, mythic, symbolic aspects of the work as if it had soared out of the body of English literature and become *sui generis*. I note that the blurb on the back cover of my Viking paperback edition of *Finnegans Wake* uses a telling quotation from the *Skeleton Key*:

> *Finnegans Wake* "is a mighty allegory of the fall and redemption of mankind...a compound of fable, symphony and nightmare.... Its mechanics resemble those of a dream, a dream which has freed the author from the necessities of common logic and has enabled him to compress all periods of history, all phases of individual and racial development, into a circular design, of which every part is beginning, middle, and end."[6]

Nevertheless an odd kind of reflection of the polarity Groden finds among some critics of *Ulysses* has also become evident in Wakean criticism over the past four decades. The apocalyptic kind of approach I have cited above has been more than balanced by "novelistic" approaches. Margot Norris probably overstates her case and certainly exhibits her party bias when she claims that Wakean critics divide into conservative and radical groups, that the conservatives "have dominated *Wake* criticism for the past thirty years [as of 1976]" and that their "approaching the work as a novel" has imposed formidable restrictions on what they could accomplish.[7] But she makes some telling points, as when she writes:

> Even the recently published *A Conceptual Guide to "Finnegans Wake,"* which aims at a comprehensive study of the work, embraces this conservative tradition by approaching the work as a novel: "along with the problem for the reader of deciphering Joyce's language goes the stumbling block of figuring out the narrative or the plot."[8]

Unquestionably there has been a paramount need for a great deal of fairly traditional grubbing about in the published text and the archival materials of *Finnegans Wake* to produce the close explication of individual passages, the careful tabulation of foreign words and the identification of hidden allusions which has gone on during the last two decades and without which valuable studies such as Norris's could not have been written—as indeed Norris would be first to admit.[9] At the same time it must be said that most of the decidedly "novelistic" studies and "novelistic" facets of studies have led only into blind alleys. I have in mind such efforts as these: Adaline Glasheen's more extreme attempts to separate characters, e.g., distinctions between Issy and her mirror image, or between the two legendary Iseults;[10] attempts at tracing a narrative sequence of events through some chapters or parts of chapters; attempts to pin down an exact date (such as June 16, 1904) on which the "dream" of the *Wake* might be supposed to have taken place,[11] or to fix precisely the identity of the dreamer or to settle once for all the historical significance of 1132 A.D. It is my impression that such extreme examples of the novelistic approach have dwindled rapidly in number over the past decade. On the other hand the recently published *Understanding* Finnegans Wake which attempts once more to follow the "narrative" of the *Wake* does have valuable observations to make since it utilizes skilfully so many of the detailed identifications made over the last couple of decades.[12]

In my judgment, however, the kinds of critical approaches which have been most successful in reaching towards comprehensive conceptualizations of the *Wake* are those which have chosen large thematic facets of the book as points of focus and been highly eclectic and selective in utilizing critical methods which the ramifications of their points of focus seemed to call for. The outstanding example of such studies, I believe, is Patrick A. McCarthy's *The Riddles of* Finnegans Wake.[13] An earlier more doctrinaire example is Margaret Solomon's *Eternal Geomater*.[14] Other instances on a smaller scale appear in the various centennial collections of essays. I should add that some very recent studies from more radically oriented critics such as John Paul Riquelme appear to be beginning at last to elucidate the complex functions and problems of the reader of *Finnegans Wake*.[15]

Despite the accumulation of Wakean exegesis over the past four and a half decades the problems facing the would-be reader of *Finnegans Wake* remain formidable. First of all, and I intend this statement literally, *Finnegans Wake* cannot really be read but only reread.[16] Even if a prospective reader owns the motivation and tenacity of the "ideal reader," says Roland McHugh, and wades as McHugh did through the *Wake*, word by word, line by line, page by page, from front cover to back, without peeking ahead and without consulting a commentary, the work he has "read" is so radically different from the work he begins to apprehend when he starts to reread that the two can scarcely be regarded as the same work. I shall attempt now to outline the features of *Finnegans Wake* that cause it to be comparatively so inaccessible to any but the most dedicated readers.

Through the long years of writing *Finnegans Wake* Joyce managed to keep its title secret since it contains in microcosm the major concerns and themes of the work. These radiate outward in widening circles of details and specificity like the spreading ripples on a disturbed pond, through the opening paragraphs, the first chapter and the whole work, to be brought back again by Anna Livia's final monologue to her husband, the title, and the first page. The first syllable of the title is a color word, *finn* being fair or blond or white in Irish. Finn is also the great Finn MacCumhaill or Finn MacCool of Irish mythology, "the hero of much medieval and early modern Irish story-telling and song. His name comes from Celtic *Vindos* (which gives Welsh Gwyn and the Gaulish god-name Vindonnus) and means 'fair, bright.' "[17] The important aspects of the Finn mythology, as far as readers of *Finnegans Wake* are concerned, are these: firstly, as an old man he loved a young woman, Grainne or Grace, who rejected him for a younger man, Dermot; secondly he gained his wisdom from a salmon; and, thirdly, he was supposed to be not dead but sleeping, ready to wake and defend Ireland in her hour of need. One meaning of Joyce's title therefore is the waking again or resurrection of the god-hero Finn to save Ireland. And since the title lacks the possessive apostrophe it can be read as an exhortation to Finn or to the dormant creative energies deep within the human psyche to arise and save man's soul or sanity. The additional fact that *fin* means man in Shelta, one of the underground languages of Ireland which Joyce frequently employs in the *Wake*, broadens the sense from the human individual to the human universal.

Finnegan is the eponymous hero of the Irish-American ballad "Finnegan's Wake," the builder's laborer who fell from a ladder to his seeming death but was revived at his wake by an accidental baptism of whiskey. In the ballad, and of course in Joyce's title, Wake is both death and resurrection. And since *fin* is French for ending, both beginning and ending are present; the title begins with an ending and ends with a beginning. Wake is also a homonym for "weak" in certain Anglo-Irish dialects and thus asserts the weakness and proneness to falling of man. The two central syllables of the title, "-egan," suggest "again" and thus the cyclical, repetitive nature of man's experience despite the vagaries of local or temporal circumstance; they are also very close to some Anglo-Irish pronunciations of "against" as in "agin the government," thus constituting in Joyce's title an opposition between the sleeper and his death-resurrection. The title then begins with a fairhaired hero or a construction worker (man as builder and creator and procreator) or simply a man and ends with a death or a rebirth. It is a clarion call to the people of the world to rouse themselves from the sleep of history and an assertion of the weaknesses and inevitable falls of the human race. Since the sleeper opposes his own resurrection he is divided against himself from the start; contradiction, conflict and paradox are essentials of the psyche and so also is a terrible drive towards individuation and resolution and definition—and towards building and creating and procreating. The grown man is like the embryo which, to attain wholeness, must begin with the juncture of two disparate elements and then grow by a process of continued splitting and sundering.

The paradoxical essence of human nature as the *Wake* presents it is also implied in the book's title in this way: it consists of a principle, its other or opposite and the tension that forever thrusts them together and apart: "*Shem and Shaun and the shame that sunders em*" (526.14). Here also in the four syllables of the title is man's Viconian history, three phases and a *recorso*. In addition the title exhibits a characteristic which I find is central to Joyce's method in *Finnegans Wake* and which I shall have frequent occasion to discuss with regard to the functioning of color patterns, namely the subversion of the equilibrium of antithesis. "Fin-" or ending balances "Wake" or beginning in a symmetrical antithesis. But "Wake," being also associated with death or ending, contains within it a qualification or contradiction which upsets the stability of the balance and suggests the inevitable untrustworthiness of man's resort to opposites, distinctions, categories, as a way of ordering. The inescapable drive in the human psyche towards unity and wholeness will have begun to sabotage such category systems from their beginnings. This drive, though healthy and "normal," is also capable of tremendous destruction as Joyce demonstrates in the *Wake* through his depiction of the drive's most dramatic embodiment, sexuality.

John Paul Riquelme finds the "aftermath" meaning of Wake in Joyce's title to be significant. Citing the phrase "as punical as finicin" (32.06) he identifies Finnegan with Punic or Phoenician and the book itself with the "Punic Admiralty Report" and therefore with the *Odyssey* and *Ulysses*. He continues:

> Joyce's title implies broadly that every act of writing reawakens earlier texts, including the author's own.... Each author necessarily follows in the wake of earlier authors and texts, and in his own wake.... The book constitutes a wake for the dead, for itself, for its author, and for the literature it resurrects only to bury, and buries only to resurrect from the midden of letters.[18]

Riquelme posits quite convincingly an adumbration at least in Joyce's title of the following themes and techniques of the work: the polyvalent pun; the Homeric connection between title, pun, hero and quest; the destructive acts the writer must commit on literature, his book and himself to bring his work to birth; the analogous quest the reader must undertake to come to grips with *Finnegans Wake*.

If I may regress for a moment, my own earlier discussion argued the presence in the title of these important concerns of the work: life, death and resurrection; the cyclical nature of man's experience and its universality across space and time; man's fateful quarrel with himself which leads to sexuality and to guilt; the inevitable cycle of weakness/fall and resurrection/triumph; man's unending quest for reconcilation and wholeness, again most dramatically embodied in his sexual drive; the instability of all antitheses and category systems by which man attempts to order his experience.

The single most important source for the structure of *Finnegans Wake* is undoubtedly the psychology of dreams, more specifically one book, Freud's *The Interpretation of Dreams*. The connections between the two books are so strong and so ubiquitous that when one goes from *Finnegans Wake* to Freud's book sentence after sentence in the latter read as if they were written to describe not the nature of the dream but the nature of the *Wake*:

> Generally speaking, words are often treated in dreams as things, and therefore undergo the same combinations as the ideas of things. The results of such dreams are radical and bizarre word-formations.[19]

> In view of the part played by witticisms, puns, quotations, songs and proverbs in the intellectual life of educated persons, it would be entirely in accordance with our expectations to find disguises of this sort used with extreme frequency in the representation of dream-thoughts.[20]

> A word, as the point of junction of a number of ideas, possesses, as it were, a predestined ambiguity.... Generally speaking, in the interpretation of any element of a dream it is doubtful whether it (a) is to be accepted in the negative or positive sense (contrast relation); (b) is to be interpreted historically (as a memory); (c) is symbolic; or whether (d) its valuation is to be based upon its wording.[21]

If we change the "or whether" to "and" to suggest all of those interpretations as simultaneously valid, then Freud's observation becomes an accurate description of *Finnegans Wake*.

At another point in the book Freud identifies one of the peculiarities of memory in dreams, "that it makes a selection in accordance with principles other than those governing our waking memory, in that it recalls not essential and important, but subordinate and disregarded things."[22] And Freud makes a comment which is of central importance to the contents of the *Wake:* "Dreams which are apparently guileless turn out to be the reverse of innocent if one takes the trouble to interpret them."[23]

For students of *Finnegans Wake* every statement of Freud's I have quoted has a ring of utter familiarity and requires no elaboration. But there is more. In his lengthy chapter 6, "The Dream Work," Freud explains distortion in dreams and the two chief ways in which it is brought about, namely, "displacement" and "condensation." There is no sufficiently brief summative description that I can find in Freud's book for either of the two so I shall quote instead an excellent description of displacement from Rose and O'Hanlon:

> Displacement owes its existence to the censorship imposed by the ego upon the unconscious; it is a method of slipping through that censorship. What happens is that some of the thoughts seeking expression in the dream are obnoxious or threatening to the ego.... By replacing the troublesome ideas by related but more innocent thoughts, the censorship ... can be bypassed.... What has been effected is a simultaneous repression and revelation.[24]

Margot Norris quite rightly asserts: "The difference between displacement and condensation is very slight."[25] The difference indeed need not concern us here.

The relevance of these Freudian ideas to Joyce's techniques in creating *Finnegans Wake* is surely incontrovertible. Indeed we must remind ourselves that the *Wake* is not the transcription of a dream but an ordered literary artifact in which every imported material has been transmuted into the stuff of art. We do not just read through the "manifest dream-material" of the *Wake* to get at its "latent" content—for the reader both surface and depth are of equal importance. And as readers within the dream of the *Wake* we still possess all the analytic tools and perceptive abilities denied to the ordinary dreamer and made available only to his analyst in retrospection. The condensations and displacements in Joyce's work do not well up higgledy-piggledy from the unconscious but have been designed and placed to effect the most far-reaching and richest possible web of contacts with other elements scattered through the book. At the same time we must realize that *Finnegans Wake* in approaching the condition of dream has moved a long way from the conventions of the traditional novel. As Margot Norris points out: "Novels are rooted in eighteenth-century empiricist notions of a unitary consciousness, while dreams are disguised messages from a censored unconscious."[26] And: "Whereas the novel requires a prose that stresses semantic precision, the correspondence of words to things, the dream technique in *Finnegans Wake* requires words that are semantically polyvalent and whose meanings are deliberately uncertain."[27]

It is in the language of the work that the prospective reader of the *Wake* meets his first challenge. First there is the distortion to which the usual English word is subjected. Then the reader's predictions are constantly undermined by the substitution of an echo word, malapropism or nonsense word for the word which the semantic and syntactic cueing systems have led him to expect. The integrity of words in the *Wake* is further violated by distortions which tamper with the divisions between them, "why 'tis" for instance or "bequiet horse." Meanings then reside not in the words themselves but in the network of echoing associations with all the other elements in the book that the words trigger in the reader's mind. Roland McHugh writes:

> A *Finnegans Wake* word is not, so far as I am concerned, the same thing as a word in the book you are now reading. It is a solid entity, a weird beautiful crystal, one of whose faces is perhaps identical with a fragment of Thom's *Dublin Directory*, but which in its totality is entirely subservient to the Wakean rules of play.[28]

What is true of the separate words is equally true of phrases, especially those that echo fragments of popular culture such as songlines, nursery rhymes, proverbs and slogans. What the reader must do is hold in suspension in his mind all the possible meanings including the contradictory ones that the text suggests to him. Of one particular sentence in the *Wake* Hugh Kenner writes:

> It is worse than useless to push this towards one or other of the meanings between which it hangs.... It is equally misleading to scan early drafts for the author's intentions on the assumption that a 'meaning' got buried by elaboration. Joyce worked for seventeen years to push the work away from 'meaning,' adrift into language; nothing is to be gained by trying to push it back.[29]

As the reader pursues meaning through the patterns of association the text triggers in his mind he is seduced into rewriting the text as Joyce wrote it, or at least into an analogous set of mental operations that reenact Joyce's composing process. And as he proceeds through the text and builds up his store of those associations that persist in drawing themselves to his attention the larger meanings begin to stand forward.

The most notable feature of the characters of *Finnegans Wake* is their uncertainty and fluidity of identity. One way of dealing with this problem and its resulting confusion for the reader is to attempt to pin down as closely as possible the character-identities of every human figure that appears. This is what Adaline Glasheen has done in her *Census*. Many of the shorter notes that have appeared in *A Wake Newslitter* over the years attempt similar tasks for one character or another. Obviously such work has provided highly useful information for all Wakeans. Yet there comes a point for every reader when such charting of identification reaches the limits of its usefulness and he must accept the "characters" in the *Wake* as different in kind to the traditional characters of fiction.

In the "novelistic" sense the primary characters of *Finnegans Wake* are the five members of one family, the father (HCE), the mother (Anna Livia), the daughter (Issy) and the twin sons (Shem and Shaun). Most of the other characters are projections of or figures cognate with one or more of the five primary characters. These secondary characters are figures drawn from history, literature, mythology, religious tradition and popular culture. But there is little consistency to this schema. Some of the primary characters may merge on occasion and some secondary figures may be associated now with one primary character and now with another. Thus in the "Russian General" chapter (II, 3) the sons appear to merge, and they may at one point merge with the father as well. And Oscar Wilde is frequently associated with the father—each had a great sexual fall—but as martyred writer he is even more frequently a cognate figure of Shem's.

A more useful way to look at the characters in *Finnegans Wake* is to view them in terms of the dream. Thus the central character is the dreamer in whose head everything takes place. That dreamer may be identified with the primary consciousness or point of perception in the book which I see as a loose amalgamation of writer, reader and first character, HCE. All other "characters" are projections that personify the concerns haunting the dreamer's mind. Margot Norris has a succinct account of this notion of Wakean character: "Wakean figures are interchangeable because characters in dreams are fictions created by the dreamer—including fictions of himself. In other words, the dreamer is invested in all of his characters in certain ways."[30] In addition the nature of dream is such that characters come into existence in dream to play out a part of the dream action; the "same" character, if required for a later action, need not be entirely true to his prior appearance. David G. Wright comments: "Joyce-personae [in the *Wake*] form themselves from apparently fragmentary matter, enact a recognizable deed, attitude or mannerism, then disintegrate, only to recur in altered form."[31] Furthermore, the overwhelming power of association in the structure of the *Wake* "bends" the characters as it shapes everything else. The Duke of Wellington provides an example of what I have in mind. He was of course the victor at Waterloo. But Waterloo is popularly remembered as an instance of defeat. So in the Wakean Waterloo Wellington is defeated or falls. And since the name of the battle brings to mind the loose waters that caused HCE's fall in the Park, Wellington's fall at Waterloo becomes a sexual fall. All of these phenomena connect Wellington with HCE. As giant redwood tree or *Sequoia Wellingtonia* and also because of the Wellington monument, the *peannlua mor* or great lead pencil in the Phoenix Park, the Duke represents the phallic authority of the father, HCE. But since these are also tree and stone they associate Wellington with the sons or the warring elements within the father's psyche.

The fall of the father, HCE, is the central event of *Finnegans Wake* and the attempts to find out how his fall actually occurred constitute the rest of the book. His fall involves every human fall—Humpty Dumpty's, Parnell's,

Wilde's, drunkenness, detumescence, depression—and is the source of his guilt and of his fear of the truth of himself, a truth that if uttered may cause him to split or fall apart. This connects HCE's fall with the failures of characters in Joyce's earlier works, the failure to achieve self-knowledge and self-realization in the face of the conflicting demands and limitations of the social environment. In the *Wake* the struggle is an internal one, taking place between the dream personae who reflect the terms of the dreamer's quarrel with himself. The fact that the primary personae of the Wakean dream are all members of the one family suggests that incestuous feelings and their repression are at the heart of the dream action. McCarthy sees the Oedipal riddle as the central myth of the *Wake* and comments:

> Because Oedipus and other riddle-solvers violate the tenuous order of the universe, they may spawn pestilence. On this level, then, it may be seen that in *Finnegans Wake* the dreamer's fascination with riddles parallels his incestuous desires, and that his refusal to answer his own questions represents his attempt to avoid the fate of Oedipus.[32]

At the same time we must remember that the fall in the *Wake* can also be seen as beneficent, as the frequently repeated motif, *felix culpa*, reminds us. Indeed the fall is often seen in the *Wake* as the first act of creation without which all subsequent acts and the phenomenal world and human civilization could not have come into existence.

A sense of guilt is all-pervasive through *Finnegans Wake*. The dreamer and those personae close to him are obsessed with guilt for some vague or rumored sin, for the incident in the Park in fact. The guilt drives them to two activities which constitute most of what "happens" in the *Wake*. Firstly they are preoccupied with the need to find out the facts of the great sin. This pursuit of the truth becomes the quest of the book. Norris writes: "Wakean speakers are ever seeking something, asking questions.... Yet these same postures of inquiry and argumentation, slander, and the like perversely reveal the very information that is sought."[33] Secondly they must project the guilt on to someone else. They do not succeed of course but a great deal of energy is consumed in the laying of blame and verbal abuse. The result is a heightening of the sense of guilt.

The dreamer's guilt is most closely associated with sexuality. *Finnegans Wake* is a very dirty book in the sense that sex, at its crudest, most physical and, frequently, most sordid, is everywhere. The reader must become rapidly sensitive to every possibility of sexual innuendo—he must become like the dreamer and have sex on his mind but he must be much more aware than the dreamer's personae that he does have sex on his mind. Sexuality is deliberately exploited by the author but not for the purposes of titillation—in this as in everything else that could contribute to his art Joyce was uncompromising.

The images that most strongly reinforce the dreamer's sense of guilt are his own genitals, sometimes the penis in a state of erection and sometimes the penis and testicles. The three soldiers who witness HCE's crime in the Park are privates; in fact, as Margaret Solomon points out, "the enemy-accusers are his own genitals."[34] Solomon notes the other, Latin, connection: testis has two meanings, witness and testicle. At another level the three soldiers in the Park are HCE and his twin sons. The publication of "privates," of the most deeply hidden and most humanly universal energies in the dreamer's psyche, is a central ongoing activity of *Finnegans Wake*. The revelation of HCE's most private and shameful sins of desire, through the metaphor of genital exhibitionism, ironically establishes his common humanity, his oneness with the rest of us.

The female genitalia are also a powerful image in the *Wake*. Most if not all pairs with female connotations or associations, especially of course pairs of women—the two temptresses in the Park, Anna and Kate, Anna and Issy, Issy and her mirror image, Snowwhite and Rosered, rose and lily—can be identified for much of the time with the bilabial female genitalia. This image provokes the dreamer, not so much into heightened awareness of his sexual desires (though it does that too sometimes), as into a recognition of the opportunity to shift guilt and the urgent need to avail himself of that opportunity. He does this in two ways, by positing the woman as active temptress who seduces him into sin (the Genesis ploy) and by hiding his guilty desires under the guise of paternal benevolence and familial love. It is in this latter tactic that his own language most frequently gives him away. And since all the primary characters are members of the same family the most striking feature of HCE's sexual desires is their incestuous nature, most often associated, as Patrick McCarthy points out, with the "insect" motif: "Earwicker's name punning on 'earwig' reveals his 'insectuous' nature."[35]

There is another dimension to the function of sexuality in the *Wake*; it is a metaphor for artistic creation and thus for the writing of the book in which it finds itself. This is to be found in the *Wake* in a rambling, loose and frequently oblique scattering of associations. The sexual fall produces not only tensions and guilt but also civilization, cities—and literature. The shooting of the Russian general is an act at once of parricide, homosexual incest and the union necessary to produce art. Joyce insists on the quotidian nature of the materials from which art must be produced, and the similarities between that production and every other kind of human production. The more sharply physical aspects of procreation and parturition (and defecation) are seen as strictly analogous to the agonies and ecstasies of the writer creating his literary work.

For the reader who has persisted into the labyrinth of *Finnegans Wake* it is probably not the language or fluidity of character identification that provides him with his greatest challenge but the mysterious relationship between author, reader and intervening personae. This characteristic does not of course suddenly appear fully fledged in the *Wake*—its roots can be traced all the way back to the ending of "The Dead." Brook Thomas examines the complexities of the writer-reader relationship in *Ulysses* in an article that draws heavily on Michael Groden's account and analysis of the evolution of the published text of that work.[36] Thomas utilizes current theories of the reading process on which to base his argument and focuses on the retroactive nature of Joyce's method of composition:

> Just as reading is no longer considered merely a passive process, so writing is no longer considered a totally active process.... As we often tell students of composition, writing is a continued process of revision, and as that master of the craft, Henry James, puts it: "To revise is to see, or to look over, again—which means in the case of a written thing neither more nor less than to re-read it."[37]

Thomas goes on to discuss Joyce's seemingly endless process of rereading, revising and adding, and concludes:

> My point is, however, that *Ulysses* has been abandoned only by Joyce, not by its readers. *Ulysses* will never be finished until it is abandoned by its readers, for each time that a reader reads and rereads *Ulysses*, he repeats with a difference the process by which Joyce created the book, thereby helping once more to bring into existence that "world without end." (*Ulysses*, 37.31)[38]

This complexity of reader-writer relationship which Thomas examines as it evolves in *Ulysses* is fully formed from the beginning in *Finnegans Wake* and all of the major features Joyce built into the latter work contribute to forcing the reader into quasi-writing activity as he reads: the deletion of consistently conventional vocabulary, of consistently normal syntax, of familiar narrative sequence and of reliable factuality; the primacy of phonetic and allusive cross-reference and of rumor and gossip; the circularity of the work and of its parts; the fluidity of narrator and character and event. The fluidity of narrator and character are, I believe, of especial importance here since the vacuum of stable identity the reader encounters pushes him into filling it to some degree with his own identity, thus causing him to abandon any detached viewpoint outside the work and thus to partake of the indeterminacy which surrounds narrator, character and, ultimately, writer.

On the other side there is the intrusion of the writer into the work. John Paul Riquelme describes it in this fashion:

> In the *Wake*, Joyce adopts a protean narrating persona. This labile teller describes a character, Shem the Penman, who writes the real author's books. As several passages suggest, these texts are self representations of Shem. Through this curious pseudonymous

fictional presentation of the author as Shem and of Shem as an author in *Finnegans Wake*, Joyce's narrator manipulates the complicated relationships among author, teller and tale with comic intensity.[39]

Riquelme goes on to connect writer with reader through Shem:

> On the one hand, the language of the *Wake* forces us to collaborate with Joyce by rewriting his text as we read it through our actively re-creative response. But more to the point about the specific presentation of Shem in 1.7, *he* is described as *both* reader and author.[40]

Riquelme's argument can readily be supported with evidence from the text, for instance at 179.26–27. Other critics have noted the existence in the book of a posited reader figure who becomes blurred with a writer figure. Manfred Putz distinguishes between this figure and the actual reader and points out the indeterminacy of his identification:

> A reader-figure haunts the pages of the *Wake*—a figure not to be confused with the actual reader, but rather a creation of the author analogous to the author-persona. And this fictitious receiver of messages to whom Joyce repeatedly talks and onto whom he projects certain reactions, is no longer an easily identifiable constant someone.[41]

Putz concludes: "A final consequence of the reader-figure's unstable and continuously shifting identity is that the rigid borderlines between reader and writer break down altogether."[42] Putz cites some specific instances in the language of the *Wake* in which the "rigid borderlines" appear to have been deliberately and pointedly broached: "But how transparingly nontrue, gentlewriter!" (63.9–10), "I can tell you something more than that, drear writer" (476.20–21): and that "letter selfpenned to one's other" (489.33–34).

In one sense this confusion of reader and writer is merely the extreme example of the persistent subversion in the *Wake* of binary opposition. Even flat contradictions when set on the page in black and white imply some degree at least of temporary equilibrium. The observer can as it were rest outside of the book and contemplate with detachment the paradoxes within it. But in the *Wake* clean-cut opposites, and identities, and categories, are deliberately blurred, driving the reader deep into the turmoil of the book and of himself.

When we proceed to examine the color patterns of *Finnegans Wake* we find, as the remainder of this study will demonstrate, that they weave an intricate web of associations through the texture of the work and constitute a significant feature of the battery of techniques employed by Joyce to give uniquely ordered articulation to his themes.

Earlier in this chapter I claimed that the title of the *Wake* contains in microcosm most of the major themes of the work. Through the first page of the text the elaborations of this vision of man radiate outward, preserving always the central kernel of truth stated in the title. Before the end of the first page the ripples have already widened to the point at which we can only focus on a fragment at a time. These opening paragraphs have received much critical attention, from Joyce himself among others, so I shall concentrate here on the patterns of colors through the first page (p. 3).[43]

This page contains a wealth of color words, being, in order of appearance: "violer," "doublin," "bland," "fair," "wroth," "Rot," "arclight," "rory end," "regginbrow," "oranges," "rust," "Green," "devlinsfirst" and "livvy." The first of these occurs in the phrase "Sir Tristram, violer d'amores." "Violer" suggests violet, viola, violent, violate. What Tristan violated was the trust of his uncle King Mark of Cornwall when he made love to the king's betrothed, Isolde of Ireland. The violation/violence is male, colorful, sexual, even incestuous, and committed by an outsider, an invader of Ireland in fact.

From the context it is clear that the next color word, "doublin," is the Dublin in Laurens County, Georgia. The name Dublin comes from the Irish *dubh-linn*, "black pool," the name given to the Viking town on the river Liffey. Dublin, Georgia is itself a double, of Dublin, Ireland, and the spelling "doublin" and the repetition of the Georgia city's motto, "doublin all the time," emphasizes this double, or split, aspect of it. The city, like the human race of which it is the reflection, has a doubling or split or potential conflict built into it from the beginning. That split widens, as it does here, through both time and space.

The next three color words, "bland," "fair," and "wroth," apply to the political rivalry of Parnell and Isaac Butt, and the amorous triangle of Jonathan Swift with Stella and Vanessa. We have already seen in *A Portrait* and *Ulysses* the pairing of red and white associated with sexuality. What better figure than Parnell could be found to illustrate the relationship of sex to politics? As public figures, Parnell and Swift had in common a doubleness, an internal contradiction of personality: Parnell, the revered leader, fell because of his illicit liaison with Kitty O'Shea; Swift, the revered churchman and patriot, had a secret penchant for intimacy with young women. And woman herself symbolizes a very early division of Adam. Red brings us to the rainbow and alcohol, both associated with Noah and his new beginning. Alcohol raises man and causes him to fall. The rainbow is the sign of God's promise and of man's fall. It also marks the point of expansion of themes beyond which we can only perceive fragments; the rainbow after all is an arc, a fragment of a circle. The first of these fragments is manifest in the final cluster of colors on the first page: the strife of the orange and the green.

The scene is "the knock out in the park where oranges have been laid to rust upon the green since devlinsfirst loved livvy" (3.22–24). "Devlinsfirst" is

"Dublin first" and "Dublin's first citizen, HCE." "Livvy" is the heroine ALP, Anna Livia Plurabelle, or the river Liffey. "Livia" has the color connotation livid, or (Latin) *lividus*, both of which denote a bluish-greyish leaden color, or the skin discoloration caused by a bruise. I should add however that popularly "livid" is often taken for angry red, a misinterpretation that, I assume, was equally common in Joyce's day and that Joyce was aware of. The "park" is of course the Phoenix Park with its Castleknock Gate not too far from which the victims of the Park murders were knocked out and HCE suffered his fall. The war of Ulster Protestants ("oranges") with Irish nationalists ("green") are equated with the shenanigans in the Park. The "green" is both Park and Ireland. These "oranges" symbolizing resistance with sword and gun have more to do with "rust" than "rest." This closing paragraph of the first page uses two analogies, the relations between man and woman and the historical strife between Irishman and invader, to pinpoint the central conflict of the novel, that within the human psyche.

E. L. Epstein argues in a recent article that "there are only two characters in the *Wake*, Man and Woman.... Therefore all the men in the book are Man, as all the women... are Woman."⁴⁴ He goes on to cite a passage from the "Inquisition of Yawn":

> —*Three in one, one and three. Shem and Shaun and the shame that sunders em. Wisdom's son, folly's brother.* (526.13–15)

This is the voice of Yawn responding to a query about the park incident. One could legitimately push Epstein's argument a final step: there is only one character in the *Wake*, man, mankind in the generic sense, in the particular sense HCE the dreamer. The drama arises from the splits within the human psyche and the manifestations of those splittings in the personae which populate the dream. Once one split occurs the splitting process is uncontainable. In the *Wake* passage quoted above the duality immediately posits a *tertium quid*. The three soldiers in the Park are three aspects of HCE's psyche, the primary warring elements within him, Shem and Shaun, and the warring relationship itself which both "sunders" them and identifies their "shame" and their sameness. What keeps the psyche from flying apart is its urgent drive to reconstitute and individuate itself. According to some of the more powerful mythologies the earliest sundering of man was the separation of the sexes, described in Genesis as the creation of Eve by the removal of Adam's rib. In *A Portrait* the earliest conflicts faced by Stephen were political and sexual, and the same is true of the opening paragraphs of *Finnegans Wake*.

Kimberly Devlin sees the central struggle of the *Wake* as that of "Self and

Other" and she traces it through certain attitudes of the hero's mind in *A Portrait* as well.[45] Her argument has considerable relevance for my thesis and I shall quote from it at some length:

> In the dream world of *Finnegans Wake*, the psyche imaginatively reconstructs the confrontation between the individual and his external authorities or models. This essential psychic concern emerges in the dream whenever a patently uncivilized figure confronts the civilizer, or in other words, whenever the primal "self" confronts the authoritative "other."...[S]elf and other are no longer easily distinguishable because the figures in a dream are often interchangeable....[46]

Of special relevance to my arguments in this chapter are Devlin's perceptions of Irish nationalism vs. British imperialism, the Irish private soldiers attacking the Russian general, and native vs. invader, as Wakean analogues for this intrapersonal conflict. Here, Devlin considers the fight with the Russian General:

> This imperialistic warfare can be interpreted as another version of the self/other conflict, because it entails a "native" or original personality defending itself against interference from external or "foreign" forces. The goals of socialization and imperialistic conquest, after all, are strangely similar.... Joyce employs the native/invader contest as a metaphorical structure for the battle between the unsocialized self and the civilized "other" throughout the Wakean dream.[47]

One further elaboration by Devlin must be added:

> In the Wakean dream, self and other are superficially represented as disparate figures, but the differences between them are continually collapsing.... An explanation for this paradoxical representation of simultaneous difference and similarity emerges if we take into account censorship, the prime mechanism for distortion in the dream process.[48]

It is my belief that Irish history with its sequence of invasions, assimilations, changes of sides, betrayals, assassinations and braggadocio provided Joyce with a significant metaphor for the struggle of self and other that Devlin describes. That many facets of the historical struggle bear color labels is a fact that Joyce will not fail to exploit in the working out of his theme.

Green is the color of Irish nationalism. It is also one of Joyce's colors of "cecity" or blindness, and Irish green in the *Wake* is consistently associated with difficulties of vision and with self-delusion. The arch-druid Balkelly-Berkeley tells us that High King Leary, as representative Irishman, is green through and through despite his varicolored outward garments and his red hair (pp. 611–12). The irony of the arch-druid's insistence lies partly in the historical fact that the native institutions are about to be defeated by the invader Patrick than whom no person or institution will be more gloriously identified in the popular mind with Irish green. Ireland is "Emerald-illuim" (62.11–12), the green Troy, but Ilium has become "-illuim," tending towards illusion. In the "Inquisition of Yawn" this exchange occurs:

—It is woful in need whatever about anything or allselse under the grianblachk sun of gan greyne Eireann.
—A tricolour ribbon that spells a caution. The old flag, the cold flag.
—The flagstone. By tombs, deep and heavy. To the unaveiling memory of. Peacer the grave. (503.22–27)

The first and third statements here are Yawn's and the central one is made by an inquisitor. Yawn is being questioned about "the Incident in the Park" and he identifies the Park with Ireland, a common enough identification in the *Wake*. The three colors of blindness, black, green and grey, are in evidence; in addition, "grianblachk" includes Irish *grian*, "sun," to make "black sun," and "gan greyne" contains not only "grey" and "gangrene" but Irish *gan ghrian*, "without sun." Echoes of the song "Alive, Alive O," in which the heroine dies of the fever, and "The Memory of the Dead" emphasize the association of Irish flag/flagstone/tombstone. No doubt the ambitions of Peter the Great contributed in his time to the ranks of widows and orphans and helped bring about that peace of the grave which in Irish oral tradition represents the result of *Murcha na dToitean's* reign of terror in Munster during the Elizabethan wars. All in all, blindness, terror, death and putrefaction are seen as the marks of the newly green independent Ireland.

"Gangrene" appears again in the phrase "through their gangrene spentacles" (397.35) in a description of the four old men in "Mamalujo" (II.4). In addition to the connotations of green, putrefaction and absence of sunlight, there is an echo of an incident in Goldsmith's *Vicar of Wakefield* in which the vicar's son, Moses, is duped with a gross of green spectacles in shagreen cases. That echo is reechoed in I.7 (Shem), where the agony of the creative artist is identified: "But with each word that would not pass away the squidself which he had squirtscreened from the crystalline world waned chagreenold and doriangrayer in its dudhud" (186.6–8). The colors of blindness are here too (the black is in the squid's ink) but I think that the dominant image, if only faintly present, is that of the greying and aging Joyce going blind in the service of the illumination his art will give the world.

A colloquial Irish phrase for naivete and lack of perception is to have green in one's eye. We may recall the "Cyclops" narrator's use of the phrase to decry the Jewish businessman: "What? Do you see any green in the white of my eye? Course it was a bloody barney. What? Swindled them all" (*Ulysses*, 12.1088–90). The same speaker uses an associated phrase to pillory the citizen's cunning in cadging drinks: "Gob, he's not as green as he's cabbagelooking. Arsing around from one pub to another" (*Ulysses*,

12.752-53). In "Jaun's Sermon" (III, 2), Dave the dancekerl is portrayed as "Begob, there's not so much green in his Ireland's eye!" (466.34-35). As well as being Irish vision, Ireland's Eye is an island off the coast of north county Dublin. As any visitor can attest whose plane has taken the northeast to southwest approach to Dublin airport, Ireland's Eye is a vivid, almost luminous green, and so, frequently, is the shallow portion of the Irish Sea surrounding it. The contradictions of Shaun's comments on Shem-Dave are even more marked in the comment made of Burrus (the Shaun figure) in I, 6: "That his seeingscraft was that clarety as were the wholeborough of Poutresbourg to be averlaunched over him pitchbatch he could still make out with his augstritch the green moat in Ireland's Eye" (162.29-32). Not only are there two of the colors of blindness present here but further doubts are cast on the vision of Burrus and that of Ireland. Burrus's clarity of vision is "clarety" or boozy, while "augstritch" is, among other things, a bird noted for sticking its head in the sand. The "green moat" is not only the Irish Sea but the "mote" of the Sermon on the Mount, symbol of hypocrisy and wilful blindness.

This blindness associated in the *Wake* with Irish nationalistic green extends to the flag of the new Irish Free State, the green, white and orange tricolor. In "Jaun's Sermon" (III, 2), we find this sentence: "Haul Seton's down, black, green and grey, and hoist Mikealy's whey and sawdust" (441.4-5). The context is the sequence of Shaun's sexual caveats and has to do with marriage, lust, stripping and underclothes. The colors to be hauled down are the colors of blindness. "Mikealy" combines Michael, the archangel, with T. P. Healy, first governor-general of the Free State. The colors of the papal flag are white and gold, close enough to "whey and sawdust." The orange of the Irish tricolor has frequently been confused with gold—I have seen miniature flags being sold on Dublin streets as souvenirs where the orange was replaced by a golden yellow. In other words, all we need to add to the papal flag to get the Irish tricolor is the green already present in the colors of blindness. That Shaun, the self-appointed guardian of civic virtues, should exhort his listeners to flag-proclamation of the new order in which Christ and Caesar will be truly hand in glove is appropriate—supplanting the old blindness with a more colorful and bombastic kind of blindness. It is also appropriate to his character that his exhortation should hint at the lowering and raising of intimate garments for intimate purposes.

The two conflicts which have dominated Irish history for the past four centuries, Irish nationalism vs. British imperialism and Irish nationalism vs. Ulster Protestant Loyalism, green vs. red and green vs. orange, provided Joyce with two suitable analogies for the conflicts that were his real concern, namely the conflicts within the individual psyche. In his self-defense (in II, 3), HCE protests aloud his attachment to all the publicly approved sentiments he can think of, including the slogan (and song title) shouted by the virago near the end of "Circe," the "Green above the red" (*Ulysses*, 15.4517). HCE's protestation carries an ambivalence typical of all absolute statements in the "Wake": "The green approve the raid" (364.8). In "Night Lessons" (II, 2) the popular charge of British duplicity is also undermined, by the improbable claim made for "our side": "Porphyrious Olbion, redcoatliar, we were always wholly rose marines on our side every time" (264.F 3). On another occasion the ambivalence of sentiment is achieved by the failure to distinguish who is which: the sleeping twins are "rosengorge" and "greenafang" and both are "Blech and tin soldiers" or murderous invading Black and Tans (563.30). And the narrator of "Jaun's Sermon" (III, 2) portrays the call of the Irish people to Patrick for conversion to Christianity, that glorious moment in Irish history, as Irish self-abasement to British expediency: "mesaw mestreamed, as the green to the gred was flew, was flown, through deafths of durkness greengrown deeper I heard a voice, the voce of Shaun, vote of the Irish, voise from afar" (407 11–14).

By the time Joyce started writing *Finnegans Wake* British red in Ireland was past history except in the North. Green vs. orange is the more important of the two struggles in the *Wake* and the two struggles are intimately related not only through historical fact but also through their colors. The ancient flag of Ulster is the Red Hand. Matt Gregory, representative of Ulster, speaks of "the rubricated annuals of saint ulstar" (520.34) and displays his native bias: "—Gently, gently, Northern Ire! Love that red hand!" (522.4). But orange is Protestant Ulster's color. Of the fifty-five or so occurrences of orange in the *Wake* about twelve have direct reference to Ulster Protestantism, especially in its intransigent and violent aspect, as when the children are "flocking for the fray on that old orangeray, Dolly Brae" (246.25–26), or when "*the pognency of orangultonia*" appears in the battles of Butt and Taff (343.1), or when Matt gives an aggressive answer involving Belfast shipyards and "yer orange garland" (140.19) to the fourth question in "The Quiz" (I, 6).

Ulster Protestantism, like everything else in the *Wake*, has its own contradictions. For one thing, HCE the first citizen of Dublin is sometimes identified with William III and the order that bears his name. In "The Quiz" (I, 6) HCE is said to be "like the prince of Orange and Nassau" (135.12) and a little further on he is clearly identified with William: "his little white horse decks by dozens our doors" (135.22). When Yawn is asked: "Did any orangepeelers or greengoaters appear periodically up your sylvan family tree?" his answer is not only evasive but calculated to cause a diversion: "—Buggered if I know!" (522.16–18). And one of the witnesses' accounts of HCE's fall in the Park suggests that he was seduced in a field by a "Lili Coninghams" (58.30). The passage has lots of aggressive reds and its Orange connections are indicated further by the name Lili from the Orange Ballad "Lilibullero." Orange Lily appears again as "Lili O'Rangans," paired with

"Iris Trees" (30.1-2), which is, among other things, green Irish trees and the Irish iris in opposition to the Orange lily. At the climax of the Prankquean scene (I, 1), HCE emerges from his castle embodying a rainbow and looking like an angry violent Orangeman as well as the Norman invader, Strongbow (23.1-2). Despite HCE's native credentials as Hill of Howth and personification of Dublin city, he also has the precarious identity of the Orangeman and his fall is due to an Orange temptress.

Like Bloom and Gabriel Conroy and Stephen Dedalus, HCE does not quite belong. In "Cyclops" Bloom's comings and goings prompt this exchange:

>—And after all, says John Wyse, why can't a jew love his country like the next fellow?
>—Why not? says J.J., when he's quite sure which country it is. (*Ulysses*, 12.1628-30)

The identity problem maliciously attributed to Bloom is actually and uncomfortably that of the Orangeman. If this fiercest of British loyalists goes to Birmingham to find work, to natives of that city he, with his Irish accent, is just another "fucking Paddy" to be abused and excoriated when there is another I.R.A. bomb threat.

I must add two other color associations made with Ulster Protestantism in the *Wake*. The first is violet, which Joyce links with "violent" and "violate," and through "ultraviolet" with Ulster violence (e.g. "ulstravoliance," 316.2). The other is blue, a color traditonally associated, at least in Ireland, with staunch, intransigent "true-blue" Protestantism. "Your tooblue prodestin arson" (328.9-10) combining true-blue Protestantism with Presbyterian predestination, can have but one result in Ireland, orange flames. A line in "Night Lessons" (II, 2) tosses Orangemen, nationalists and Irish fascists of the 30s, known as "Blue Shirts," into one unholy Irish stew: "You were republicly royally toobally prussic blue in the shirt after" (305.14-15).

Through diminution of the pretensions associated with the new Irish flag and its conflation and confusion with the flags of other nations, Joyce ridicules all patriotic aspirations and portrays the outcomes of independence-seeking and international conflicts as a matter of Tweedledum and Tweedledee: "—A tricolor ribbon that spells a caution. The old flag, the cold flag.—The flagstone. By tombs, deep and heavy. To the unaveiling memory of. Peacer the grave" (503.24-27). The significations of Ireland's tricolor are coldness, fear, graves, futile dying for a cause, and echoes of death songs. At another point (582.10-11) the Irish tricolor is identified as "green-mould upon mildew over jaundice." Shaun is the one who cloaks himself in the virtues of the national flag. When Glugg has guessed wrong in the "Colors Game" (II, 1), the girls turn to his model brother, Chuff, and exclaim: "Candidatus, viridosus, aurilucens [Latin: white, green, gold], sinelab? Of all the green heroes everworre coton breiches [Bog-latin: green], the whitemost, the goldenest!" (234.8-10). As well as being patriotic hero Shaun is also Catholic hero, as the substitution of gold for orange reminds us. But Shaun's heroic posture is undermined by his gluttony so that when he is envisioned as HCE's splendid successor (in III, 1) he appears clothed in "a starspangled zephyr with a decidely surpliced crinklydoodle front with his motto through dear life embrothred over it in peas, rice and yeggyolk" (404.27-30). And when Shaun-Kevin in the "Recorso" is described as "feed up to the noxer with their geese and peeas and oats upon a trencher" (602.35-36), not only is the tricolor trivialized but also Dublin's General Post Office, glorious symbol of Easter 1916, revered in the New Ireland. Shaun regularly and predictably proclaims his patriotism. In "Jaun's Sermon" (III, 2), he says "Down with the Saozon ruze!" (411.30) and "Like the regular redshank I am" (411.33). "Sazon ruze" is both British red (in Breton), and English duplicity. "Redshanks" was a term applied by early invaders of Ireland to the natives who resisted them since their lower limbs were bare, without armor. Nevertheless the echo of the British red in the second phrase clouds the neatness of the polarity and muddies to some degree the sincerity of Shaun's patriotic proclamation. Even Shem, when he strives to defend himself by aping Shaun's self-proclaimed virtues, reaches for the tricolor, truly the last refuge of a scoundrel. He envisions himself as an opera singer "better than Baraton McCluckin with a scrumptious cocked hat and three green, cheese and tangerine trinity plumes" (180.8-9).

The climactic scene of the clash of flags occurs in the "Shem" chapter (I, 7) in the passage describing Shem's cowardice on Bloody Sunday:

> Now it is notoriously known how on that surprisingly bludgeony Unity Sunday when the grand germogall allstar bout was harrily the rage between our weltingtoms extraordinary and our pettythicks the marshalaisy and Irish eyes of welcome were smiling daggers down their backs, when the roth, vice and blause met the noyr blank and rogues and the grim white and cold bet the black fighting tans, categorically unimperatived by the maxims, a rank funk getting the better of him, the scut in a bad fit of pyjamas fled like a leveret for his bare lives. (176.19-27)

Bernard Benstock's comments on this passage capture the aspects of it important to my concerns:

> Much is then made of Shem's cowardice as he parallels Joyce in avoiding both the Irish Insurrection and the First World War.... The flags of the various combatants are the red, white, and blue of both France and England against the black, white, and red of imperial Germany, while the Irish green, white and gold fought against the British Black 'n' Tans.

Benstock adds that Joyce's fight against the American, Samuel Roth's, piratical publication of *Ulysses* is the reason for the inclusion of the U.S.A.'s red, white and blue.

The clash of the flags subsumes all wars, and one flag is much like another. Their only real significance is the terror they strike into the heart of the artist, Shem. Which flag happens to be allied with which, or to be winning or losing, is irrelevant. A similar mangling of flags and their colors occurs in the pedant's lecture (I, 5): "Billiousness has been billiousness during milliums of millenions and our mixed racings have been giving two hoots or three jeers for the grape, vine and brew" (117.21–23). The imperial flag of Britain and of all empires and the respect paid to it in far-flung lands is reduced to the drunken actions of rum-sodden natives and British administrators whose couplings have produced the "mixed racings" and are merely another parallel to the incident in the Park. When Shaun appears in the "Recorso" as HCE's reincarnation he is associated with "the gren, woid and glue" (596.21), a mixture of Irish and English flags. Native and invader have coalesced.

In my discussion of *Ulysses* in chapter 1, I noted a tendency of Joyce's to avoid the polarity of black and white and to pair instead colors such as red and white whose antithesis is less clearcut, less balanced. In the *Wake* Joyce does use black and white but in ways which undermine any simple polarity the reader may attempt to attribute to them. A large part of the conflict of native and invader is worked out through a tangled patterning of black and white especially conducive to ironic amd satiric perceptions.

The most consistent identification made throughout the *Wake* for its hero HCE is with Finn Mac Cumhaill. For instance the answer given to Question #1 of "The Quiz" (I, 6) which asks about HCE over thirteen pages is "Finn MacCool!" (139.14). Of course, the identification is also present in the book's title. The identification is so pervasive as to make Finn practically an alternative name for HCE. "Finn" means "fair" or "white" and is connected with fair hair or white cap. In his manifestation as Hill of Howth, HCE is also white-capped either because of Howth's white heather or, sometimes it seems, because of Howth's occasional snowcap. HCE refers to himself in a sympathy-seeking speech as "—Old Whitenowth he is speaking again. Ope Eustace tube! Pity poor whiteoath!" (535.26–27). And since Howth is a peninsula, it is an "albutisle" (17.18), which contains the Latin *alb*-. Oddly enough the ancient name "Elbana" given to Dublin in Ptolemy's map can be distorted slightly to give the Latin *alb*-, which distortion indeed occurs in the *Wake* at 364.22, "Analbe." Dublin being HCE's or Finn's town can be called white town or "Finntown" as it is at 265.28. And the great park so central to the happenings of the *Wake* does not derive its name from the word "phoenix" but from the Irish *fionn uisce*, white or bright or clear water. The Phoenix Park is white because it is HCE-Finn's park ("Finn his park," 546.08), and also because that is the origin of its name. Finally, the viking founder of Dublin was Olaf the White with whom HCE is identified in the *Wake* (e.g., 100.26 and 134.27).

HCE then is closely identified in the *Wake* with Dublin city to a degree that makes it reasonable to claim that he is Dublin city personified. Much of that identification and personification works through patterns of "white." But Dublin is black; its name in Irish means literally "black pool." And that meaning is frequently in evidence in pages of the *Wake* when Dublin is called "Pool-black" (35.16–17), "blackpool" (85.15), "Black-pool" (88.34–35) and "pool in the dark" (135.14). The name Dublin, with its two elements in Irish, constitutes almost exactly the Irish word for Guinness's stout, *lionn dubh*. Such a reversal occurs in the *Wake*, for instance, in the "Pool-black" cited above, and the double Dublin-Guinness meaning hinted at, as in the phrase "my granvilled brandold Dublin lindub" (553.26–27).[51] Guinness's stout is the symbol in the *Wake* of male potency, though weaker and less obtrusive than the female symbol, white wine/urine. HCE's inextricable relationship with Dublin city is like one of those black bordered white lines in the Book of Kells which loops in and out, backwards and forwards, over and under until its exact path is untraceable by the naked eye.

This black and white patterning extends beyond the city of Dublin. An area around Dublin city encompassing parts of counties Wicklow, Dublin and Meath has been known for centuries as "the Pale." It was the stronghold and center of British power in Ireland and was a number of times the only part of Ireland in which the British monarch's writ did run. The origins of the word "Pale" have nothing to do with color but rather with fence-paling. Nevertheless its mention in the *Wake* inevitably evokes echoes of pale/pallid/white. On at least one such occasion we find that echo deliberately emphasized: "stocks dry pudor for the Ill people and pinkun's pellets for all the Pale" (128.12–13). Part of north county Dublin, the rich plain between the Liffey and the Boyne, is known as Fingal or Fingall, so called because it was dominated by Norwegian vikings, fairhaired foreigners or *finn gaill* in Irish, in contrast to the Danes, dark foreigners or *dubh-ghaill* who settled to the south of the city. "Fingal" also suggests Macpherson's *Ossian* to which there are frequent references in the *Wake*—Ossian or Oisin was Finn's son. Fingal is frequently almost a synonym for Dublin, especially in contexts of strife and invasion. Thus at 329.14 we find "Fingal of victories." In the "Inquisition of Yawn" (III, 3) Fingal is Dublin's Phoenix Park, scene of the Park murders and HCE's fall (503.13), and armed strife and viking rapine haunt this phrase in ALP's final monologue: "the lodge of Fjorn na Galla of the Trumpets!" (622.6). The connection of Fingal with HCE-Finn is frequently underscored in the text as in the distortion "Old Fincoole" (569.23). In the "Inquisition of Yawn" HCE is the fox chased by a pack of hounds, "the fingall harriers" (480.33–34), and in "Jaun's Sermon" (III, 2) HCE is Finn, native, Dubliner, invader, rapist and an Irish political party: "the bould one that quickened her the seaborne Fingale" (469.14–15).

Fingal is fully entangled in the black-white ambiguities of Dublin and HCE. The washerwomen in the "ALP" section (I, 9), recalling a time when "all that was was fair," refer to HCE as "Dear Dirty Dumpling, foostherfather of fingalls and dotthergills" (215.13–14). HCE is Dear Dirty Dublin with his dumpy and dumplinglike figure and his propensity for Humpty Dumpty-like fall. He is father, foster father and fumbling (Anglo-Irish *foosther*) father of fair foreign sons and bright (Irish *geal, gill*) daughters. Black begets white in fishy fashion. In the "Inquisition of Yawn" (III, 3) a voice from deep within Yawn's psyche responds to the question "whu's within?" with the answer: "—Dovegall and finshark, they are ring to the rescue!" (500.4). The main action here, either carried out or posited, is running or riding to the rescue. "Dovegall" is dark foreigner or Dane, black rooster (Latin, *gallus*), and the Irish missionaries, Columba (dove) and Gall. "Gall" also suggests bitterness, impudence, soreness, while "dove-" is both Irish "black" and white, peaceloving dove. "Fin-" is white in antithesis to the flawed black of "dove-" and also HCE-Finn. "Shark" points to violent predacity, but *searc* in Irish (pronounced "shark") is love or affection, especially between the sexes. The juxtaposition of "dove-" and "-ark" suggests Noah and his ark and inevitably the raven of that story, symbol also of violent viking invasion. But in addition to invasion we have two prominent figures of that peculiarly Irish "evasion," the Christian foreign mission from Ireland. St. Columba founded the monastery of Iona and St. Gall that Swiss monastery now the site of the town which bears his name. What we have here in fact is an intensive complex of the black-white, war-peace, invasion-resistance themes, qualified, modified, twisted into an incredible knot.

Two further variations of the black/white/HCE/Dublin tangle merit brief discussion. The first is a phrase in Hosty's Ballad: "some dub him Llyn and Phin" (44.11). Red is present here with black ("dub") and white ("Phin"). "Llyn" is primarily the eponymous mock-hero of the ballad "Brian O'Linn" with whom HCE is frequently identified. But "O'Linn" means "of Flann" and "flann" in Irish means "ruddy." This is the red of our first father, Adam: HCE is Finn and Dublin and Adam. My second instance comes from Question #3 of the "Twelve Question Quiz" (I, 6). The question asks for the motto of HCE's pub, "that Tick for Teac thatchment painted witt wheth one darkness" (139.29–30). The answer given is a distortion of Dublin's motto. "Teac" and "Tick" are Irish "house"; "thatchment" is the thatched roof and hatchment or escutcheon; "witt" is Dutch "white." There is HCE's black and Dublin's white but also Shem-Joyce, the artist, with white fearful face and black eyepatch, lurking about in the shadows of his house firing off literary projectiles to the world.

The black-white identification of HCE and Dublin also extends to the nation of Ireland. As Finn's land, Ireland can be referred to as "Finnyland" (245.15) and "Fyn's Insul" (510.24-25) or Finn's Island. When Butt exclaims "Guards, serf Finnland, serve we all!" (340.24), he is shouting not only the German slogan of the Great War, *Gott Strafe England*, but also a line from a patriotic Irish song: "God save Ireland, say we all!" But Ireland is also black-dark. Two patriotic-sentimental names for Ireland for at least two centuries have been "dark cow" and "black rose." The latter, originally *Mo Roisin Dubh*, anglicized by Mangan as "My Dark Rosaleen," appears in the *Wake* as "dark Rosa Lane" (93.27) and "durck rosolun" (351.9).

The black-white play extends to various antagonists in HCE's and Ireland's struggles. *Sinn Fein* is sometimes distorted to include "finn": the slogan *Sinn Fein Amhain* becomes "Fennsense, finnsonse, aworn!" (614.14), and "sinfintins" (624.18). The customers in HCE's pub, who are both his supporters (as customers) and detractors are "Finnfanntawners" (309.9-10)—vagrants, enthusiasts for the Irish language, feeble fellows, Sinn Feiners, and fawners on the goodwill and credit of HCE. Those who oppose *Sinn Fein* have the "Pale" mentality and are "palesmen" (42.34) and "palers" (323.30). On at least one occasion the strife of Orange with Green is portrayed as a fight between whites and blacks: "men on the two sides in New South Ireland and Vetera Uladh, bluemin and pillfaces, during the ferment With the Pope or On the Pope" (78.26-28). "New South Ireland" is the Free State; "Vetera Uladh" is ancient Ulster (Latin and Irish); "pillfaces" are pale faces and sickly faces; "bluemin" are blacks—in Irish a black is *fear gorm*, literally "blue man." We are not allowed to determine which side is white and which black—because it doesn't matter. A couple of lines later their historic struggle is diminished to a pair of dances: "Bellona's Black Bottom, once Woolwhite's Waltz" (78.31-32). The Sullivani, Sully's thugs who are enemies of HCE, and the Doyles who prosecute the Honuphrius case both have (Irish) "black" in their names. The former are identified by ALP with the "Black Hand," the Serbian secret society responsible for the assassination of Franz Ferdinand at Sarajevo, and the Sicilian "mafia" (495.2). In the dialogue of Mutt and Jute (I, 1), Mutt finds a similar pattern in the struggles of Ireland's earliest settlers: "mearmerge two races, swete and brack. Morthering rue" (17.24-25).

In addition to the complex of black and white associated with the struggle of native and invader, the theme is generally colorful as it apears in the *Wake*, as indeed was the case with the same theme in Stephen's thoughts in "Proteus." One group of invaders, the infamous Black and Tans, have a color label and that label is often used to designate all invaders. Thus the viking warrior is a "black and tan" (46.16). Strongbow, the Norman leader, is also "a tan" (288.15). It should scarcely surprise us that HCE himself is prominent among the Black and Tan invaders. In "The Ballad of Persse O'Reilly" he is both viking and Black and Tan sailing into Dublin Bay, and he is frequently identified with Strongbow (e.g., 46.14). In ALP's final monologue, HCE "in your bark and tan billows" is incoming tide and both territorial and sexual invader at Liffey mouth (626.21-25).

A brief passage in the "Norwegian Captain" section (II, 3) constitutes one of those intensive displays of major related themes that occur fairly regularly through the *Wake*, and it also displays the colorfulness associated with the native-invader theme: "That with some our prowed invisors how their ulstravoliance led them infroraids, striking down and landing alow, against our aerian insulation resistance, two boards that beached ast one, widness thane and tysk and hanry" (316.2-5). What is ostensibly going on here is the return of the Norwegian Captain to Dublin but his arrival drags in its train all of Ireland's historical invasions. The "prowed invisors" are the "proud invaders" from the song "Let Erin Remember," a song that emphasizes native disunity and treachery in the face of the vikings. "Invisors" are also those who lack vision as the invaders fail to foresee the consequences of their actions, for instance the process of assimilation to Irish life which will absorb their descendants. Other consequences of their actions will be Ulster violence ("ulstravoliance") and struggle of Irish with Britain's imperial red ("-raids"). The rainbow and the limits of the spectrum visible to the human eye are present in "ulstravoliance" and "infroraids." The rainbow is the sign of promise and the sign of fall. The limits of the rainbow spectrum suggest that all nuances and ambiguities and variations of human actions are perceptibly present in the native-invader clash. While the invaders aim down, pragmatically, at the immediate action, the natives appear to have their heads in the clouds—but this in the final result will make little difference; they are both as one. The "two boards that beached ast one" suggest a built-in disunity among the invaders themselves, especially since these "boards" are not only ships but birds, namely the white dove and black raven which Noah sent out from the Ark. But the "boards" are also the two "birds" in the Park who with Tom, Dick and Harry as witnesses contribute to the central fall of the *Wake*.

Another passage with some strikingly similar functions appears in the "Porters' Bedroom" scene (III, 4). HCE is in bed, as Mr. Porter, and the second vision of his buttocks is given in topographical terms as a description of the Phoenix Park. The passage runs on for more than a page (564.1-565.5) but these few lines are of particular relevance to my discussion here: "A scarlet pimparnell now mules the mound where anciently first murders were wanted to take root. By feud fionghalian" (564.28-30). The invaders at this point are merely tourists, "grekish and romanos," interested in colorful myths and scandals rather than ancient history. But the final phrase of the piece I quoted is very interesting. I have already examined "Fingal" as part of the color patterns associated with the native-invader theme. Fingal is present here too but its spelling replicates exactly the spelling of the relatively obscure Irish word *fionghal*, defined by Dinneen as "fratricide; the slaughter of a fellow-tribesman or relative; murder, treason."[52] The only real enemy is the one within us; native and invader are its dream manifestations.

The climax in the *Wake* of the clash of native with invader is the druid-saint confrontation in the "Recorso." It is a brief scene encompassing some two pages of text (611.4–613.4), and it contains more color references by far than any other two-page passage in the book. Clearly of major significance, the scene has received more critical attention than any other brief scene in the *Wake*.[53] Campbell and Robinson's account of the scene still has general acceptance from the critics. Here is part of it:

> The druid's strictly idealistic philosophy... is strongly Berkeleyan in character, with a flavouring of Kant. Practical, hard-headed St. Patrick on the other hand... knows well enough how to give a popular reply.... He simply cuts the gloriously involved Gordian knot.... With that stroke, the deep night of druidical brooding is dispelled and the way is open for the day of progressive action. The logic of *Finnegans Wake* itself, which is the logic of slumber and druidic myth is overcome by St. Patrick's blow.[54]

William York Tindall's interpretation of the scene is in my judgment fairly representative of the critical opinions of the past two decades:

> Berkeley... confronts a foreign invader, this time Patrick.... The veil of illusion, says Berkeley, hides the "hueful panepiphanal" world of Lord Joss from vulgar eyes; for each object in the "heupanepi" world, absorbing six of the seven colours of solar light, reflects the obvious seventh. To the heuristic "seer" however the absorbed colours are apparent.... At this point... Patrick, ignoring subtleties... disposes of the Irishman's "ruinboon"... Patrick kneels before the three-sided Balenoarch [a whale of a God] and hails him....[55]

Despite the general critical agreement as to the main outline of events in the Berkeley-Patrick confrontation, the passage is disturbingly reminiscent of what appears to me to be its counterpart at the beginning of the book, the Prankquean incident. In both cases the comparative clarity of the action serves to hinder rather than help the interpretation of its significance. For the Patrick-Berkeley passage I shall try to focus on the patterns of color, their relations to the events, and their relations to the patterns of color that have, up to this point in the book, marked the clash of native and invader.

The arch-druid wears a seven colored or rainbow mantle. This identifies him not only as the High King's chief "ollave" or wise man but as HCE, representative man guilty of the seven deadly sins and capable of falling to the temptation of the seven rainbow girls. He is also the dreamer and champions the rainbow colors of dream vision against the harsh conventionally perceived colors of day. Most critics accept him as the champion of artistic integrity against philistinism, or in Paul Anghinetti's words, "the artist who engages the predatory world of fact."[56] As "Balkelly" the druid is "kelly-green" and a devotee of the Celtic god Baal. His insistence on the visibility of the seventh, absorbed color of objects to the perception of the seer seems a reasonable metaphor for the penetrating vision of the artist-dreamer until we come to his further insistence, repeated almost hysterically, on green as the only inward reality of High King Leary. This is a signal that Balkelly is being treated ironically. The arch-druid is with Yeats and Lady Gregory and the others of the Irish Dramatic movement who, in Joyce's view, turned their backs on Europe to restrict their vision to Irish peasant confines. We are back to Mulligan's "new art color for our Irish poets: snotgreen" (*Ulysses*, 1.73). Our recognition of this obsessive nationalism in Balkelly should open us to perception of his other contradictions. As representative of Irish druidic mysticism Balkelly is surely an odd figure. George Berkeley after all was a member of the Anglo-Irish ascendancy, a Protestant bishop and defender of the Established Church of Ireland, in Irish terms an invader if ever there was one. And yet he is here portrayed as the champion of Celtic druidism and in addition he is "pidgin fella," pidgin-speaker, dove of peace and a type of Colmcille, scion of Celtic royalty and greatest of Irish missionaries.

Patrick ignores all appearances and argument and goes for the jugular. In contrast to the druid's blaze of color Patrick is in white ("alb") and his companions in grey, but he calls the druid "shiroskuro blackinwhitepaddynger" or black-and-white-stupid-Irishman. Patrick will use any tactic to sway the crowd; he represents a Christianity of the marketplace that recognizes political realities and manipulates the ignorance of the populace. Opposed to the arch-druid's "viriditude" or Irish green is Patrick's "eruberuption" or violent British red. At the heart of his "Christianity" is power and its classic manifestation in British Christian imperialism. Nevertheless he shows no hesitation in using the green shamrock of Ireland to wipe at least his nose and the eyes of his hearers. His response to the druid is clumsy, vulgar and confusing. At least some of that confusion seems to me to be due to the narrator's loss of detachment and his dangling syntax. The narrator intrudes so far into the discussion as to make it quite difficult for the reader to ascertain who is speaking or to what degree editorial interference on the narrator's part is distorting what is being said. The narrator through his partisanship of Patrick constitutes a third character in the drama and the blurred identities of the three give us the classic intra-individual triangle of conflicts: "*Shem and Shaun and the shame that sunders em.*"

It is generally agreed that Patrick's populist response wins the day and that in the *Wake* scene as in historical fact Christianity is triumphant. The one who exults in that triumph is the narrator: "That was thing, bygotter, the thing, bogcotton, the very thing, begad! Even to uptoputty Bilkilly-Belkelly-Balkally. Who was for shouting down the shatton on the lamp of Jeeshees"

(612.31–33). The tone here is strongly reminiscent of the "Sirens" narrator with his contemptuous wordplay or the "Cyclops" narrator who relished the discomfiture of the loser in every exchange in the pub. More exactly the narrator's voice here is the voice of the mob.

Critics have rightly questioned the reality or finality of Patrick's victory; it is full of contradictions. In addition to suggesting "whale-god" (as Tindall notes above) "Balenoarch" includes the Celtic pagan god Baal, Noah and his ark and rainbow, and the Italian for rainbow, reversed, *arco baleno*.[57] The shamrock is synthetic and the "four three two agreement" is "seeming-such."[58] The "murk-blankered" superstition of the druid is closer to Patrick's obscurantist "monkblinkers" than either would wish to admit. Patrick is, historically, a figure of most delicious ironies. He was British by birth and was originally brought to Ireland against his will as part of the spoils of an Irish cattle-raid on Britain. His return to Ireland as Christian missionary was the most successful invasion of Ireland ever completed. He later became the symbol of the narrowest and most sentimental strain of chauvinistic Irish nationalism. That his emergence as that symbol was due in large part to the new-found separatist tendencies of the eighteenth century Protestant ascendancy—George Berkeley's people—and that the cult was taken over by nineteenth-century sentimental Catholic nationalism, add to the irony. Further irony is added by the presence in the background of this scene of that slogan from the early Christian period which became Ireland's proudest boast: Island of Saints and Scholars. In the *Wake* scene, they are at each other's throats. The saint wears British imperial red, in his complexion if not in his clothes, and represents Christ and Caesar most happily hand in glove. The wise man, unwise in the ways of the world, champions the blind, superstitious, snot-green. In one sense this is a playing out at the climax of Joyce's final work of the Christmas dinner confrontation in *A Portrait*. What happens to the arch-druid now is that he goes underground and fires off verbal missives written in his own excrement to the great embarrassment of the Shaun in all of us. Invader and native resister are linked forever and their most violent struggles bind them all the more tightly.

A persistent thread running through Ireland's history of invasions is division and treachery on the part of the native resistance. We know that the idea of treachery was important in Joyce's life as it is in the thoughts of his protagonist, Stephen Dedalus. Such treachery is frequently referred to in the *Wake* in allusions such as those to the song "Let Erin Remember" and "feud fionghalian." The white in Ireland's national flag officially symbolizes peace between Orange and Green. The actual relations between Orange and Green since the foundation of the states provide such an ironic commentary on the white/peace symbolism as Joyce could hardly resist. In the *Wake* white becomes a symbol of strife, although the point is rarely made overtly. The closeness of pronunciation of "white" and "fight" in some Irish dialects is exploited by Joyce for his purpose as in "fight niggers" (40.13) and Festy King's "fight shirt" (85.34). The invaders are no less prone to division and treachery than are the natives, as we can see in such phrases as "black fighting tans" (176.24-25). It is the complex of ironies built into the native-invader conflicts of Irish history that makes that theme such a superb metaphor for the conflicts within the psyche. In Irish history as in the druid-saint confrontation the invader always triumphs. But Ireland's propensity towards assimilation of its invaders is legendary. In Ireland the native is always a past invader, give or take a few generations, and the successful invader by dint of that very success is a future native. We are all boat people. One of the livelier ironies of Irish history is that Trinity College, founded by Elizabeth to anglicize and protestantize Ireland and sustain the West Briton mentality has through the centuries provided among its graduates the educated leaders of rebellions against the very establishment Trinity was founded to preserve, revolutionary leaders removed in some cases only one generation from their invading status. In the dream world of the *Wake* where Time has been collapsed native and invader are one—and that one at war with himself. HCE is "the unnamed nonirishblooder that becomes a Greenislender overnight" (378.10-11)—not only viking and green-islander but one who is prepared to lend out or export his Irish vision, on a missionary basis, no doubt.

At one point in Jaun's sermon he exclaims: "When will the W.D. face of our sow muckloved d'lin, the Troia of towns and Carmen of cities, crawling with mendiants in perforated clothing, get its wellbelavered white like l'pool and m'chester?" (448.11-14). Shaun's elimination of the essential black (Shem's color) from Dublin is matched by his removal of "liver" and "man," of humanity and human frailty, from his vision of the English cities. Dublin is "pig-loved" (Irish, *muc*) and a sow or harlot (Italian, *troia*).[59] Its beggars are insects crawling on its body. Shaun wants to deny the reality of Dublin and to give it a proper coat of whitewash to match his vision of the respectable English cities. Since Dublin and HCE are one, what Shaun really wants is to deny his father's Shem-like qualities and clothe him in antiseptic respectability. Shaun must condemn, reject, repress the Shem element of their combined nature. He cannot tolerate the acceptance of mysterious and warring uncontrolled forces deep within the psyche that his creator Joyce insists upon.

In his paper at Padua, "The Universal Literary Influence of the Renaissance," Joyce wrote:

> Giordano Bruno himself says that every power, whether in nature or in the spirit, must create an opposite power, without which it cannot fulfil itself, and he adds that in each such separation there is a tendency towards reunion. The dualism of the sublime Nolan reflects faithfully the phenomenon of the Renaissance.[60]

This doctrine as it applies to the "spirit" is enunciated in the *Wake* through Joyce's insistence on the inextricable entanglement of native and invader in Irish history and of the colors that mark them. His refusal to allow clearcut polarities, his insistence on the presence in every antithesis of an element that unbalances it, is effectively communicated through his manipulation of colors, and constitutes one chief way through which he attains what Fritz Senn calls "the Principle of Disrupted Pattern,"[61] and John Gordon calls "Joyce's old habit of having things both ways."[62]

3
A Chameleon at Last: Colors of the Male

If colors are important in *Finnegans Wake* then we may expect its hero, HCE, to be a colorful figure. He is. Not only does he have special relationships to certain colors but he is frequently linked with the spectrum of colors and with color in general. The girls call him "our Farvver" (93.20), both "our father" and (in Danish) "our colors." The colors here hint also at the girls' underwear and sexual secrets. God the Father—HCE in a more dramatic manifestation—is the "farbung" (235.5), "tint" or "dye" in German. In the washerwomen's gossip HCE is "the quare old buntz" (215.13), *bunt* being "bright color" in German. In one of his self-defensive speeches HCE refers to some dubious sexual occasion and relates his confusion or weakness or upset thus: "all the colories fair fled from my folced cheeks!" (365.36); even if his cheeks are false or tearful (Irish: *folc*) his identity and vitality are bound up with his colors. And in the "Inquisition of Yawn" (III, 3) Yawn, or more likely one of his inquisitors, tosses out the phrase, "—And his shartshort trooping its colors!" (360.20). This is almost certainly the incident in the Park and the trooping of the colors HCE's exhibiting of his sexual crime on that occasion.

I shall first examine those color associations of HCE which are relatively minor but do have some importance for the novel as a whole, namely blue, yellow, green, grey and brown. In Joyce's scheme of things blue is a woman's color; nevertheless HCE, by my count, has eleven blues.[1] I find two patterns of significance running through those blues. In three of the "blue" instances (76.32, 328.9-10, 542.3), HCE is "true-blue," the true-blue of Orange Ulster's intransigence on the one hand, and on the other of the heroic O'Donoghue, who, legend has it, sleeps beneath Lough Lein, ready to wake and fight at the hour of Ireland's need. As the hero of a resurrection myth (even if the resurrection is deferred), O'Donoghue like Finn and Finnegan is an entirely appropriate *alter ego* for HCE. The second blue pattern is blue and buff (511.10 and 567.25), the colors of the Duke of Beaufort's hunt according to McHugh.[2] This association connects with the hunt which wanders in and out of the pages of the *Wake*, and in which HCE is usually the hunted fox or *madairin rua*. Indeed, that mysterious "old sexton, red-Fox Good-man" receives the kicking that results in contusions of "black and bufetteer blue" at 511.10. I shall have more to say of this hunt later.

Only eight greens properly belong to HCE and only one significant pattern is evident to me among them.[3] That is an association with life and growing things, especially with returning to life or resurrection. Thus his feet are "swarded in verdigrass" (7.30); in one account of the Park incident he is "high chief evervirens," everliving and evergreen (88.2); and at the end of I, 3, before the hero's burial in I, 4, that is, he is "Greenman's Rise O, (lost leaders live! the heroes return!)" (74.2–3).[4] This sense of resurrection is also present in the green bough in this account of HCE's fall: "They have waved his green boughs o'er him as they have torn him limb from lamb" (58.6–7). As McHugh points out, this is the ritual murder of the divine king to ensure his continued life or resurrection as described in Frazer's *The Golden Bough*.[5]

HCE has only half a dozen or so yellows of little consequence—yellow is Shaun's color—and only a handful of golds and goldens, but there is one gold pattern of some significance involving white and gold. The "white soul of gold" mentioned by HCE in his protestation of innocence probably has reference to himself (538.13); "Helius Croesus, that white and gold elephant in our zoopark" is certainly HCE (564.5–6); and gold is present by implication in this image of HCE as hill of Howth: "shows one white drift of snow among the gorse-growth of his crown" (128.20–21). It is my contention that the white and gold of the papal flag are present in the background of each of these images and that paternal authority and the tyrannical rule of the Church in Ireland are being jointly attacked. It is interesting to note that the official residence of the papal nuncio to Ireland is situated in the Phoenix Park, "our zoopark" since the Dublin zoo is also situated there. And one may confidently identify "Monsigneur of Deublan" as HCE at the king's visit in III, 4, with "his goldwhite swaystick aloft ylifted" (569.19–20). Not only is church-papal pretension being ridiculed here as it defers to the British monarch but also the phallic authority of the father, and all three are tainted by association with Nazi fascism ("swaystick" = swastika).

Grey, surprisingly enough in view of its status as one of the colors of blindness and its significance in *Ulysses*, *A Portrait of the Artist* and *Dubliners*, is of comparatively minor importance in *Finnegans Wake*. HCE has two interesting sets of grey association. One links him as middle-aged patriarch with the middle-aged father/author, James Joyce—when HCE is described as "*the grogram grey barnacle gander*" (399.5) he is identified with the husband of the barnacle goose or Nora Barnacle. Through the grey of the title *The Picture of Dorian Gray* the fall of the hero and of the author of that work are linked with the fall of HCE as at 241.9. That thread of association eventually reaches to the persecuted artists Shem and Joyce, and possibly to that other symbol of persecution, the grey donkey.

The color brown is more obviously associated, as in Browne and Nolan, with the sons than with the father in *Finnegans Wake*. Nevertheless HCE has some brown associations worthy of note. In Shaun's sermon Issy is warned against a potential rival of Shaun's for her affection, "a man in brown about town," clearly identified in the context as the father figure, HCE (443.20-21). In what seems to be an exchange between Kate and HCE in the "Norwegian Captain" or first "Pub" scene (III, 3), this curious conglomeration of defensive father figures occurs:

> —This is time for my tubble, reflected Mr. 'Gladstone Browne' in the toll hut (it was choractoristic from that 'man of Delgany'). Dip.
> —This is me vulcanite smoking, profused Mr. 'Bonaparte Nolan'.... (334.6-10)

At the least, Gladstone, Parnell, Bruno, Napoleon, Wellington (tip) and Joyce himself are jostling for position here.[6] The "smoking" is interesting since the Cad, HCE's antagonist, is frequently identified as a pipe-smoker and HCE as a smoker of a big brown cigar as at 95.16-17, "puffing out his thundering big brown cabbage!" No doubt, Dublin's ancient name of Hazel-wood-ridge, which appears a number of times in the *Wake* (e.g. 372.15), gives the city's personification, HCE, a legitimate brown connection.[7] But HCE's strongest brown connection is with "brown bear." When HCE is a red fox being hunted through the townlands of county Dublin he displays a tendency to turn into a brown bear, or a black-brown bear, "a bruin of some swart" (97.6). This tendency is also apparent when HCE masquerades as Brian O'Linn, comic hero of the ballad of that name, and we find him to be "Bruin O'Luinn" (382.2). It is evident also in his role as Brian Boru, defeater of the vikings: "Bruinoboroff, the hooneymoonger, and the grizzliest manmichal in Meideveide!" (340.20-21). What all of these occasions have in common is that HCE is under great pressure, is in danger, is being attacked, and is being pushed towards that splitting of personality with which Browne and Nolan and Shem and Shaun are so intimately connected.

As I explained in chapter 2, HCE has a great many white and black associations, the chief link for the former being his identification with Finn Mac Cumhaill, *finn* being (Irish) "white," and the chief link for the latter being Dublin which HCE personifies, *dubh-linn* being (Irish) "black pool." The further ramifications of these associations I shall now trace. More than fifty times in the book HCE is called by the name Finn or distortions thereof. Frequently the distortions extend HCE's identification beyond Finn to other personae. Thus HCE is Finnegan of the ballad and of the *Wake*'s title (531.28); he is the American novelist Fennimore Cooper (24.16, 28.34); he is Huckleberry Finn (346.26, 616.1); he is a Sinn Feiner (614.14), Fr. Finn, writer of books for boys (440.10), Old King Cole (569.23), Adam Findlater, the prominent Dublin grocer (619.3) and Saint Fintan (624.18). Despite the ubiquity of these "finn" references it must be admitted that Joyce usually makes little play with the color aspect of the connection. Indeed the use of the name Finn for HCE seems generally to function merely as a reminder to the reader of HCE's identity with all men, especially authority figures and father figures. Two exceptions to this generalization are important, HCE/white-horse and HCE/white-hat.

The association of HCE with white-horse involves his identification with the Duke of Wellington and is concentrated in the "Museyroom" episode (I, 1), though some further instances are scattered through the book. Whatever else the "Museyroom" episode may be, it is certainly the famous incident in the Park recreated in terms of the Battle of Waterloo. In the Phoenix Park version of the battle HCE-Wellington is the loser not the winner. His name is reduced to a passive "Willingdone." His horse "Copenhagen" becomes the shapeless heap "Cokenhape," and as "big wide harse" becomes mixed up with his master's posterior (8.16–21). The toppling of the hat at the end of the episode signals "How Copenhagen ended" (10.21–22) and is the signal also for the observation of HCE's exhibitionism in the Park incident and the collapse of his reputation that follows on it.

Of the dozen or so white-horse references that appear outside of the "Museyroom" episode, HCE can be detected as an immediate presence or vaguely in the background in almost all of them while Wellington is clearly present in five.[8] An examination of these five instances and the six instances that occur in the "Museyroom" episode leads me to the conclusion that these four elements constitute the chief characteristics of the HCE/Wellington/white-horse motif: the joke about Wellington's Irish birth;[9] the joke about the child's question in the waxworks museum: "which is the Duke and which is his horse?";[10] sexuality, especially sexual exhibitionism, and a fall; and the notion of common humanity cutting across individual differences, a notion explored in this sentence of the pedant's in I, 5: "If a negative of a horse happens to melt enough while drying, well, what you do get is, well, a positively grotesquely distorted macromass of all sorts of horsehappy values and masses of meltwhile horse" (117.27–30). It seems to me that the significance of the white-horse web of associations lies in its insistence on the universality of man's fall, on the similarities of victors and losers, of the great and the humble. As ALP says in her final soliloquy, "all men has done something" (621.32).

The etymology of Finn Mac Cumhaill's name involves white hair/head or white cap/hood—no one is quite sure which. Joyce plays with this doubt in his use of the music-hall slogan "Take off that white hat!"[11] Thus hat sometimes becomes head as at 311.24 and 607.3. Distortions or part renditions or exact renditions of this slogan occur in the *Wake* a total of ten times by my count.[12] On all occasions the slogan applies to HCE or an HCE-type. On three of the occasions there is threat and insult implied—all three involve the Norwegian Captain.[13] In two other instances, HCE speaking injects references to Wilde into his discourse.[14] Oscar Wilde's frequent identification in the *Wake* with HCE is obviously appropriate when we consider that he was a great Irishman who fell because of sexual indiscretion. But he has a special additional tie with HCE/Finn/white in that one of his names was "Fingall," and that Oscar in the Fenian sagas was Finn's grandson.[15] The first occurrence of "Take off that white hat!" is at the naming of HCE by the king (32.23) and it can be said that because of Finn and the etymology of his name and HCE's identity as Finn and Finnegan the slogan on every one of its occurrences raises questions of HCE's identity. This is accentuated by the confusion of white-head and white-hat as if head and hat and name were all equally matters of arbitrary personal choice. One particular distortion of the slogan, "tuck upp those wide shorts" (614.14), drags in the notion of sexual display again and the fall which inevitably accompanies it in the *Wake*. In fact one can say that the HCE whites, despite their number and intricate patterning all have an air of ambiguity about them, all tend to cast some doubt on the very identification they ostensibly assert.

I have already examined, in chapter 2, some of HCE's associations with the color black. I propose to pursue that discussion further here. As personification of Dublin or *dubh-linn* or "black pool," HCE is naturally black. As Dublin innkeeper he is Mr. Porter of Guiness's stout or porter, Ireland's national drink brewed at James's Gate, Dublin. Porter of course is black and to this day in the pubs of Ireland porter is not simply poured into a glass like common beer but is skilfully and lovingly built into the specially shaped twenty-ounce glass. When properly built the pint of Guinness has a solid creamy or off-white head which protrudes a quarter-inch or so above the glass edge in a *cruach*, a name also commonly applied in Ireland to a ridge or mountain. As Dublin's incarnation HCE is black but has Finn's white head or cap like the pint of Guinness. In the *Wake*, Guinness's stout is also Genesis and has the generative properties appropriate to a father. It is in fact the weak male correlative to the powerfully generative and regenerative white/wet/urine/ wine/tea of the woman which I shall discuss in chapter 4. The Irish for porter is *lionn dubh*, only one letter away from *linn dubh* or *dubh-linn*, Dublin. The two are joined with HCE's male sexual prowess in a boast of his achievements that he makes through the voice of Yawn: "I brewed for my alpine plurabelle, wigwarming wench, (speakeasy!) my granvilled brandold Dublin lindub, the free, the froh, the trothy freshener, puss, puss, pussyfoot, to split the spleen of her maw" (553.25-28). The image of the pint of Guinness is frequently in the background of Wakean scenes as on the occasion in the "Porters' Pub" section (III, 4) when Issy sees HCE's erect member exposed and he is twice referred to as "duffgerent" or black-ruler-bringer forth (566.21, 24) or in ALP's final version of HCE's conquering sea: "you'd rush upon me, darkly roaring, like a great black shadow with a sheeny stare to perce me rawly" (626.24–25). Two further phrases which display I believe the same phenomenon appear in the list of HCE's exploits in Question #1 of the "Twelve Question Quiz" (I, 6): "passed for baabaa blacksheep till he grew white woo woo woolly" (133.25) and "his porter has a mighty grasp and his baxters the boon of broadwhite" (136.4–5). But the generative powers of Guinness are at least matched by its capacity to cause a fall as we are reminded in the description of HCE in his cups after closing time in the pub: "overwhelmed as he was with black ruin" (381.17).

I have also examined briefly in chapter 2 the black aspects of HCE's connection with Doyles and Sullivans but must expand on that examination now. The etymology of Doyle is *dubh-ghaill* or black foreigners, in other words Danes; that of Sullivan is *suil-dubhain* or black-eyed. Question #7 of the "Twelve Question Quiz" (I, 6) describes the twelve customers in HCE's pub as "the Morphios," "component partners of our societate" (142.8) and identifies them as "doyles when they deliberate but sullivans when they are swordsed" (142.26–27). Adaline Glasheen perceives "the Twelve" as "ordinary,"[16] and identifies them with the Doyles and the *Dail* (Irish Parliament).[17] She associates "the Twelve" with "the Sullivani" but also describes the latter as "a band of mercenaries, led by Sulla or Sully the Thug."[18] Both Doyles and Sullivans in my view represent manifestations of facets of HCE's psyche that are aggressive and destructive, that he wishes to conceal from his own consciousness. The Doyles at least appear to function by conventional criteria of behavior and they come into their own in the Honuphrius trial (III, 4) in which judge, expert legal witness, jury, one defendant and the defendant's address are all Doyles and the evidence is given in "doylish" (557–76). The results of their efforts, presumably to get at the truth, are to mire the case hopelessly in legal technicalities so that it is finally dismissed. The Doyles, I believe, represent a Shem-aspect of HCE which seeks to reveal truth. The judge in the Honuphrius case is referred to at one point as "Judge Jeremy Doyler" (575.32). "Jerry" is a Shem name and black is Shem's color, black because he is in opposition to Shaun's "whitewashing" and faith in fair outward appearance.

The Sullivani are a more fearsome threat to the personality since they are clearly capable of and tending towards physical violence. ALP accuses Sully and his gang of responsibility for all the troubles of HCE which in one sense is true since they are projections of the deeply self-destructive and anarchic parts of his psyche. ALP, in defense of HCE's reputation, goes on the attack:

> The said Sully, a barracker associated with tinkers, the blackhand, Shovellyvans, wreuter of annoyimgmost letters and skirriless ballets in Parsee Franch who is Magrath's thug and smells cheaply of Power's spirits, like a deepsea dibbler, and he is not fit enough to throw guts down to a bear. (495.1–5)

There are contradictions built into ALP's diatribe—for instance among the knowledgeable Power's Gold Label whiskey is considered among the finer Irish whiskeys. Naturally Shaun detests the Sullivan gang, portraying them as predators of the night: "The Sully van vultures are on the prowl" (435.29). At one point in the "Recorso" the three soldiers in the Park Incident are called "three Sulvans of Dulkey" (616.10-11), obviously three members of the Sullivan gang. In the *Wake*, Doyles and Sullivans represent the darker, more disturbing, less rational and conscious, the subversive and threatening depths of the dreamer's psyche.

As father of all of us HCE is also the first father, Adam, whose name is generally accepted as having derived from words for "red earth" or "red clay." Three of HCE's "red" associations in the *Wake* provide evidence of Joyce's awareness and use of that etymology. Among the exploits and qualities attributed to HCE in Question #1 of the "Quiz" (I, 6) is this phrase: "pink sunset shower, red clay cloud, sorrow or Sahara, oxhide or Iren" (127.25-26). Shaun in the "Sermon" (III, 2) refers to men as "the wandering sons of red loam" (469.3). The third instance is more complex. It occurs in Mutt's discourse on history: "This ourth of years is not save brickdust and being humus the same roturns" (18.4-5). This earth of ours, the earth on which we walk and of which our bodies ("Dust thou art...") and our history ("years") are composed, is naught save the dust of past civilizations ("brickdust"), which being human ("humus") is caught in the cycle of death ("rot-") and resurrection or return. The red-clay Adam is to be found in the brickdust which is red and in the red character (*rot*, German) of the cycle itself.

In Yawn's dream within a dream (III, 3) a passage, which conflates the Genesis account of Adam's fall with Vico's explanation of the beginning of civilization and mixes the identities of the protagonists into a Joycean stew, suggests a further dimension of the HCE/Adam/red identification, a dimension which is echoed elsewhere in the book:

> —Well, he was ever himself for the presention of crudities to animals for he had put his own nickelname on every toad, duck and herring before the climber clomb aloft, doing the midhill of the park, flattering his bitter hoolft with her conconundrums. He would let us have the three barrels. Such was a bitte too thikke for the Muster of the hoose so as he called down on the Grand Precurser who coiled him a crawler of the dupest dye and thundered at him to flatch down off that erection and be aslimed of himself for the bellance of hissch leif. (505.36-506.8)

One thread of the many thoughts here is that Adam, for the rest of his (and our) life, will be ashamed of sexual arousal and even the beauty and romance ("bellance") that can inform relations between man and woman. The "dupest dye" is not only the foolish death to which Adam is condemned but also the red blush of his shame and guilt. This red of shame attaches to HCE at many points in the book. We are told in I, 1 that he has a "blushmantle upon him from earsend to earsend" (24.9-10). The Ballad of Persse O'Reilly suggests that "he ought to blush for himself, the old hayheaded philosopher, / For to go and shove himself that way on top of her" (47.1-2). Even one of his defenders claims "it would be skarlot shame to jailahim" (60.4-5), once again combining red (scarlet) with sexuality (harlot) with shame with HCE. Kate, in accusing HCE of having made sexual advances to her, describes him as "braising red in the toastface with lovensoft eyebulbs" (531.8) while the four old men watching the copulating Porters say of him: "Derg [Irish, "red"] rudd face should take patrick's purge" (582.28-29), meaning that he should atone for the red crimes, whose evidence is in the blush of shame on his face, by making the pilgrimage to St. Patrick's Purgatory or Lough Derg. Two lines further on they reemphasize the point: "Redspot his browbrand" (582.31). Even his wife in her spirited defense of HCE in the "Inquisition" (III, 3) lets slip: "I will confess to his sins and blush me further" (494.30-31). When HCE is the accused Pegger Festy in the dock, he is "the rudacist rotter in Roebuckdom" (90.26-27), a phrase which contains three reds. And one version of the Park incident finds him with "his alpenstuck in his redhand" (85.11-12), i.e., caught redhanded in exhibiting himself or masturbating. The emphasis on red flush of shame for sin in these examples suggests for the name "Adam" a false etymology of the sort that appealed to Joyce's fancy.

The profusion of reds that attend HCE and the tangled web of associations and identifications they provide are so striking as to make red HCE's definitive color. He is "ruddy blond" (559.24-25) and has "ruddycheeks" (493.8). He is gossiped about as "Allan Rogue" (*rouge*) (588.28) and "whiggissimus incarnadined" (79.3). His penis (or possibly buttocks) is "how rood [Dutch, "red"] in norlandes" (564.23) and he is also referred to as "ruddy old Villain Rufus" (122.16-17) or William the Red. On his bottom he has a "scarlet pimparnell" which in addition to being an angry red pimple and Baroness Orczy's "Scarlet Pimpernel" is also the sign of the pimp for the scarlet transgressions which brought Parnell low. In his cups he is "toastified by his "cheeriubicundenances" (382.2-3) or flaming red face. Reds attend his role of invader of woman: "he would redden her with his vestas" (536.18), and by his own account he will tame the Liffey "with three plunges of my ruddertail" (539.18-19).

The primary significance of the HCE-red set of references is, I believe, the identification with Adam, but there are at least ten other associations that merit discussion. The final pages of the "Pub-scene" (II, 3), pp. 380-82, identify the about-to-fall HCE with Roderick or Rory O'Connor, last high king, i.e., last native king, of Ireland.[19] "Rory" means "red" as Joyce pointed out in his "Key" to the opening paragraphs.[20] Of the two dozen or so appearances of Roderick-Rory listed by Glasheen, almost all can be connected with HCE, but there appears to be little use made of the color aspect of Rory's name.[21] The one clear exception is the very first occurrence of "rory" (3.13) for which Joyce's "Key" tells us that this is the red extreme of the rainbow. Clearly it is also, in "rory end to the regginbrow," the end of the native highkingship, the end of a cycle symbolized by the name of the last high king.

Another of HCE's reds attends him as great life-tree described in I, 3: "the gigantig's lifetree, our fireleaved loverlucky blomsterbohm, phoenix in our woodlessness, haughty, cacuminal, erubescent (repetition!) whose roots they be asches with lustres of peins" (55.27-30). This is at once the symbolic tree of life, a real tree at the site of the Incident in the Phoenix Park, HCE's erect and shameful-red-blushing ("erubescent") penis, and that very phallic monument also to be found in the Phoenix Park, the Wellington monument. The connection with Wellington is strengthened by HCE's position prior to the king's arrival and HCE's naming: "saving daylight under his redwootree one sultry sabbath afternoon" (30.13-14). This is the giant redwood or sequoia brought to England in 1853 and named Wellingtonia. This in turn hints at further red connections, as Adaline Glasheen suggests in her *Third Census* entry for Sequoia:

> Sequoia...—the "big tree" or "red wood" of California. One of its kind was brought to England, 1853, and named Wellingtonia..., and the same species is called Washingtonia in America. I think Joyce mixes the giant redwood with Washington's cherry tree and with the Tree of Liberty...whose political colour is "red."[22]

The Phoenix Park connection is interesting for another reason. In his note "Phoenicians and Phoenixes," J. Mitchell Morse writes:

> Liddell and Scott tell us that *phoinix* as a noun means "*a purple-red, deep purple or crimson*, because the discovery of this colour was ascribed to the Phoenicians";...as an adjective, *phoinix* means "*purple-red, purple* or *crimson, red*";...also like Lat. *fulvus* of the colour of fire. The words *phoinix, phoinikeos*, etc., included all *dark reds*, from crimson to purple.[23]

Thus red links HCE, tree, Wellington, phoenix, phallus in one strand of association.

In one of those fascinating coincidences that prove language, as someone has remarked, to be in collusion with James Joyce, it happens that the Irish for "earwig" is *deargadaol. Dearg* is the Irish for "red." Thus in the "Pub-scene" (II, 3) HCE is a dearagadye" (313.18) or red color and earwig. And since the Dargle is a Dublin river—Issy mentions it at 460.15—"the Dargul dale" at 327.18 connects Dublin, red, HCE-Captain and ALP-Issy.

On a few occasions HCE is associated with Roth and with Rothschild. As a man of property and an entrepreneur, no doubt HCE is entitled to have "some dub him Rotshield" (129.20). The red (German: *rot*) is emphasized in this spelling. And in I, 1, HCE has "seven wrothschields" (10.35) designed no doubt like his seven garments to shield him from the wrath of his enemies, among whom is Samuel Roth, the piratical American publisher of parts of *Ulysses* and *Work in Progress*. Roth is almost certainly present at least three times in the *Wake* in contexts in which anger, dissension and hostility are aimed at a surrogate figure of HCE's (3.12; 176.23) or at HCE himself (58.30–31).

HCE is frequently a fish in the *Wake*, not to say fishy. He is especially associated with the king of fish, revered in ancient Ireland, the salmon. In his "Sermon" (III, 2) Shaun dreams of a future in which he will fish at leisure and lists some of the fish he intends to catch, among them "the finny ones, . . . the big Gillaroo redfellows" (450.4–6). Finn, the finny one, gained his wisdom from the salmon of knowledge and his reincarnation HCE is a fishy red fellow—*giolla rua* is literally "red fellow" and also a kind of trout. Shaun's real target is the father whom he hopes to replace in the future. At the wake of HCE-Finnegan in I, 1, the corpse is both the sacrificial feast and the Christ-fish; in the midst of a series of fish images he is "almost rubicund Salmosalar" or red salmon (7.16). The salmon is a logical incarnation for the invader of the mouth, or vagina, of the Liffey. But the salmon identification has one further and interesting junction. When the dead man is more or less quietly in his grave the imminent arrival of his replacement-reincarnation is announced thus: "For, be that samesake sibsubstitute of a hooky salmon, there's already a big rody ram lad at random on the premises of his haunt of the hungred bordles" (28.35–29.1). Here the red salmon is identified with the Duke of Wellington whose nickname was "Old Hooky" and whose phallic redwood tree is also, as we have seen, a manifestation of HCE.

One quite minor and tenuous red association of HCE's merits mention, namely that with the Dublin of Laurens County, Georgia, which features largely on the first page of the book. Adaline Glasheen observes: "I suppose Joyce picked this Dublin . . . because Laurens is near St. Laurence O'Toole, Dublin's patron saint, and near the St. Lawrence family of Howth. . . . It may also have appealed because of Georgio [*sic*] Joyce."[24] I can suggest another reason, namely that Georgia is famed for its red earth, which connects with HCE through Adam. I have not found, however, that Joyce makes any play with red and Dublin's Georgia. What I have found is that Peter Sawyer, Joyce's assigned founder for Dublin, Georgia, connects on at least one occasion with an HCE surrogate who has his own red associations. The instance occurs in the "Butt and Taff" episode (II, 3): "Sans butly Tuppeter Sowyer, the rouged engenerand" (372.6–7). The Russian general, as we shall see in a moment, is very "rouged" indeed. On another occasion in the same episode Peter Sawyer may also be present with Tom Sawyer and the Iron Duke of Wellington: "when that man d'airin was big toptom saw tip side bum boss pageantfiller" (338.26 27). What "pageantfiller" Balkelly is doing here is intriguing but beyond me. One final point is worth making in this connection. One of the descriptions of the hero in Question #1 of the "Quiz" (I, 6) runs as follows: "pink sunset shower, red clay cloud, sorrow or Sahara, oxhide or Iren" (127.25-26). The last three words constitute one of the many distortions in the *Wake* of the song title "An Exile of Erin," and also suggest, among other things, "oxide of iron," which is red, as indeed is the sandstone of the Sahara, and Adam ("red clay") and the state of Georgia, site of the other Dublin. HCE's red has a universal human or at least masculine dimension that transcends place as well as time.

The Russian general may be of Crimean War vintage but his red is as pronounced as that of any Russian communist leader of our day. This red is emphasized at almost every opportunity in the book. He is the "rudskin gunerally" (220.15), "the rosing girnirilles" (346.21) and "the rouged engenerand" (372.6-7). The word "Crimean" is distorted towards "crimson" as in "crimosing balkonladies" (569.2), and the battle scene is a blaze of blood red: "flashing and krashning [Russian: "red"] blurty moriartsky blutcherudd" (338.8-9). In the battle he wears "scarlet manchokuffs" (339.12) (a reference to Generals Scarlett and Menshikov) and the temptresses have become "scharlot runners" (352.6). The red is the mark of HCE-Adam, of man who carries the guilt and shame of past falls and crimes and who will certainly fall again.

The final red association of HCE's I wish to discuss is "red-fox," an association that I can trace but can make little sense of. HCE beset by his enemies is frequently pictured as a quarry hunted through the townlands of county Dublin. HCE is not always a fox on such occasions; sometimes he may be a bear, sometimes a deer as in ALP's final monologue (622.29). But the hunters generally hunt him with a pack of foxhounds. On at least three occasions HCE is identified or at least closely associated with the song title *Madairin Rua*, literally, "Little Red Fox."[25] But on another occasion *Madairin* is distorted towards "little mother" and applied to ALP (558.29-30). There is the further mystery of Fox-Goodman. Glasheen lists eleven occurrences for Fox-Goodman's name in the *Wake*.[26] On only one of those occasions does it seem likely that Fox-Goodman is HCE (603.32). In at least one case he cannot possibly be HCE (35.30). In only two cases, 511.9 and 515.2, is "red" explicitly named with Fox-Goodman. And yet Fox-Goodman strikes at least this reader as very much an HCE-type figure, but I have failed to find a coherent pattern to substantiate such a view.

The phrase I have chosen to head this chapter, "a chameleon at last," appears on the last page of III, 4, that is, it comes just after the last act of night, the vain attempt at sexual intercourse, has concluded or been abandoned, and just before the "Recorso" begins. Dawn has already arrived. Here is the passage in which the phrase appears:

> They know him, the covenanter, by rote at least, for a chameleon at last, in his true falseheaven colours from ultraviolent to subred tissues. That's his last tryon to march through the grand tryomphal arch. His reignbolt's shot. Never again! (590.7–10)

"Covenanter" is the Scots covenanter, the only successful invader of Ireland in the sense that he remains to this day the only invader whom Ireland has failed to assimilate, witness the ongoing Troubles in Ulster. He could of course also be regarded as the only *un*successful invader since he is as it were still on the beaches. But "convenanter" is also Noah, the sign of whose covenant with God was the rainbow. "Rote" is red, HCE's primary and most obvious color. But his red like his nature is continually changing; he is a chameleon whose color changes. His colors, full seven and Fall seven, change even as we look at them; the seven girls who seduce him and the seven deadly sins of which he is guilty are real enough, yet they fail to define him. His fall is no more real or true than his pretensions. "Ultraviolent to subred tissues" indicates the rainbow, the sign both of God's covenant with man and of man's fall. The phrase also suggests the violence that continues to be part of man's nature and behavior and the flesh of which his body consists. The final two words claim that he is finished forever, but as so often happens in Joycean absolutes, the absolute contains its own qualification; in this case, the finality of "never" is weakened by the "again" which is tagged on to it. "Reignbolt" is the rainbow of promise and fall, and HCE's "reign," while "the grand tryomphal arch" is the rainbow, the *arc de triomphe*, and Noah's ark. But all of this latter part can be read in a sexual sense, especially in view of the unsuccessful sexual intercourse HCE has just concluded with ALP. In this sense "tryon" suggests an attempt at "hardon" or erection; the arch is the woman's pubic arch or the arch formed by her thighs and genitalia. But this sense contains many contradictions: were his bolt shot (we are told he never wet the tea) his intercourse could be regarded as being successful. But the narrator or narrators of the *Wake* are no more trustworthy than the narrators of *Ulysses*. The narrator here revels in what he claims is the final fall, the final failure. But the chapter ends twenty lines later in a paradigm of the endless cycle: "Tiers, tiers and tiers. Rounds" (590.30). What the passage we are examining really propounds is that doubt is the only certainty; that not even identity is knowable or even fixed; those who are certain at least of HCE's human masculine red find at last that all they have is a pattern of ever-changing colors.

A minor and scattered but persistent pattern of color that attaches to HCE is the combination and contrast of red and white. This particular pattern demonstrates neatly the effectiveness of colors in establishing the paradoxical Wakean vision of "Identity and Difference" while extending the implications of that paradox to various themes and personae of the book.[27] To show red and white with HCE fulfilling this function I shall examine five separate passages.

Here is the first passage: "... the white ground of his face all covered with diagonally redcrossed nonfatal mammalian blood as proofpositive of the seriousness of his character" (84.19-21). This is part of a lengthy sentence describing the wounds of one antagonist in one of the park confrontations given in I, 4. This person is certainly HCE. Both red and white are the colors of HCE and here they are the marks of the violent external conflict in which he has just been engaged as well as outward symbols of inner struggles tearing his psyche apart. They also suggest both life and death as in Mulligan's "the white death and the ruddy birth" (*Ulysses*, 10.1073-4). But they also indicate a union, the union of white skin and red blood, or, in other words, the hypostatic union of Christ's body and blood, of his deity and humanity, symbolized in the white bread and red wine of the Last Supper. Both union and conflict are given a sexual dimension by the abrupt change at the end of the sentence of one or another of the antagonists into a female: "her whacking. Herwho?" (84.27).

My second example is taken from the opening pages of the "Norwegian Captain" chapter (II, 3) where the publican is preparing a drink of O'Connell's ale for a customer: "That host of a bottlefilled, the bulkily hulkwight, hunter's pink of face, an orel orioled, is in on a bout to be unbulging an o'connell's" (310.26-28). HCE is the host of the filled bottle, the host of a battlefield or a man at war with himself. He is also the arch-druid Balkelly and bishop Berkeley. Though he is pictured as a bulky hulking and skulking white, his face is the bright pink of a huntsman's jacket, well on its way to the red which will signify his guilt, his manly exertions and his eventual inebriation. He is an eagle (Slavic, *orel*) about to be brought down by time (*oriole:* Italian, "clock")[28], the same weapon which he will use to oust his customers, and which threatened himself in the Park. Yet at the same time, as Communion host and "bottlefilled" he is once again the unity of Christ incarnate symbolized in bread and wine.

The "Colours Game" (II, 1) is the source of my third passage, one of those scenes in which one of the sons, in this case the Shem-type Glugg, merges under pressure of hostility and accusations back into the father figure HCE whose proper function it is to bear all such nastiness on his broad shoulders: "Collosul rhodomantic not wert one bronze lie Scholarina say as he, greyed vike cuddlepuller, walk in her sleep his pig indicks weg femtyfem funts" (241.8-10). In the dream world man is as guilty of his crimes in other people's dreams as in his own. Here the dreamer is Issy (Italian *scolarina*: "little schoolgirl"[29]) and the crime is sexual molestation of her vulva with finger or penis (pig indicks... funts). On the one hand HCE is what Lady Campbell called Wilde, "a great white slug," here a great white caterpillar. The "greyed" reflects his paternal authority and echoes Dorian Gray. "Vike" is both vice and (Greek: *nike*) victory. "Cuddlepullar" suggests at least surreptitious caresses but hints too at masturbation or fellation. He is also the Colossus of Rhodes, is rosecolored and is associated with romantic roses. In other words the fever of illicit sexual urges, manifested in the clash of red and white in the dream, is leading HCE to a colossal fall—and erection.

My fourth example occurs near the end of I, 1: "Creator he has created for his creatured ones a creation. White monthoid? Red theatrocrat? And all the pinkprophets cohalething? Very much so!" (29.14–16). Despite the obscurity of the passage and its context a number of observations can safely be made, I believe, about the colors. If we take the reiterated "creation" to be God's seven-day creation then we have on the one hand monotheism, unity, the white light of eternity, the spirit. On the other hand we have theocratic, aristocratic, theatrical forms of organization. "Theatr-" has to do with vision; "red" sometimes suggests the rainbow in the *Wake* and may suggest here the rainbow vision of dream. Red is, as we have already seen, the physical world and man. One reading of this is to see it as the creation of the individual when God breathes the white immortal soul into the red clay and flesh of the body. When the two coalesce to form pink, the color of living skin, we have life. But "cohalething" also contains "Lethe," the river of forgetfulness and death. Every heartbeat, every struggle of the individual signifies life but brings him one step closer to the dissolution of death. The overriding image of the passage is that of the creation of order and government and includes man as creator with God.

My fifth and final example of the red/white/HCE set of associations consists of a parenthetical passage in what appears to be a drunken dissemination of Hosty's ballad:

> (it seemed he was before the eyots of martas or otherwales the thirds of fossilyears, he having beham with katya when lavinias had her mens lease to sea in a psumpship doodly show whereat he was looking for fight niggers with whilde roarses) (40.9–13)

I shall concentrate my attention on three phrases: "a psumpship doodly show" is a Punch and Judy show or a battle between the sexes and a urinating exhibition ("pumpship"). "Fight niggers" is white niggers, white knickers or panties and fighting. "Whilde roarses" is wild roses, white roses, wild red roses, wild red arses, white and red arses, wild horses, Wilde and buggery. HCE may be urinating. The two girls almost certainly are. HCE is watching the girls who are watching him. The three fusiliers are watching him and them. HCE tries to spy the girls' white knickers and white bottoms and red genitalia. What actually occurs in the Park incident is as uncertain here as it is in any other version. Nobody is innocent; voyeurism, exhibitionism, masturbation, titillation both homo- and heterosexual occupy the collective minds of the one, the two and the three. Red and white mark the tension between male predacity and female provocation. The black in "doodly" (Irish, *dubh*) and "niggers" serves to unbalance the symmetry of tension and to insist on the instablity that every antithesis in *Finnegans Wake* must contain.

A color pattern of the greatest ubiquity and highest importance in the *Wake* is the juxtaposition of raven and dove with their black and white implications. I shall examine the sexual and female aspects of the dove-raven motif in chapter 4, but since many occurrences of dove-raven are particularly and intimately connected with HCE, I must engage in a preliminary discussion of the matter here.

There is one article which outlines cogently the broad significances of the raven-dove motif in the *Wake*, namely Wilhelm Fuger's "Ravens and Doves." Fuger outlines the Genesis story of the raven and three doves which Noah sent out from the Ark, and the traditional Western symbolism associated with raven and dove, namely the raven as representing black/evil/war and the dove as white/goodness/peace. He goes on to assess Joyce's use of raven and dove in *Finnegans Wake*:

> These contraries are nothing but the two sides of the one medal that is reality in its inseparable union of good and evil.... This idea of duality seems to be the ultimate reason why raven and dove are so often and so insistently combined with each other. Words like 'ravenindove' (354.28) or 'dovesandraves' (363.07), which put this *coincidentia oppositorum* in a nutshell, can thus be regarded as programmatic expressions of one of the book's central ideas.[30]

While agreeing entirely with Fuger's general outline of this motif's significance I must add one point of which Fuger seems unaware but which his point of view can assimilate quite readily, namely that the Irish word for "black," *dubh*, is pronounced almost exactly like the English word "dove." Thus in classic Joycean fashion the dove-raven antithesis carries within it an element which qualifies its simple polarity and upsets its balance.

The doves and ravens which attend HCE and some of his surrogate figures function very much as Fuger's thesis would suggest; they emphasize the degree to which good and evil, high ideals and venal tendencies are inextricably entangled, melded even, in the human psyche. They also insist on the likeness and brotherhood of man and man by providing a fragile chain of echoes to link human figures far removed in time and space and circumstances. I shall trace some of those links.

Among the insults to which HCE claims to have been subjected in the gate incident (I, 3) is "*Hraabhraab, Coocoohandler*" (72.13). *Rab* is German "raven" and "coo-" is of course the dove. *Raab* is also Danish for "shout," according to McHugh.[31] What we have is cheek-by-jowl accusations of aggression and peace, roughness and gentleness, black and white, a reminder that all of these things exist side by side simultaneously in the heart of HCE. But the "good" side of the equation has built-in qualifications. *Kuhhandel* is German "shady business,"[32] while "coocoohandler" suggests "shit-handler" (*ka-ka*) and also a fondler of girls. In Question #1 of the "Quiz" (I, 6) it is said that HCE "bears a raaven geulant on a fjeld duiv" (136.12–13), which combines in one coat of arms the raven of viking ferocity, and the dove of peace. The difficulty of defining and separating the opposite qualities symbolized in the phrase I quoted is further complicated if the reader recalls that *duiv* is Irish "black" and that in heraldry "gules" is red, a red represented in black-and-white engravings by alternating vertical black and white lines. This alternation of black and white in location or field is balanced a few lines further on by an alternation in time and mood: "the pigeons doves be perchin all over him one day on Baslesbridge and the ravens duv be pitchin their dark nets after him the next night behind Koenigstein's Arbour..." (136.29–32). Ballsbridge and Kingstown (now Dun Laoghaire) are both suburbs of Dublin. Their similarity rather than their difference is emphasized by the spelling "Baslesbridge" which suggests the (classical) Greek *basileus*, "king." Incidentally this is one of the passages that demonstrates Joyce's consciousness of Irish *dubh* as he plays with the dove-raven motif.

As we trace the threads of the dove-raven motif as it relates to HCE through the *Wake*, we can see the author continually punning and distorting the phrases in which the motif occurs to create new imbalances and asymmetries within the basic antithesis. In the first Pub-scene (II, 3) the drunken customers fantasize their host's death by execution: "And a free for croaks after. Dovlen are out for it. So is Rathfinn" (377.22). "Croaks" are the ravens. But in Irish the "th" of "Rathfinn" is silent, moving that word very close to the English "raven." That "Rathfinn" also contains *finn* or "white" further complicates the entanglement of opposites. In the "Museyroom" (I, 1) HCE as Wellington is attended by dove and raven who are quite clearly here the temptresses in the Park: "The jinnies is a cooin her hand and the jinnies is a ravin her hair and the Willingdone git the band up" (8.33–34). Typically, dove-raven does nothing to distinguish one girl from the other but merely suggests white hands and black hair—maybe. Sometimes in HCE's relationship with ALP she is the dove and he is the raven: "Hold the raabers for the kunning his plethoron. Let leash the dooves to the cooin her coynth" (579.14–16). Two pages earlier the same identifications occur: "peg of his claim and pride of her heart, cliffscaur grisly but rockdove cooing" (577.16–17). But such a simple category of identification is not consistently allowed. At one point raven and dove are both applied to HCE while ALP is associated with neither: "The boss made dovesandraves out of his bucknesst while herself wears the bowler's hat in her bath" (363.6–8). The ducks-and-drakes here further accentuates the similarities and the commonalities of dove and raven.

At one point in her final monologue ALP, speaking directly to her husband, says: "Or the birds start their treestirm shindy. Look, there are yours off, high on high! And cooshes, sweet good luck they're cawing you, Coole! You see, they're as white as the riven snae" (621.35-622.2). Among other things going on here this much is clear: the "cooshes" are the doves even if they caw like ravens. "Coole" as well as being HCE-Finn is also the Coole Park of Yeats's swans which of course are as white as the driven snow. Dove and raven here are effectively merged. In addition the change of "driven" to "riven" puts us within one phoneme of "raven," a phoneme supplied by the change of "snow" to the dialect "snae." This is a particularly important sound to have changed since a significant feature of the dove-raven polarity is the alpha and omega to be found in their names and in the call each makes, "coo" and "caw." *Finnegans Wake* continually challenges the uniqueness and originality of beginnings and the uniqueness and finality of endings.

Chief among HCE's surrogates associated with dove and raven is of course Noah himself, and with Noah his counterpart in the Greek deluge myth, Deucalion. "Jukoleon" is the protagonist in a distorted version of the Genesis story in the first Pub-scene (II, 3) and the birds are "the fionnling and dubhlet, the dun and the fire" (367.22-23), and "coold by cawld" (367.28). "The dun and the fire" are the dun and the fair as well as the wicked and the true (Irish: *dona, fior*). In the "Inquisition of Yawn" (III, 3) another version of the Genesis story runs: "He sent out Christy Columb and he came back with a jailbird's unbespokables in his beak and then he sent out Le Caron Crow and the peacies are still looking for him" (496.30-32). According to McHugh "Le Caron Crow" is Henri Le Caron who betrayed the American Fenians' plans to invade Canada.[33] Certainly treachery is a characteristic of the raven in the Genesis story and popular tradition. The "peacies" who seek him are the seekers of peace symbolized by the dove, police constables, and the Irish police force or "peace guardians" (*gardai siochana*). Christopher Columbus is an appropriate dove figure both because his name, Columbus, is Latin for "dove," and because he was an adventurer and explorer who returned faithfully and triumphantly. Constancy is an important quality associated with the dove. Columbus thus turns up a number of times in association with dove. In the "Inquisition of Yawn" (III, 3) a voice which may be Shem's or that of some Shem-Shaun mixture claims: "I'm of the ochlocracy with Prestopher Palumbus and Porvus Parrio" (484.31-32). If we compensate for the Irish p/k split we have "Crestopher Calumbus" and "Corvus Carrio." "Palumbus" also echoes (Spanish) *paloma*, "dove," while *corvus corone* is Latin for carrion crow. Further on in the same "Inquisition" section two occurrences of Columbus with dove and raven show a merging of the opposites into one name: "— Crestofer Carambas!... Vulturuvarnar!" (512.7-8), and "Crashedafar Corumbas!" (513.6). "Varna" is Lithuanian, "crow."[34] The raven has become a vulture-crow. The introduction of the raven's *r* and *a*'s into Columbus unbalances the polarity. This merging is even more pronounced in the second example with "Coru-" being only one letter away from *corvu*, the Latin "raven."

Columbus is sometimes, possibly always, combined with the name of the Irish missionary Columba, or *Colm Cille*, literally "dove of the church." Columba is almost certainly present in the drunken customer's rehashing of HCE's misfortunes when they talk of "another doesend end once tale of a tublin wished on to him with its olives ocolombs and its hills owns ravings" (335.27-29). On the one hand there are the raven and hell's own ravings and on the other Columbus and the dove of peace. "Olives" is the olive branch of peace as well as the Irish *ollamh*, "scholar," symbolizing the blend of learning and Christian love on which Ireland in the Dark Ages prided itself and of which Columba is the outstanding personification.

Columbus's dove is sometimes opposed by Poe's raven. Among the attributes of HCE in Question #1 of the "Quiz" (I, 6) is this: "what Nevermore missed and Colombo found" (129.30-31). I cannot pretend that I understand the point of this phrase. Certainly Edgar Allan Poe with his troubled life, his lugubrious and often violent fiction and his gloomy raven makes an appropriate contrast to the American dreams of opportunity symbolized by Columbus. Poe's raven also appears in another dove-passage, an obscure piece describing how those responsible for spreading Hosty's ballad met with bad ends. Here are the relevant phrases: "after which the cawer and the marble halls of Pump Court Columbarium, the home of the old seakings, looked upon each other and queth their haven evermore for it transpires that on the other side of the water it came about that on the field of Vasileff's Cornix"(49.9-13). "Vasileff's Cornix" is King's Crow (Greek and Latin). The "cawer" is also the raven while "Quoth the raven 'Nevermore'" is the repeated line in Poe's poem "The Raven." "Columba-" is the dove and Columba-Columbus. I suspect an obscure play is going on here between the name "Poe" (meaning chamber pot), and "pump ship" or "urinate," but I can't quite follow it or find its significance.

The single most noticeable color feature in *Finnegans Wake* is the rainbow. Its presence is usually indicated in the book in one of three ways, by a simple direct use of the word rainbow or a word cognate with it, by designation of the first and last bands of the rainbow, namely red and violet, or, more elaborately, by a working into the text of all seven colors in a cluster. Obviously the last of these devices is the one that most calls attention to itself. By McHugh's count it occurs twenty-eight times in the *Wake*.[35]

It is well known that rainbows in the *Wake* have a special connection with HCE. Adaline Glasheen sees seven as HCE's number, most frequently displayed in his seven garments and in the seven Rainbow girls who tempt him.[36] The rainbow has a dual significance for mankind: as well as being a promise, God's covenant with Noah that there will not be another deluge and that man will be sent a saviour, it is also a reminder or threat: that man *has* fallen and that he will fall again. Indeed the *Wake*'s rainbows are regularly associated with occasions of man's fall—woman, pride, guilt, alcohol.

The first appearance of the rainbow is in the second paragraph of the book; it does not occur as a listing of the colors, i.e., it is not an item in McHugh's list, but through reference to violet and red. This paragraph begins, "Sir Tristram, violer d'amores" (3.4) and ends with the sentence: "Rot a peck of pa's malt had Jhem or Shen brewed by arclight and rory end to the regginbrow was to be seen ringsome on the aquaface" (3.12–14). In a letter of November 15, 1926 to Harriet Weaver, Joyce gave what he called a "key" to these first two paragraphs or rather to an earlier version of them.[37] In a series of five articles in *A Wake Newslitter* Adaline Glasheen uses Joyce's "key" to make a close analysis of the opening paragraphs of the *Wake*.[38] A good deal of her discussion focuses on the rainbow in paragraph 2 and some of her observations are germane to any discussion of rainbows in the *Wake*.

Glasheen sees the first paragraph of the book as "part of a circle, an arc, and it is about the arc-shaped trip of the Ark." She adds that the second paragraph "is another arc, the rainbow, and also a circle of viconian history."[39] What I think is important to remember about the rainbow in this connection is its duality. On the one hand it is, as arc, part of a putative circle. On the other we ordinarily see the rainbow only as an arc, that is, a broken circle. And this aspect of it is pointed out in the second paragraph in "rory end to the regginbrow" (3.13–14). It is the rainbow's end that we associate with illusions and false promises such as the pot of gold. Glasheen reminds us that according to Joyce's "key" the final line of the second paragraph contains a human face with eyebrows, itself "a very neat emblem of the arc and circle."[40] Since the first and last colors of the rainbow also mark the limits of human perception this rainbow-connected face may reasonably be seen as the human face of the book's protagonist, writer and reader, fallen man's vision of himself.

Glasheen makes a good deal of "violer" as Viola of *Twelfth Night* and "rory end" as Rosalind of *As You Like It*. She considers the transvestism of both heroines and concludes: "The simple and important thing about them is that they are prime examples of—illusion."[41] She pursues the ideas of illusion and ambiguity in the rainbow's symbolism:

> Accepting the pledge [of the rainbow], man ventures out on to dry land and falls almost at once, right at the start of the third paragraph, and after the fall comes the hundred-letter-word which is a thunderclap. Man should have known his etymology—Latin "arcus" (bow) is akin to Greek "arkys" (net or snare). The rainbow is like drink (raging brew) or women, a trick to lure man to his fall again.[42]

In the final article of the series, Glasheen develops that argument to a conclusion: "The rainbow promise is a bloody lie which lures man to his fall.

This is amply borne out, for as soon as the red band is formed, we come to 'The fall...' and the ominous roar of thunder."[43]

The first full listing of the rainbow colors in the *Wake* occurs at the climax of the Prankquean incident (I, 1) and describes the angry Jarl von Hoother emerging from his castle (R #1):[44]

> For like the campbells acoming with a fork lance of lightning, Jarl von Hoother Boanerges himself, the old terror of the dames, came hip hop handihap out through the pikeopened arkway of his three shuttoned castles, in his broadginger hat and his civic chollar and his allabuff hemmed and his bullbragggin soxangloves and his ladbroke breeks and his cattegut bandolair and his furframed panuncular cumbottes like a rudd yellow gruebleen orangeman in his violet indignation, to the whole length of the strength of his bowman's bill. (22.30-23.3)

This is quickly followed by the Jarl's defecation, shutting up and the thunderword, followed by the emergence of peace, literature, alcohol, and order, civilization in short: "And that was the first peace of illiterative porthery in all the flamend floody flatuous world" (23.9-10). The passage is preceded by the Prankquean's action: "And she made her wittest in front of the arkway of trihump" (22.28). There are anger and aggression in "lance," "lightning," "Boanerges," "terror," "chollar," "bullbragggin," "soxangloves," "bandolair," "rudd," "yellan," "orangeman," "indignation" and "bill." The presence of Strongbow, first and fiercest of Norman conquerors, adds to the air of violence. And yet the result of this explosion is the beginning of Vico's civilization—the thunder, the beginnings of language, the retreat to the cave (i.e., the shutting of the door). There are also echoes of the Noah's ark story in rainbow, "arkway," "floody," "porthery," "peace." What provokes the thunder in Vico's myth is sexuality and what provokes it here is the sexual challenge of the Prankquean's "witting." In a sense HCE/von Hoother is God provoked into a peace "betoun ye and he" (23,12). Possibly the most important aspect of this first rainbow is that it signals von Hoother's emergence, his manifestation. If, as I shall argue, it is true that the rainbow marks the dream-vision as opposed to the harsh, white, conventional light of day, then it is appropriate that the rainbow should signal the emergence into the open of figures which represent normally repressed complexes of the dreamer's psyche. As the dreamer falls deeper and deeper into sleep the daytime censor becomes weaker and the more threatening elements of his pysche surface in the disguises of a variety of personae. In that sense the book to this point has consisted of the half-awake prologue to the deeper sleep. But in this deep-dream drama the emergence of the father as von Hoother is triggered by the triple attack of the Prankquean on his fortress. That attack is sexual and it leads to sexual exposure. The Prankquean's wit/wet/urine provokes "the arkway of trihump" or the telltale excitation of the dreamer's genitalia. The anger and aggression of the released von Hoother represent the explosion of the normally censored possessive and incestuous aspects of the father's protective love of his children, especially Issy.

Sevens in the *Wake* suggest the rainbow and mark the kinds of revelation I have been discussing above. We can readily see this in the case of HCE's seven garments. Clothes in the *Wake* do more to reveal than conceal and what they especially reveal is that central exposure of the book, namely HCE's leaving his pub and walking out into the Phoenix Park to meet his destiny. Obviously this can be interpreted at one level as HCE's unbuttoning his fly and displaying his penis, especially since this is the particular exposure that appears to bother HCE most, judging from the accusations of the other personae. In the passage I have just examined above, the emergence of von Hoother from his castle is, essentially, HCE's walking out of his pub into the Phoenix Park. In the first clear account of the Cad's confrontation in the Park with HCE (in I, 2) HCE "was billowing across the wide expanse of our greatest park" (35.7–8) clothed in seven odd garments of one of which we are given the color—blue. Another version of the Park incident, or the earlier of the Park incidents if there were two, again shows HCE walking out in his seven garments. This time we are given the colors of two of them, "gingerine hue" and "finndrinn" (52.23–28). In the same section (I, 3), a particularly obscure version of the Park incident has a wandering poet who studies the seven signs of the zodiac (56.21–25). At the trial of Festy King, the defendant, another persona for HCE, is wearing seven garments, one of which is white. Obviously this is another potential revelation of hidden truth although the confusion of witnesses and judges makes it impossible to discern just what is revealed.

Frequently the HCE-figure who sports the seven garments or is otherwise associated with sevens and rainbows is a fearsome, violent figure, for reasons I have discussed earlier. This is true of the Russian general as Butt describes him in his seven garments with the appropriate red well to the fore (339.9–13). On the same page the general is given a fully detailed rainbow (R #21) in which rage and threat predominate (339.27–29). As we have seen in connection with the first rainbow in which the seven colors are listed (R #1: 22.30–23.3), the Norman invader, Strongbow, can also function as the threatening figure being revealed in the dream. He is present again as "Arcoforty" with "iridescent huecry" in highly suspicious circumstances at 68.19–20. As Glasheen notes: "Biblical scholars sometimes suggest that the rainbow was God's war-bow, the lightning his arrows."[43] In the ramblings of the four old men in III, 4, HCE appears again as a fearsome invader. He is not identified with Strongbow here but he wears the seven garments (387.3–6).

Some other examples of rainbows and sevens that fit into this pattern of the emerging HCE are worth considering briefly. One of the titles given to HCE in the "mamafesta" (I, 5) is "*Arcs in His Ceiling Flee Chinx on the Flur*"

(104.13–14). *Arc-en-ciel* is French, rainbow. What the title primarily points to is the contrast between the rainbow pretensions and the personality's flaws which lurk beneath the surface. But the closeness of "arcs" to "arse" suggests flaws in the pretensions themselves that provide an imbalance in the polarity and the tendency of the poles to coalesce. There is a strong hint of fall here and the rainbow, free drinks (on the floor rather than on the house) and flowers (or girls) connect with that fall. In the version of the ballad of Persse O'Reilly given in the Shem chapter (I, 7) occurs the line: "*Not yet his Arcobaleine forespoken Peacepeace upon Oath*" (175.16). This line looks back to the opening paragraphs ("not yet") and forward to the saint-Arch-druid confrontration ("Balenoarch"). *Arcobaleno* is Italian, "rainbow." The promise of peace upon earth is undermined by the echo of "foresworn" in "forespoken," the change of "earth" to "oath" (also "Howth" or HCE) and the suspicion of "piss-piss" in the doubled "peace." The deepest fear of the dreamer is that the perceptions revealed by the rainbow vision of the dream may prove horrifying.

Shaun's dreams of grandeur generally picture him stepping into his father's shoes and displaying himself as a popular success. Such a dream is outlined at the beginning of III, 1, and in it Shaun is resplendent in the father's seven garments with papal white and gold and the Irish flag conspicuously in evidence (404.16–30). On one of the rare occasions on which his artist-brother dallies with similar dreams of worldly success he sees himself as an opera singer in receipt of adulation from swooning women and enveloped in his brother's tricolor and his father's seven garments (180.1–15). These two dreams within a dream are not so much revelations of hidden conflicts as they are fantasies of alternative scenarios for the future, or in Freudian terms, wish-fulfilment dreams. During Shem's frustration with mathematics in the "Night Lessons" (II, 2), his discussion veers off towards the incident in the Park and we get two rainbows in rapid succession. One is fragmentary and obscure but seems to have overtones of sexual indiscretion (R #18, 284.27–285.3) while the other is made up of foodstuffs and is, for this reader at least, disconnected with the text (285.F6). Some pages earlier in the same section there is another seemingly disconnected rainbow (R #17, 277.F4), while on the same page occurs the sentence "His sevencolored's soot (Ochone! Ochonal!) and his imponence one heap lumpblock (Mogoul!)" (277.1–3). Death is very much present in this latter context. Shem's mathematical foray is going to lead to disclosure to the children of the mother's sexuality and to signal the coming of age of the next generation and therefore the tolling of the bell for the present generation personified in HCE. It is the deeply terrifying nature of those ideas that makes the "Night Lessons" section so discontinuous and cryptic. The censor is desperately struggling to assert his authority in the face of these hints of horrifying revelations, and is being partially successful. The rainbows and seven-references remain stillborn, immobilized, obscure, but visible.

St. Kevin is involved with sevens as well as nines (605.26–606.12). Kevin is essentially the Shaun-aspect of HCE and manifests the triumph of the ideal of Irish monasticism at Glendalough. The arch-druid wears a seven-colored garment and is much involved with rainbows. He represents an earlier ideal than Kevin's but his voice is that of dream, art and deepest truths—about to be overwhelmed by Patrick's muscular and cynical Christianity, the light of day in fact. HCE himself likes to boast of his achievements as being manifested in sevens, the seven hills of Rome and Edinburgh (541.1-4), the seven wonders of the world (553.9-12) and the taming of the Liffey at Dublin with seven dams (215.15).

Another set of associations between HCE and the seven-colored rainbow is carried out through "arch," "arc," and "ark." In the "Inquisition of Yawn" (III, 3) a question is asked which identifies Finnegan of the ballad and Toucher Tom and Thom's as "our arc of the covenant" (507.33). A little later in the same question the same figure is identified with "the Arch" pub (508.1). The spelling "arc" for "ark of the covenant" brings to mind the earlier covenant of Noah signified by the rainbow and, of course, Noah's ark as well. Some pages further on in the same chapter one of the seemingly endless questions asked by the Four concerns a man "carrying his ark, of eggshaped fuselage and made in Fredborg into the bullgine, across his back" (529.21-22). The man appears to be wandering out to the Park and he wears seven garments, so there is little doubt of his identity. But the odd thing about this ark is that it appears to be a Zeppelin and HCE is carrying it.[46] The bow has become a much more sophisticated weapon but whom it threatens or may save is an open question. What is certain is that the HCE-personae associated with the rainbow are powerful and fearsome and desperate.

This point is borne out in other instances of "ark" and "arc." An obscure reference in Jaun's sermon points to the father figure HCE: "Let flee me fiacckles, says the grand old manoark, stormcrested crowcock and undulant hair, hoodies tway!" (468.29-30). HCE here is Gladstone (grand old man) and Noah (man of ark) as well as king (monarch). But the dominant image of "stormcrested crowcock" with "hoodies tway"—German *hode* is testicle[47]—is one of the erect penis, obviously the most threatening, guilt-producing image that can appear in the dream. In an obscure part of that obscure chapter, the "Night Lessons" (II, 2), part of the review of history goes: "Rents and rates and tithes and taxes, wages, saves and spends. Heil, heptarched span of peace! Live, league of lex, nex and the mores!" (273.3-5). Here are seven items followed by the seven-arched span of peace—the rainbow. But "heptarched" is also Greek for "seventh ruler" or "ruler of one seventh" or "ruled by seven" and "Hail!" has become the Nazi "Heil!" The exhortation "Live" to the league of Mick, Nick and the Maggies suggests the "Colours Game" (II, 1) but is distorted to the league of law, murder and custom (Latin). The peace of the rainbow promise and of the dream-vision are regarded with cynicism and fear.

An image of some importance that crops up in connection with HCE and rainbow is *arc de triomphe*. It occurs in a passage which runs in part: "That's his last tryon to march through the grand tryomphal arch. His reignbolt's shot. Never again!" (590.9–10). The primary signification of the passage is that HCE is sexually finished, that he will never again attempt to enter the pubic arch or indeed to challenge woman's hegemony. But like every defeat in the *Wake*, this too is ambiguous. It may also mean that man is freed of the tyranny of his sexuality, that he need never again fall, need never again be cheated by the promise of the rainbow—or at least not until the next night's dream. In any event *Ulysses* has demonstrated that man no longer capable of sexual intercourse may be still very much a man and far from finished. The *arc de triomphe* also appears in a footnote in the "Night Lessons" (II, 2): "Valsinggiddyrex and his grand arks day triump" (281.F1). As in "the arkway of trihump" (22.28) of the Prankquean incident this is probably a belittling reference to HCE's genitalia.

The most prominent and consistent identification of the rainbow colors in the *Wake* is that with the seven flower girls who tempt HCE. In fact they personify his deepest sexual desires. This is spelled out in the second detailed rainbow (R #2): "He spenth his strenth amok haremscarems. Poppy Narancy, Giallia, Chlora, Marinka, Anileen, Parme. And ilk a those dames had her rainbow huemoures" (102.25–27). We are told in the Honuphrius case (III, 4) that "Gillia,... with Poppea, Arancita, Clara, Marinuzza, Indra and Iodina, has been tenderly debauched... by Honuphrius... " (R #26, 572.35–573.2). In the case of such assertions however the reader must remind himself firstly that the *Finnegans Wake* narrator is not reliable, particularly if given the opportunity for denigration, and secondly that these are the events in a dream. HCE's debauching of the girls is real in that it exists deep in his subconscious mind and emerges as act in the dream. Its relationship to things that happen in daylight is convoluted and tenuous.

The customers ousted from HCE's pub at closing time (II, 3) are well aware of his predilections and shout them for the world to hear. They call him "the mannork of Arrahland" (378.6), that is monarch of Ireland and man of rainbow (arc), ark and Ararat. A little further on they specify the implications of the charge:

> With seven hores always in the home of his thinkingthings, his nodsloddledome of his noiselisslesoughts. Two Idas, two Evas, two Nessies and Rubyjuby. Phook! No wonder, pipes as kirles, that he sthings like a rheinbok. One bed night he had the delysiums that they were all queens mobbing him. Fell stiff. (379.14–18)

The seven whores are perpetually present at the apertures of his sensory organs—he has in fact little else on his mind. He stinks like a billygoat and is frequently in a state of arousal. In the first question of the Quiz (I, 6) we are told that HCE "had sevenal successivecolored serebanmaids on the same big white drawringroam horthrug" (126.19-20). The "seven" has almost become "several," and the juxtaposition of the seven colors with white hints that they may all be merely projections of the one Anna Livia. Rainbow #7 occurs in Shem's chapter (I, 7) and is clearly Shem's: "to ensign the colours by the beerlitz in his mathness and his educandees to outhue to themselves in the cries of girlglee: gember! inkware! chonchambre! cinsero! zinnzabar! tincture and gin!" (182.7-10). According to McHugh, *educande* is Italian "girl boarders in convent schools."[48] Berlitz identifies Joyce himself; Shem the writer is fantasizing his usurpation of his father's place; Joyce joins those personae of the father such as Swift and Lewis Carroll who are attracted to little girls.

Rainbows are also involved with HCE's relations with his wife, especially in the ALP chpater (I, 8) and more especially in connection with ALP's earliest sexual experiences. In the well-known paragraph beginning "Ah but she was the queer old sheowsha anyhow," R #9 runs: "He married his markets, cheap by foul, I know, like any Etrurian Catholic Heathen, in their pinky limony creamy birnies and their turkiss indienne mauves. But at milkidmass who was the spouse?" (215.19-22). There is both a contrast and a confusion here between the rainbow colors of the seven "hores" and the white ("milk-") of ALP. I am reminded of Glasheen's comment: "At times they are HCE's seven whores and are opposed to Anna Livia's unity; at other times, they are opposed to, or gathered up in, white light."[49] My point is that the opposition and "gathering up in" are both going on simultaneously; that the seven are splinterings of Anna, just as the seven rainbow bands are the splinterings of white light.

A few lines earlier in the same paragraph we find this passage:

> And sure he was the quare old buntz too, Dear Dirty Dumpling, foostherfather of fingalls and dotthergills. Gammer and gaffer we're all their gangsters. Hadn't he seven dams to wive him? And every dam had her seven crutches. And every crutch had its seven hues. And each hue had a differing cry. (215.13-17)

HCE is brightly colored (German, *bunt*). His children are fair sons and dark daughters, thus demonstrating the basic split and color polarity of his psyche. But, in the same way that we saw with dove-raven, this polarity too is compromised in that one pole contains its opposite within it; "-gill" means "bright," or "shining" in Irish. There is clearly evident here too Joyce's fondness for conflating the two words "hue" in the riddling rime "As I was Going to St. Ives." Despite all the sevens the answer to the riddle "How many were going to St. Ives?" is "one." And despite all the rainbows they all blend eventually into the one Anna Livia. And, as McHugh points out, Joyce explained this passage to Harriet Weaver in a letter by saying that the seven dams represented the splitting up of the river Liffey for the building of the city.[50]

There are two other passages in the ALP chapter which merit discussion here. The first is one of these sentences in the *Wake* that periodically draw together many of the book's themes: "Was it waterlows year, after Grattan or Flood, or when maids were in Arc or when three stood hosting?" (202.16–18). The point at issue is the occasion of Anna's earliest sexual experiences. The two girls and three soldiers bring in the Park incident which subsumes all incidents of an overtly sexual nature. It also implies that HCE is the male actor and perpetrator in all sexual incidents—all sexuality touches the dreamer's guilt. The names of Henry Grattan and Henry Flood recall the history of Ireland, especially the independence struggles against England. "Waterlows" suggests "Willingdone" and his erection and the "maids" or "jinnies" who provoked it (and the Park incident) with their loose waters. "Arc" suggests Noah's ark and the arc of the rainbow, as well as, quite possibly, the arc of a stream of urine and the rainbow which that could create. The idea of sexual initiation suggests loss of virginity and therefore fall and guilt; all the figures in the sentence above fell or failed.

The second passage contains a rainbow (R #8) and further explores ALP's early sexual experiences:

> You know the dinkel dale of Luggelaw? Well, there once dwelt a local heremite, Michael Arklow was his riverend name, ... and one venersderg in junojuly, oso sweet and so cool and so limber she looked... he plunged both of his newly annointed hands, the core of his cushlas, in her singimari saffron strumans of hair, parting them and soothing her and mingling it, that was deepdark and ample like this red bog at sundown. By that Vale Vowclose's lucydlac, the reignbeau's heavenarches arronged orranged her. Afroth-dizzying galbs, her enamelled eyes indergoading him on to the vierge violetian. (203.17-29)

Michael is the HCE figure and through Kevin and Luggelaw, the righteous Shaun, whose sexual fall occurs only because of the extremity of temptation deliberately offered by the woman. The hair in which he plunges his hands is pubic hair; "strumans" is streaming and, Latin, swelling. The most obvious reading of the passage is the picture of the hermit plunging his hands in the Liffey's water with the rainbow in the sky above. But I believe a better reading is the envisioning of the young river running through little rapids and waterfalls, "afrothdizzying," i.e., tumbling and frothing as well as aphrodisiac, creating numerous rivulets and numerous rainbows. ALP breaks into the seven rainbow girls to provide the sexual provocation and then reunites to flow peacefully on her way.

Towards the end of *Finnegans Wake* the rainbows as they associate with HCE display symptoms of the dissolution of the dream-vision and the onset of the rule of day. As early as the "Inquisition of Yawn" (III, 3), we find an example of this tendency: "the spectrum of his prisent mocking the candiedights of his dadtid, bagpuddingpodded to the deafspot, bewept of his chilidrin and serafim, poors and personalities, venturous, drones and dominators, ancients and auldancients, with his buttend up" (498.31-35).[51]

"Spectrem" contains spectrum and specter—the colors and apparitions of dream-vision. "Prisent" has present and prism. "Candiedights" and "dadtid" contain white light and daytime and that time. What we have here, I believe, is a disturbance of the dream and a premonition of the dawn and awakening when the dreamer's perceptions in a timeless present will be replaced by the tyranny of daylight "realism." This is very similar to the central idea in this passage in the "Recorso": "Obning shotly. When the messanger of the risen sun, (see other oriel) shall give to every seeable a hue and to every hearable a cry and to each spectacle his spot and to each happening her houram" (609.19–22). The "-anger" of "messanger" is the symptom of the repression by tyrannous, conventional daytime wisdom which attributes to every object its color (snow always white) and imposes stern limitations on our perceptions.

Finally, two other passages, both of which I have already examined in some detail, exemplify this rainbow-characteristic towards the end of the book. The first occurs on the last page of III, 4, that is, just before the "Recorso": "That's his last tyron to march through the grand tryomphal arch. His reignbolt's shot. Never again!" (590.9–10). All of the possibilities, which dream, with its collapsing of past and future, allowed HCE to hold in a kind of suspension of limitations (as in "Circe"), will now be eliminated in favor of those dictated by the insistence of daytime fact. As I suggested earlier, the "tryomphal arch" is in one sense the female pubic arch—daylight will reveal HCE to be an aging, impotent man whose abilities to "rain" and "reign" are over. But there is irony too in the "Never again!" We know that at the end of the *Wake* all contradictions will coalesce in the impersonal unity of the sea to begin all over with "riverrun" and "Eve and Adam." The second passage is that which deals with the confrontation of Patrick and arch-druid. All that are left in the book after this confrontation are a final version of the letter, that vain but persistent attempt at direct communication, and Anna's monologue reconciling all differences. The druid, representing night, dream and those subconscious rainbow impulses which fire the artist's vision, is defeated by Patrick, proponent of cut and dried, black and white certainty. But we know that such a victory is hollow and temporary.

Balkelly and Patrick are also Shem and Shaun, the sons who represent the warring factions of HCE's psyche. Shem's color is a satanic black. In the "Shem" chapter (I, 7) his blackness is reiterated and elaborated upon again and again. It is the black of Guinness stout, potent but not fit, in Shaun's opinion at least, for printer's ink and printing, "such porterblack loweness, too base for printink" (187.17–18). Justius, the Shaun-figure, always eager to point out the worst about his brother, announces: "It is looking pretty black against you, we suggest, Sheem avick" (188.4–5), and this when he is trying to draw Shem out in the open, "in your true colours" (187.33). Some lines further on Justius calls

Shem "a nogger among the blankards" (188.13), that is a nigger among the white men. But Shaun's repressed doubts surface in this speech, since "blankards" are also blackguards and blankminded or stupid people while "nogger" could be one who uses his "noggin" (slang, "head"). The passage continues:

> You have become of twosome twiminds forenenst gods, hidden and discovered, nay, condemned fool, anarch, egoarch, hiresiarch, you have reared your disunited kingdom on the vacuum of your own most intensely doubtful soul. Do you hold yourself then for some god in the manger, Shehohem, that you will neither serve not let serve, pray nor let pray? (188.14-19)

Shaun cannot abide doubt or disunity but requires the certainty of things as they are supposed to be. The possibility of two acceptable but antagonistic points of view, "twosome twiminds," must be denied at any cost. What he wishes to impose on the rebellious parts of the psyche is conventional wisdom, outward respectability, "stupid realism." The dark satanic Shem-like depths of the personality, "neither serve not let serve," simply cannot be admitted. And according to Shaun, the father is exactly what he seems and what Shaun will seem as his successor, a prosperous civic-minded burgher.

In speaking "of hisself" Shem as Mercius is hardly less harsh than is his brother: "you who ever since have been one black mass of jigs and jimjams" (193.34-35). Here he identifies his color, black, and associates himself with the sacrilegious and satanic Black Mass. He also accuses himself of bad nerves and alcoholism—"jigs" is slang for *delirium tremens*—and identifies himself with James Joyce ("jimjams"). It would be oversimplifying to identify Joyce throughout the *Wake* with Shem; what seems to be true is that Joyce-as-writer is Shem, but we must remember that Joyce is more than writer; for instance as father of a family he is HCE. The narrator of the "Shem" chapter joins the brothers in denigrating Shem: "Talk about lowness! Any dog's quantity of it visibly oozed out thickly from this dirty little blacking beetle" (171.29-31). And though the word "black" does not appear in this next accusation, blackness is heavily implied: "the shuddersome spectacle of this semidemented zany amid the inspissated grime of his glaucous den making believe to read his usylessly unreadable Blue Book of Eccles, *edition de tenebres*" (179.24-27). "Glaucous" is that blue-grey color attributed by the Greeks to Pallas Athene's eyes, but rather disliked by the Greeks. Through "glaucoma," and "*tenebres*"—darkness and blindness are the same word, *dorchadas*, in Irish—this description of Shem connects with Joyce's blindness just as the mention of *Ulysses* identifies Shem once more with Joyce the writer. The narrator repeats this pair of identifications when he says of Shem's house: "The house O'Shea or O'Shame...known as the Haunted Inkbottle, no number Brimstone Walk...with his penname SHUT sepiascraped on the doorplate and a blind of black sailcloth over its wan phwinshogue" (182.30-34). Here are collected

Shem's writing, his shame, his blackness, his satanism (brimstone) and Joyce's eye trouble and black eye patch—"phwinshogue" is very close to Irish "window."

Through parts of the book outside of the "Shem" chapter (I, 7) the black and satanic associations of Shem are frequently reiterated, often with the identification with Joyce's eye trouble and Joyce's writing. As Mutt in I, 1, Shem has "One eyegonblack" (16.29) or Joyce's troubled eyesight and black eye patch. Glugg, the Shem-character in the "Mime" (II, 1), is "the bold bad bleak boy of the storybooks" (219.24). "Bleak" brings "black" to mind and the "storybooks" are Joyce's writings. A few pages later we are told that "the duvlin sulph was in Glugger" (222.25), that is Irish, black (*dubh*), Dublin, devil himself, and the sulphur popularly associated with hell. After his first failure at the "Colours Game" (II, 1) the narrator says of Glugg: "Cokerycokes, it's his spurt of coal. And may his tarpitch dilute not give him chromitis! For the mauwe that blinks you blank is mostly Carbo" (232.1-3). Among other things going on here the blacks stand out: coke, coal, tar, pitch, carbo. After Glugg's second failure at guessing the colors, when the girls turn to the angelic twin, Chuff or Shaun, Glugg tries public recantation of his past, "born of thug tribe into brood blackmail, dooly redecant allbigenesis henesies" (240.12-13), and declares for sportsmanship, goodness and the white and gold that properly belong to Shaun. The attentive reader will notice however that Shem's black is in one instance above qualified by the presence of white ("blank") and that his recanting of the Albigensian heresy and of his consumption of Guinness's stout and Hennessy's brandy is undermined by the distortion of "recant" to "redecant" (Latin, "repeat"), and the presence of white, Latin *alb*-, in Albigensian.

Two further instances of Shem's blackness are worth looking at. The first is a revealing statement of Shaun's: "I was meeting on the Thinker's Dam with a pair of men out of glasshouse whom I shuffled hands with named MacBlacks— I think their names is MacBlakes—from the Headfire Clump" (409.21-24). The blacks and the Hellfire Club identify Shem. "Glasshouse" according to McHugh is army slang for "prison."[52] Mention of the poet Blake hints at Shem's, and Joyce's, writing. But what is particularly interesting is Shaun's confusion of singular and plural in connection with escape from prison—in a roundabout way Shaun is being forced to admit in the dream-vision the existence of Shem, of those parts of the psyche in other words of which he so heartily disapproves and makes a practice of denying.

The second instance is part of the narrator's description of the sleeping children in the "Porters' Pub Scene" (III, 4):

> He will be quite within the pale when with lordbeeron brow he vows him so tosset to be of the sir Blake tribes bleak.... Whatever do you mean with bleak? With pale blake I write tinting face. O, you do? And with steelwhite and blackmail I ha'scint for my sweet an anemone's letter with a gold of my bridest hair betied. (563.11-18)

The early part of this paragraph clearly identifies the twin being talked about as Shem. Probably the speakers are two, or more, of the Four Old Men. Shem's black is clearly in evidence as is his writing, in Lord Bryon, Blake, write, "tintingface" (German, "inkpot") and letter. What is odd is the appearance of "pale," "pale," and "white-." Black and white are in some senses at least Shem's writing and the truth that writing tries to get at. But with the appearance of gold, we have Shaun's colors, white and gold. It seems to me that Shem's writing is the means in the dream for the revelation of the truth about the dreamer's psyche and that that is why the very mention of Shem's writing brings out the very worst in Shaun, the censor.

In his "Sermon" to Issy (III, 2) Shaun warns her to avoid predatory men while he is away. The men, naturally, turn out to be Shem-types, but as so often happens at the height of Shaun's denunciations of his brother, some of his own characteristics bleed into the portrait of Shem despite Shaun's best efforts. Shaun warns Issy to

> never lay bare your breast secret (dickette's place!) to joy a Jonas in the Dolphin's Barncar with your meetual fan, Doveyed Covetfilles, comepulsing paynattention spasms between the averthisment for Ulikah's wine and a pair of pulldoors of the old cupiosity shape. (434.26-30)

The names of Dickens and at least three of his novels point to the writer Shem, whose writings like Joyce's may well reveal breast secrets and worse. Shem's black is present in "doveyed," *dubh* being Irish black. But "dove" is also the white dove which is also the meaning of the name "Jonas," and white is a color of Shaun's not Shem's. A few pages further on Shaun says, still addressing Issy: "I am well voiced in love's arsenal and all its overtures from collion boys to colleen bawns so I have every reason to know that rogues' gallery of nightbirds and bitchfanciers, lucky duffs and light lindsays" (438.32-36). Here Shem's "duffs" or "blacks" are mingled with "light" or bright, "bawns" (Irish, "white") and yellows (Irish, *bui*), which are Shaun's colors. The same kind of ambivalence is apparent in phrases in the sermon such as "fair man and foul suggestion" (445.9) and "those vigilant who would leave you to belave black on white" (439.32). To be led to believe black on white is anathema to Shaun's tightly categorized set of attitudes and yet it is this mingling of the two that his subconscious keeps thrusting to the surface of his discourse.

In the part of the "Inquisition of Yawn" (III, 3) in which Shaun most passionately lambastes his brother's reputation and wishes him dead, this phrase constitutes one of his final insults: "that benighted irismaimed, who is tearly belaboured by Sydney and Alibany" (489.31-32). "Irismaimed" is Irishman, Irishman maimed by his own country and "iris-maimed" or blinded. Iris is also the goddess of the rainbow. Among other things going on here there is clear reference by Shaun to Shem-Joyce, the benighted Irishman cast on a foreign shore, plagued by eye trouble and the rainbow of the *Wake*'s dream-vision, belabored to tears and dearly loved by the daylight world of the marketplace ("Alibany"), the world of bourgeois respectability and order to which we all kow-tow in our worst moments. On the page previous to the one on which this statement occurs there is another interesting color reference made by Shaun to his brother: "poor Alby Sobrinos, Geoff, you blighter, identifiable by the necessary white patch on his rear" (488.29-30). What is especially of interest to me in this phrase of Shaun's is the attribution of white to Shem, "Alby," and "white patch." I judge this to be symptomatic of the ambivalence of Shaun's attitude to Shem. On the one hand he wishes to blacken, discredit and disown him and finally to deny his very existence. On the other hand he wishes to whitewash him, claim him as identical twin and deny any rift or difference between them. Here we have a ludicrous example of the latter tendency. The black eye patch has been transformed into a white patch on Shem's rear. Since he is "poor" Alby we may judge the white to be the skin of his backside peeping through the rents in his pants.

In his attacks on Shem Shaun does not confine the color references to black though black is predominant. He claims that Shem is "boasting always of his ruddy complexious!" (4210.34)—Paddy Dignam's alcoholic complexion shared by Shem and HCE. But Shaun also claims that Shem has "falls feet" and a "tanbark complexion" (423.28-29), while the negative blacks also crop up in this passage: "*Negas, negasti*—negertop, negertoe, negertoby, negruntur!" (423.33-34). Shaun claims of Shem that "he was grey at three, like sygnus the swan, when he made his boo to the public and barnacled up to the eyes when he repented after seven" (423.21-23). This identifies Shem with Joyce (through Nora Barnacle) and with the grey ass and Wilde's Dorian Gray. But it is Shem's writing that brings out Shaun's worst vituperation, and he adopts contempt as his best weapon: "I am altogether a chap too fly and hairyman for to infradig the like of that ultravirulence" (425.34-35). Shem's writing is "infradig" or beneath Shaun's dignity—it includes poison, violence and is "beyond a stench" (Latin). A few lines earlier he refers to Shem's productions as "what the bogus bolshy of a shame, my soamheis brother, Gaoy Fecks, is conversant with in audible black and prink" (425.22-24). It is Shaun's deep unease about the black and white revelatory nature of Shem's writing that slips in "prink" for white. "Prink" is ink, printer's ink, print, pink (next door to white) and, no doubt, the abusive "prick." Pink suggests too the colors of the dream-vision and the rainbow itself surfaces in Shaun's abuse of Shem's writing in "infradig" and "ultravirulence"—the visible spectrum's limits of infrared and ultraviolet.

The narrator (or narrators) of the *Wake* has no such ambivalence and flails away at Shem without compunction. He hints at scandals in Shem's past (connected with his backside) by saying that "his back life will not stand being written about in black and white" (169.7-8). The echo of Shaun's "black and prink" in connection with Shem's writing is conspicuous. In one sense it signifies the kind of revelation that the censor, Shaun, and the dreamer-narrator most fear, namely, the dragging into the white light of day of the dangerous images that parade through the world of the dream. In another sense it suggests the coexistence or even the coalescence of the white-Shaun and black-Shem elements of the psyche and thus the much-feared admission of Shem's existence and legitimacy.

Shem of course is not confined to the color black. At one point in the "Shem" chapter (I, 7), the narrator portrays Shem as "a nightlong a shaking betwixteen white or reddr hawrors" (184.7-8). This combination of red and white immediately suggests the father, HCE, and attaches to Shem at such points as this when he is most clearly participating in the personality struggles and guilts of the father. In this particular case he is struggling with the shackles of alcoholism and he is also the dreaming father shaking nightlong at the terrible revelations of the dream. The same kind of thing is apparent in the narrator's description of the failed, self-pitying, sexually disappointed Glugg after his second set of guesses in the "Colours Game" (II, 1): "There end no moe red devil in the white of his eye" (252.33-34). But the narrator's malicious accounts of Shem keep coming back to blackness and darkness. In the "Shem" chapter we are given this revealing incident: Shem places bright and Shaun-like colors in his alchemical furnace but the final result is that "with each word that would not pass away the squidself which he had squirtscreened from the crystalline world waned chagreen-old and doriangrayer in its dudhud" (186.6-8). Green, grey and the essential black (the ink squirted by the squid) make up Joyce's colors of blindness, or, in Irish, darkness. It almost seems, in a kind of reversal of the story of Dorian Gray, that as Joyce's exterior world falls into darkness and night as his eyesight deteriorates, the rainbow colors of his inner world, his artistic vision, his dream, flash ever more brightly and richly and revealingly.

In the most abusive part of the "Shem" chapter, the narrator gives Shem one dove-raven image and one rainbow that merit brief examination. The crucial terms in the dove-raven image are "for Duvvelsache" and "a corves" (178.35-36). As frequently happens with the dove-raven polarity there is no attempt here to associate any specific elements with either pole. Instead dove-raven appears to function essentially as a reminder that though Shem is a splinter of his father's psyche he carries within him the certainty of further splintering, that certainty displaying also an imbalance that promises another, even further split. I have pointed out earlier in this chapter the qualifications which "dove" carries within it, namely Irish *dubh*. "Duvvel-" here is also "devil" in a phrase where the reader's expectation posits God—"for God's sake." As it happens, Duvel is Romany "God."[53] What we have then is Shem's satanic black inextricably entwined with the whiteness of God and eternity and virtue.

The rainbow in question (R #6) requires a lengthier quotation:

> The tragic jester sobbed himself wheywhingingly sick of life on some sort of a rhubarbarous maundarin yellagreen funckleblue windigut diodying applejack squeezed from sour grapefruice and ... they found ... it came straight from the noble white fat, jo, openwide sat, jo, jo, her why hide that, jo jo jo, the winevat, of the most serene magyansty az archdiochesse, if she is a duck, she's a douches and when she has feherbour snot her fault, now is it? artstouchups, funny you're grinning at, fancy you're in her yet, Fanny Urinia. (171.15–28)

This describes Shem's drink, Joyce's favorite tipple, the Swiss white wine "Fendant de Sion," as well as Shem's drunken behavior while under the influence of that drink. That Shem's inebriation rates a rainbow is appropriate since that is one of the skulking writer's few emergences into view and is also the commonest cause of his fall. But there is another cause of fall also present. That Joyce referred to the wine in question as "the piss of an archduchess" is a commonplace of Joyceana. Here the "winevat" is the "why hide that" or "white hide" or private parts of a Hungarian "archdiochesse" or "douches." "Feherbour" is Hungarian "white wine" or "white skin." This of course is the female-sexual white which I discussed in the first chapter and which I shall examine in relation to *Finnegans Wake* in chapter 4. In the passage I have just quoted the bodily position of the archduchess is made quite explicit. It is the female vision fantasized by Bloom in "Circe," "with divaricated thighs ... with ... well uplifted white sateen coatpans" (*Ulysses*, 15.3425–27), and realized by Molly in "Penelope" as she makes "chamber music" (*Ulysses*, 18.1142–48). And the Hungarian *jo*, repeated five times, is very close to Molly's "yes."

Not only does Shem's writing bring out the worst in Shaun and the narrator but it also evokes a kind of confused braggadocio from Shem himself. But we must keep in mind that anything attributable to Shem is filtered through the narrator who uses an unknowable degree of editorial discretion. After his first failure in the "Colours Game" (II, 1), Shem-Glugg boosts his battered ego by fantasizing the bold strokes with which he will astonish the world, and especially the girls: "He would jused sit it all write down just as he would jused set it up all writhefully rate in blotch and void.... a most moraculous jeeremyhead sindbook for all the peoples" (229.26–32). Shem is more sore than sorry and he has the instinct for the jugular. The book he writes will be his revenge; it will expose in black and white the truth that will cause his enemies/family to writhe. It will be a complaint or Jeremiad and will jeer. It will be a book of people's sins as well as a scapegoat (German, *sundenbock*).[54] It will be miraculous, not divinely miraculous, but Shem's satanic black— "moraculous" is black-haired (Italian) and black-arsed (Italian and French). A little further on in the same sentence Shem fulminates "about whose told his innersense and the grusomehed's yoeureeke of his spectrescope and why he was off colour and how he was ambothed upon by the very spit of himself" (229.36–230.2).

There is little doubt as to the reader's distance from Shem's self-pity here. Shem's complaint concerns the occupational frustrations of the writer, which he blames on the thief of his inner sense and innocence—as if Shem were ever innocent. He also sees as theft the failure of his writings with the reading public, the revelations of his rainbow vision that stink (reek) and are gruesome and cruel. A spectroscope is a device which analyzes light into its constituent colors. Here it also raises and identifies specters from the recesses of the personality. Shem as always prevaricates in naming his twin as his censor and oppressor, although "the very spit of himself" points clearly enough towards his identical twin, Shaun, and "ambothed" contains Latin *ambo,* "both," and the English word "both," hinting again at his double. Shem's black is here in "-s ambo-"; his artistic vision is seen as rainbow or spectrum; his frustration and failure are his being "off colour." Like a great deal more in this "Shem" chapter, Shem's self-pity reflects the feelings of frustration of Joyce through those years of his wrangles with the potential publishers of *Dubliners.* Shem skulks in his house, feels himself a scapegoat and blames the world, but what the reader senses of the author's posture is not sentimental self-indulgence but sympathy informed with irony.

When Shem feels most put upon, as when he immures himself in his inkbottle house in the "Shem" chapter (I, 7) or when he contemplates his failures in the "Colours Game" (II, 1), his favorite tactic is to clothe himself in the virtues of his father and his brother, and the colors that attend those virtues. He glories drunkenly in his writings,

> turning over three sheets at a wind, telling himself delightedly, no espellor mor so, that every splurge on the vellum he blundered over was an aisling vision more gorgeous than the one before t.i.t.s., a roseschelle cottage by the sea for nothing for ever, a ladies tryon hosiery raffle at liberty, a sewerful of guineagold wine with brancomongepadenopie and sickcylinder oysters worth a billion a bite. (179.29-35)

Branco is Portuguese "white"[55] and with "guineagold" gives us Shaun's colors. A little later he fancies himself as a great operatic singer with "enthusiastic noblewomen flinging every coronetcrimsoned stitch they had off at his probscenium" (180.1-3) while he squeals "the topsquall in *Deal Lil Shemlockup Yellin*" (180.5-6), dressed in seven garments including "a scrumptious cocked hat and three green, cheese and tangerine trinity plumes on the right handle side of his amarellous head" (180.8-10). "Yellin" is Shaun's yellow as is *amarello* (Portuguese).[56] "Green, cheese and tangerine" constitute the Irish tricolor associated primarily in the *Wake* with Shaun's nationalistic fervor. The seven garments are HCE's trademark. The narrator's response to such pretensions is to put Shem right back in his proper (i.e., black) place: "such lowdown blackguardism" (180.31-32). In the "Colours Game" Shem tries very similar tactics, seeking to clothe himself in "sporticolorissimo," "polentay rossum" ("gold" and "red-gold" in Amaro), "bianconies" ("silver," "white" in Amaro). Ambivalence sneaks in when he claims to be Shaun-like, the "weedhearted boy of potter and mudder" (240.15-23).

Part of the advice given by Justius-Shaun to Mercius-Shem in I, 7 is this: "And remember that golden silence gives consent, Mr. Anklegazer!" (193.11-12). Shaun is trying to foist his own characteristics on Shem and thus deny the Shem-reality. Shem can neither possess gold nor be golden, for he cannot be silent but must write. "Though he shall live for millions of years a life of billions of years, from their roseaced glows to their violast lustres, he shall not forget that pucking Pugases" (231.18-21). Despite the resentful and abusive overtones ("pucking," "puga," Latin for buttocks), Shem cannot reject the rainbow vision of the winged horse.

As I have pointed out in my discussion of Shem, the chief colors associated in the *Wake* with Shaun are white and yellow, or white and gold. Shaun's white is usually given in the form of "fair" or "finn" or "fine." In III, 1 the Four address Shaun as "O phausdhcen phewn" (412.9), fairhaired child in Irish; in the "Sermon" section (III, 2) the narrator refers to Shaun as "finfria's fairest" (430.24) and wishes him: "May your bawny hair grow rarer and fairer, our own only wideheaded boy!" (472.4-5). "Bawny" is Irish white; "wideheaded" is whiteheaded. In the "Mime" (II, 1) Shaun is fawned upon by the girls as "the finehued, the fairhailed, the farahead" (234.26-27). The introduction of Chuff or Shaun among the *dramatis personae* of the Mime indicates his position in the triumvirate: "the fine frank fairhaired fellow of the fairytales, who wrestles for tophole with the bold bad bleak boy Glugg, geminally about... chuting rudskin gunerally or something" (220.12-15). Shaun's white wrestles with Shem's black for control of the father's position and personality (HCE's red).

Shaun's yellow almost always appears in conjunction with white with the notable exception of the "Sermon" chapter (III, 2) in which Shaun is consistently referred to as "Jaun," (French, "yellow"). I have mentioned earlier that Shaun's white and yellow are the colors of the papal flag—Shaun represents repressive and obscurantist ecclesiastical authority—he is Catholic Ireland's version of prudish and prurient Victorian respectability. When green joins Shaun's colors to form the Irish tricolor we have the perfect exemplar of Christ and Caesar hand in glove. The girls in the "Mime" perceive him as "Candidatus, viridosus, aurilucens, sinelab? Of all the green heroes everwore coton breiches, the whitemost, the goldenest!" (234.8-10). As authoritarian churchman (Mookse) and founder of the monastic settlement at Glendalough, Kevin-Shaun is a blaze of liturgical colors, but most prominent among them are white and gold and green. In preparation for "violet vesper" he is "girded" in "sable *cappa magna*" (606.4-5). He comes "in alb of cloth of gold to our own midmost Glendalough-le-vert" (605.10-11)—white, gold and green, suitably liturgical. The "green" of Glendalough is that green valley in the Wicklow mountains and the green of nationalist pride in the history of the Island of Saints and Scholars. Kevin is sometimes, as well as being the saint, the nationalist hero Kevin Barry executed by the British during the Troubles: "nicechild Kevin Mary (who was going to be commandeering chief of the choirboys' brigade the moment he grew up under all the auspices) irishsmiled in his milky way of cream dwibble and onange tustard and dessed tabbage" (555.16–19). The tricolor here is an edible one—almost all of Shaun's color associations reflect his gluttony. Shaun's one rainbow (R #22) occurs in his sermon and is appropriately liturgical: "Is it rubrics, mandarimus, pasqualines, or verdidads is in it, or the bruiselivid indecores of estreme voyoulence and, for the lover of lithurgy?" (432.30–33). Bruise-livid intercourse and indecorum and esteem for extreme voyeurism and violence indicate the sadistic tendencies that lie beneath Shaun's respectability. That this rainbow appears in the text on p. 432 is presumably an unintended irony!

Shaun and his personae are given lots of bright colors, as when "Yawn" is a great colorful fish whom the Four are trying to net (477.11–30) or a blaze of potatoes and astronomic color display (475.7–17), but only two patterns of these colors are of sufficient significance to be discussed further here, namely, the colors of Tristan and of Dave the Dancekerl. In "Who is Who When Everybody is Somebody Else," Glasheen lists Tristan of Lyonnesse in both the Shem and Shaun columns.[57] However, I believe few Wakeans would disagree with my placing him squarely in the Shaun column, if only for his *active* role and his "lady-killing." Tristan appears in the second paragraph of the book: "Sir Tristram, violer d'amores... had passencore rearrived from North Armorica... to wielderfight his penisolate war" (3.4–6). He is both Sir Amory Tristram, successful invader of Ireland, and Tristan of Lyonnesse, violater of the love-trust, but it is the violence and violation that are of most importance in the case of Tristan. He is "violet," a color associated in the *Wake* with one extreme of the rainbow spectrum but especially with virulence, voyeurism, violation and violence, and particularly with the violence and virulence of sectarian life in Northern Ireland (ultraviolet and Ulster-violence). The only other occasion in the book on which Tristan is given important color connections occurs in II, 4, as the four old codgers watch Tristan and Isolde making love. There Tristan is Isolde's "gaelic champion, the onliest one of her choice, her bleaueyedeal of a girl's friend... with his sinister dexterity, light and rufthandling ... the brueburnt sexfutter" (384.23–28). Tristan is a Shaun-like "Gaelic champion," a six-foot rugby player, an acrobatic and masterful lover, a Boylan-like phallus figure ("sex-," fucker; and "futt" is, vulgarly, vagina).[58] And like Boylan he is "penisolate," or isolated from humanity except for his forays of the penis. Like Boylan too he is given the color blue ("bleaueyedeal," "brueburnt") an unusual color for a male figure in Joyce's works. One reason for this I believe is the narrator's tendency to have his vision colored by the participants he describes. The language of this second Tristan passage is Gerty-Issy-sexy talk and there is a transfer of the girlish blue to the girl's male sex object. Another reason is the surfacing set of contradictions of the Shaun-type male, that occurs in the passage not only in such phrases as "sinister dexterity" but in the whole clash of sex-as-love with sex-as-violence.

These contradictions are rife in the portrayal of Dave the Dancekerl. Dave is the successor whom Shaun welcomes as he himself is leaving. Thus Dave is the Holy Ghost. He is also St. Patrick since he arrives on the 4.32 train. But he is also Shem-Joyce, who can't "stop tippling" (462.20), "with his blackguarded eye" (464.12). Shaun calls him "the sneaking likeness of us, faith, me altar's ego" (463.6-7) and identifies Dave and Shaun as "Got by the one goat, suckled by the same nanna" (463.15-16). At the same time he attributes to Dave "semicoloured stainedglasses" (463.14) which conflates James Joyce's glasses with that prototypical Shaun-type, Stanislaus Joyce. In addition some reds in these pages hint at HCE's and Dave's "showing the three white feathers" (463.3-4) which points to the incident in the Park, in terms of both exhibition of male genitalia and the three watching soldiers. This confusion of identification reflects, I believe, the surfacing in the dream of Shaun's ambivalence about his brother. Here he tries to deny the aspects of Shem's character that he cannot accept and to paint him as the perfect Shaun-like successor. But denial cannot bring about resolution, only, in the final event, revelation. Shaun is caught in a dilemma: "I hate him about his patent henesy, plasfh it, yet am I amorist. I love him" (463.17-19).

It is my contention that colors play an important part in the delineation of the divisions within the dreamer's personality and his efforts at reintegration, as these conflicts are worked out in terms of the warring twins, Shem and Shaun. There are many pairs of figures in the *Wake* cognate with Shem and Shaun—the Mookse and the Gripes, Justius and Mercius, Butt and Taff and so on. Yet, with the notable exceptions of Glugg and Chuff in the Mime (II, 1) and saint and druid in the "Recorso," colors play very little part in the struggles of the cognate pairs generally. This is true even of those pairs such as Burrus and Caseous and Browne and Nolan where color connotations are built into their names from the beginning.

The Browne-Nolan antithesis is so prominent in the *Wake* as to merit further discussion here. It is true that Mr. Browne in "The Dead" does have some limited antithesis of color with Freddy Malins and Gabriel Conroy but not even that limited degree of color use is applied in the *Wake* to Browne and Nolan. To the best of my detective abilities there is only one instance in the *Wake* of Joyce's attributing a color value to the Nolan side of the Browne-Nolan equation and on that occasion he adds a black to the Browne side to yield a black-white polarity: "a white noelan...a bruin of some swart"

(97.5-6). Joyce inflicts all kinds of wordplay and distortion on Browne and Nolan, such as "Mr 'Gladstone Browne'" (334.6-7), "Mr. 'Bonoparte Nolan'" (334.9-10), "noland's browne jesus" (300.29), "bronnanoleum" (391.21), "Mr. Nobru" and "Mr. Anol" (490.26-27). But not one of them plays with color. It seems to me that the function of Browne and Nolan in the *Wake* is simply that of a mnemonic tag. Since the booksellers Browne and Nolan are one firm and one establishment, the memory of the eponymous founders long since having disappeared, and since Bruno of Nola was indeed one man, we are continually reminded that even the most crisply defined contraries are at bottom merely different aspects of the one human nature.

Earlier in this chapter I declared red to be HCE's primary color characteristic, though with white a close second. One could, I think, mount an argument to demonstrate that red is the color of HCE as representative of men (*aner*) and white his color as representative of mankind (*anthropos*), but that is not my concern here. A passage in the ninth question of the "Quiz" (I, 6) epitomizes, I believe, the method by which Joyce demonstrates through the colors of the male the paradox of unity and diversity of human consciousness of itself, of the tension of integrative and disruptive forces that constitutes the human psyche. The question is quite short, twenty-five lines or so, but nevertheless too lengthy to quote in full here, so I shall quote it in part:

> If a human being duly fatigued by his dayety in the sooty, having plenxty off time on his gouty hands and vacants of space at his sleepish feet... were at this actual futule preteriting unstant, in the states of suspensive exanimation, accorded, throughout the eye of a noodle, with an earsighted view... could such a none... byhold at ones what is main and why tis twain, how one once meet melts in tother wants poignings, the sap rising, the foles falling, the nimb now nihilant round the girlyhead so becoming, the wrestless in the womb, all the rivals to allsea... then *what* would that fargazer seem to seemself to seem seeming of, dimm it all? Answer: A collideorscape. (143.4-28)

Ostensibly, this question is about the seven rainbow girls but alert readers have perceived that it is in fact exploring the *Wake* itself and the act of reading it.[59] Question #9 is about the *Wake*'s dreamer-reader and enquires as to the nature of the vision of human life he finds in the book. The dreamer-reader is pictured as a middleclass man "fatigued" from his day's work in the city, his duty to his deity and the general, seemingly endless, effort of maintaining his middleclass respectability and appurtenances. The *Wake* is probably indicated by "the eye of a noodle" which is a good deal more difficult to pass through or see through than the eye of a needle, especially "with an earsighted view," when one is attempting to be a "fargazer." The question asked is: What does he see? But at this level it answers itself. Since what he sees is also what he seems, then what he sees is himself, or what seems to be himself. But the "himself" is "seemself." Seer and thing seen are equally matters of probability and doubt. The question contains a rainbow (R #4) which is not so much a reference to the seven temptresses, though these too are no doubt on the dreamer's mind and therefore part of his vision, but the mark in the dream of epiphany or revelation or emergence of deeply buried elements of the psyche. The answer, being by its nature less important to the revelation of truth than the question, is very brief, two words in fact, but it too has a contribution to make. My *Concise Oxford Dictionary* defines kaleidoscope: "Tube through which are seen symmetrical figures, produced by reflections of pieces of colored glass, and varied by rotation of the tube; (fig.) constantly changing group of bright objects."[60] "Collideorscape" also includes "coll" or mountain (HCE), "kale" or beauty (Greek), "lide" or game (Greek, *lude*), "collide," "deor" or tear (Irish), "door," "corridor," and "-scape" as in escape or landscape. It includes the pair of alternatives, "collide or escape." What is to be collided with or escaped is the dreamer's vision of himself—a collide-o-scope is in one sense a mirror.

But the aspect of the question that chiefly exercises the attention of the dreamer comes a little earlier in the question. "by-hold at ones what is main and why tis twain, how one ones meet melts in tother wants poignings." "By-hold" contains "behold," "twice hold" and "boy, hold!" "Ones" is "once," "one's," "one," and the plural of one, i.e., two. "Main" is the chief or central event or factor; it is also *mein* or "mine" and "men" or "man." "Why tis" is "why it is" and "white is." "Twain" is "two" and Mark Twain the writer. "One once meet" is "one man's meet," what is meet or appropriate for one, and how the "ones" or splinters within one's personality are reconciled. "One man's meat" is also his "help meet" and, vulgarly, the female he desires or captures sexually. "Tother" is "the other" and the female genitalia (Irish). "Wants" is "one's" in some Irish dialects. "Poignings" is, among other things, "poison" and "poignancy" and derives from Old French and Latin words meaning to prick or pierce. Obviously, this is one of those Wakean passages (of less than two full lines), the echoes and ripples of which reecho and recombine to an extent that is simply inexhaustible.

The features of the question most germane to my discussion can be teased out readily enough. What is man? Why is his nature inevitably split against itself? Why is the white daylight vision of man, so clear and unified at first glance, splintered and modified as soon as we examine it closely? The commonest mental picture of Mark Twain derives from that well known and most frequently reproduced picture of him in later life with his white mane of hair. He is of course an excellent exemplar of man's duality, not only because of the duality in his name, "Twain," but also because that was his pen-name and not his "real" name, Samuel L. Clemens. Even such a persistently felt drive as man's sexual desire for woman is modified by the vagaries of personal taste and the corollary of homosexuality.

The paradox of man's nature resides in the tension of his always being at odds with himself and in his need to continually try to reconcile his conflicting parts. The example of the rainbow is instructive here. Its very existence depends on fleeting atmospheric conditions as they strike the human retina. The perception of its seven bands depends on arbitrary cultural determinants. Yet it is always imminent in the white light of day and can symbolize a nicety of discrimination beside which conventional daytime vision is glaring and crude and conventional, and presents only superficial appearances. *Finnegans Wake* is a book of night and dream; its vision bypasses daylight clarity and aims at darkness and the rainbow and truth.

4

Whiteyoumightcallimbs: Colors of the Temptress

Anna Livia Plurabelle or ALP, woman and river, heroine of the *Wake*, does not appear in the book's title but hers is the first word of the text, "riverrun," and the last, "the." To a much greater degree than is the case with the male figures in the *Wake*, ALP is distanced from us, difficult to pin down, impossible to separate from the other female characters who are projections of her. And the details given of her character and physical appearance are often at odds, as are her colors. Margot Norris convincingly explains "these diverse forms and functions of Anna Livia Plurabelle—old, young, ugly, beautiful, faithful, treacherous, brutalized, manipulative, rejected, desired, redeeming, tempting," as projections of the male dreamer's unresolved guilts, fears and desires towards the woman.[1] It is instructive to consider Norris's view along with Suzette Henke's appraisal of the female characters in *A Portrait of the Artist:*

> They pervade the novel, yet remain elusive.... Like everything in *A Portrait*, women are portrayed almost exclusively from Stephen's point of view. Seen through his eyes and colored by his fantasies, they often appear as one-dimensional projections of a narcissistic imagination. Females emerge as the psychological "other," forceful antagonists in the novel's dialectical structure. They stand as emblems of the flesh—frightening reminders of sex, generation, and death.[2]

In the Christian mythology of man's beginnings the first split in the first man's psyche occurred when God took a rib from Adam's side and formed it into a woman, Eve. She was his first "other," and became the antagonist of the first struggle of self and "other." This polarity is suggested in the very first line of *Finnegans Wake* by the phrase "Eve and Adam's," the first landmark, or first obstacle, the river must run "past." That "duality of being" that Clive Hart perceives as "perhaps the most important of all the basic structural concepts in *Finnegans Wake*" is most notably present in the ambivalence and ambiguity of the Wakean male dreamer's attitude towards woman.[3] Since every voice in the

Wake is a projection of the dreamer, every voice, including the voices of women, exhibits the duality. The disposition of colors attendant on the *Wake*'s female figures demonstrates this bias.

"Livia," or "Livvy," as Anna is often called, has a color connotation of its own, one that is probably always present when the "liv-" part of Anna's name is mentioned. Both the English "livid" and Latin *lividus* mean a bluish, leaden color, or the skin discoloration caused by a bruise. Joyce reminds us of that connotation when he associates ALP with the blue of the night and with bluebells (7.1–2) or when he refers to *Ulysses* as "the tome of *Liber Lividus*" (14.29–30). On the whole, however, the blue implications of Anna's name are not extensively exploited by Joyce—far more is made of such noncolor associations as life/leaves/lies, as in "the river of lives" (600.8). Blue is not a prominent color of ALP's, except in her final monologue.

ALP's dominant color is that of her hair, auburn. In one of her marathon defenses of HCE ALP says: "He cawls to me Granny-stream-Auborne when I am hiding under my hair from him" (495.18–19). And so he does: "my sweet coolocked, my auburn coyquailing one" (552.22). ALP is "An auburn mayde" (13.26), is "flirty, with her auburnt streams and her coy cajoleries" (139.23–24), and is "Sweetsome auburn" (265.6–7). Her "aulburntress" is "lymphyamphyre" or Liffey-afire (137.23–24) and she recalls of her youth, "Our shape as a juvenile being much admired from the first with native copper locks" (617.33–34). Also in her final monologue, "a correspondent paints out that the Swees Aubumn vogue is hanging down straith fitting to her innocenth eyes" (617.35–618.1). In many of the instances I have cited Anna's auburn hair is clearly associated with Goldsmith's poem "The Deserted Village," which begins "Sweet Auburn...."[4] I am unaware of any special reason for Anna's association with the Goldsmith poem other than the sense of impending doom, of disintegration of personality, of profound loneliness, which attends Anna's portrayal, especially in her final monologue, a sense very close to the air of melancholy which informs the poem.

Goldsmith however is not the source of Anna's auburn. Ellmann as usual has the whole story.[5] Briefly, Joyce thought of the Liffey's waters as stained reddish by the dye-works on its banks. He therefore modelled Anna's hair on the "reddish-blond hair" of his friend Signora Schmitz, wife of the novelist Ettore Schmitz (Italo Svevo). Signora Schmitz's given name was—Livia! But she was a somewhat reluctant model.

In accordance with the duality of vision that especially marks the dreamer's attitudes towards women and of which I have spoken earlier in this chapter, Anna's hair is not only auburn or reddish-blond but also the much duller "brown." As it rises in the Wicklow mountains the Liffey is seen to have a color almost identical with the Clongowes bogwater in *A Portrait*:

> the most unconsciously boggylooking stream he ever locked his eyes with. Out of the colliens it took a rise by daubing itself Ninon. It looked little and it smelt of brown and it thought in

narrows and it talked showshallow. And as it rinn it dribbled like any lively purliteasy: *My, my, my! Me and me! Little down dream don't I love thee!* (153.2–8)

Here in addition to "brown" there are "boggylooking," "daubing," "down," (Irish, *dann*, "brown,") and the parody of the song "Little Brown Jug, Don't I Love Thee." At other points in the book ALP is "Donauwatter" or brown river (578.19–20), "Brounemouth" (578.25), and we are told that "she's even brennt [browned] her hair" (578.28) and that "Her hair's as brown as ever it was" (28.32–33). The browns generally tend towards the vaguely pejorative, as in the passage I have quoted above or in the image of the Porters copulating where she is "his bucky brown nightmare" (583.8–9). In the latter phrase "bucky brown" is "bucking down" as well as "boggy brown," and the phrase and its contextual passage sneer not only at ALP's sexual response but by implication at all human sexuality. These negative browns are especially noticeable in the aged-Anna figure, Kate the Slops, of whom nothing praiseworthy or even kind is intimated at any point in the book: "The swabsister Katya to have duntalking and to keep shakenin dowan her droghedars" (566.10–12). "Dun" and "dowan" are Irish "brown." The image of the old harridan shaking down her brown drawers is a formidable one.

The contradictions in Anna's colors are primarily due to the ambivalent vision of the dreamer, but they can also be traced all the way back to the author. In a letter to Harriet Weaver, Joyce wrote of ALP: "Her Pandora's box contains the ills flesh is heir to. The stream is quite brown, rich in salmon, very devious, shallow."[6] And Ellmann tells an anecdote interesting in this connection when he notes of the publication of *Anna Livia Plurabelle* in 1928 that "the book had to be published in a tea-colored cover because the Liffey was the color of tea" and gives Sylvia Beach as his source.[7] The trouble with the word "tea-colored" is that it could mean the color of cognac, which I suppose is more or less auburn or the muddy color of tea heavily milked as it still inevitably is in Ireland.

Two points made by Margot Norris are of interest in this regard. Firstly, she sees Anna's color discrepancies as constituting a range of colors related to the degree of romanticizing going on in the particular viewing of her:

> When Anna Livia is romanticized, her muddy waters become auburn waves.... The flotsam and jetsam of the river become lovely ornaments... when seen in this rosy glow....
> When its red color becomes truly fiery, the waves of river and woman are described like the burning lava of a volcano.... From Jaun's jaundiced point of view, smoking is unseemly for a woman.... ALP, "puffing her old dudheen" (200.18), is therefore a polluted, industrial Liffey.[8]

Secondly, Norris goes on to show how Anna's ambiguous image is produced, and color of the sort I have been discussing has a good deal to do with it:

Joyce depends on odd, double meanings of words to produce both the simultaneous beautiful/ugly and simultaneous river/woman effect. For example, Anna Liva's [sic] complexion is modulated between fair and dark. The four old codgers remember it as 'solid ivory' (396.10).... Shem calls her 'turfbrown' (194.22), but most often she appears to be in-between or 'frickled' (204.23), like a river dappled in light and shade.[9]

ALP's identification with river is much more thoroughly and consistently carried out than HCE's identification with mountain and this is partly the cause of the variations in the colors of her appearance—like a river she is always changing and always the same. Thus when the "correspondent paints out that the Swees Aubumn vogue is hanging down straith fitting to her innocenth eyes" (617.35–618.1), we have an image of the woman with auburn hair hanging straight down to her "-bumn" or her thighs ("-th eyes"). But we also have an image of the river, with its long streams of water and weeds, its deep reaches, its auburn water, the bright autumnal leaves hanging over it and floating on its surface. Margot Norris claims that "Joyce's description of the woman virtually reflects a naturalist's observation of the river"[10] and whether or not one is prepared to go quite that far it is certainly true that some of the varied color details of Anna's appearance are due to her river nature. Shaun, speaking to Issy, describes the mother as "our—as you so often term her—efferfreshpainted livy" (452.18–19), and he announces his intention to "leip a liffey and drink annyblack water that rann onme way" (451.15), this latter comment identifying ALP with Munster's chief river, the Blackwater, and many other lesser Irish rivers of the same name. It is likely also that Anna is the subject at 371.33 where "Awaindhoo's a selverbourne," that is, where Blackriver (Irish) is a silver stream, an apt enough description of the river at night. This is echoed in HCE's comment on Dublin, Georgia, and its river, the Oconee, as "the tawny sprawling beside that silver burn" (549.28–29). One of the washerwomen in the "ALP" chapter (I, 8) describes her as "pretending to tibble a roody derg on a fiddle" (198.25), an allusion to Anna playing the violin and to Lough Derg or "red lake," the name of two quite famous Irish lakes. Later in the same chapter as ALP emerges into public view she has a slapdash selection of colors to match her slapdash outfit: "guildered pin," "owlglassy bicycles," "nude cuba stockings...salmospotspeckled," "a galligo shimmy of hazevaipar tinto," "bloodorange bockknickers," "natural nigger boggers," "blackstripe tan joseph" and "wavy rushgreen epaulettes" (208.9–18). These constitute not only a bizarre woman's outfit but also typical debris that the river "wears" as it carries it to the sea. And the rainbow-colored assortment of "geegaws" and "pretty novelties" and "lumineused luxories" that HCE claims to have presented to his bride (548.19–549.5) smack more of a river's treasures than a woman's. A couple of pages further on HCE speaks of his "civicising" ALP in terms that mix woman's toilette with river-dredging: "and to my saffron-breathing mongoloid...I gave Biorwik's powlver and...unguents of cuticure, for the swarthy searchall's face on her . . . and a carrycam to tease her tussy out, the brown but combly" (550.17-20). Signora Schmitz's unease about her immortalization as Anna Livia was not entirely unfounded. Generally speaking the river aspect of Anna gives her the muddier, darker, browner and ill-assorted colors although in the same speech of HCE's from which I have quoted above he also calls her "faithful Fulvia" (546.30) and "Fluvia, amber whitch she was" (546.35). *Fluvia* is Latin, "river," while *fulvus* is Latin, "blond, yellow, or reddish yellow."

In addition to being river and woman ALP is also frequently a bird, not only the hen which digs up the letter, a bird given practically no color references, but also the dove of peace. This fits well with the mother's role in nurturing and reconciling. ALP first appears in the *Wake* as a "peacefugle" or peace bird on the battlefield of Waterloo. Among the goodies in her sack are "peewee and powwows" and "pacts' huemeramybows" (11.10-12)—peace and ceasefire in a variety of ways and the rainbow, the sign of God's peace. On a few other occasions through the book ALP is pictured as a dove. In the Porters' Pub section (III, 4) he and she are "cliffscaur grisly but rockdove cooing" (577.17), in which although there is no explicit mention of "raven," the pattern of sounds clearly posits the dove-raven antithesis. When HCE refers to ALP in the "Inquisition" section (III, 3) as "my shopsoiled doveling, when weeks of kindness kinly civicised" (550.22-23), he is unwittingly casting doubt on the efficacy of his "civicising" and calling Anna his little dove and little devil, *-een* being the Irish diminutive. It is worth noting that "dove-colored" is a specific color in English, namely a bluish grey quite close to the color signified by Latin *lividus*. But little important use is made in the *Wake* of "dove," "dove-colored," and "livid" connections as far as ALP is concerned.

ALP is sometimes "dappled." To Margot Norris this suggests "a river dappled in light and shade."[11] John Gordon has a good deal to say about "apple" in *Finnegans Wake*, connecting it with the initials of Alice Pleasance Liddell and with those initials as an anagram of ALP.[12] Although Gordon has many interesting and enlightening things to say in this connection, for instance HCE's "medding with fruit" being "connected with his fall,"[13] he does not make the association that is of particular interest to me here, namely, that of ALP, APL and apple with "dappled." Evidence of such an association seems to me to be strongly present in at least seven instances in the book and to constitute a significant pattern of which color is an important part. The context of the first instance is the fall of Finnegan: "But so sore did abe ite ivvy's holired abbles" (5.29-30). This brief passage is dense with allusions, the most important among them for the purposes of my discussion being Eve, the apple of temptation, Livia, Abel, and the dappled Liffey in which one may dabble one's feet. Finnegan's fall from the ladder and HCE's fall from grace in the Park, with which the discussion of the former fall merges, are caused, as was Adam's fall in

Eden, by a red apple proffered by a woman.[14] The presence of the name of Abel, Adam and Eve's offspring, suggests that their sexual congress was part of the fall. But dapple-dabble, since it describes the river, and "apple," also containing ALP's initials, *are* in a sense, ALP. What she proffers is herself, possibly her breasts or her buttocks. By some manner of sexual temptation ALP seduces HCE to his fall. Of course this version of the fall is due in large measure to displacement brought about in the dream-vision by the male dreamer's evasions. To bypass his guilt he pictures himself as the innocent, passive victim and the woman as the active, lusting temptress. The effect of this sense of the dreamer's awareness on the part of the reader leads, uncomfortably, to reflections on traditional male responses to crimes against women—"she asked for it!"—and casts the Genesis version of Adam and Eve's fall in an ironic light, a dappled light in fact.

The other six instances of "dappled" to which I referred above exhibit the same pattern. In the first section of the book ALP is waking the fallen giant, "all the livvy-long night, the delldale dalppling night, the night of bluerybells" (7.1–2). ALP is the dappled river, probably seen by moonlight, and her Livia-blue is the blue of night. Near the end of this first section the mourners attempt to mollify the reluctantly buried giant by describing all at home as being well in his absence, including his wife relaxing after her supper of "kanekannan and abbely dimpling" (28.19). This is "colkannon and apple-dumpling" but it also has Cain and Abel and sensuous overtones in "abbely dimpling"—not the most likely notions to lull the dead giant. And in the version of the letter examined by the pedant (I, 5) ALP clearly identifies herself, through apple-dapple, with the rainbow girls who tempt HCE to his downfall: "With apple harlottes. And a little mollvogels.... Honeys wore camelia paints. Yours very truthful. Add dapple inn" (113.16–18).

In a footnote in the "Night Lessons" section (II, 2) one of Issy's salacious remarks runs: "I was so snug off in my apholster's creedle but at long leash I'll stretch more capritious in his dapplepied bed" (276,F5). The bed referred to is the father's and therefore also Anna's: "capritious" is (Latin) "goatish," while "dapplepied" contains the dappled mother-river and the apple pie of sexual temptation. A little further on in the same section Shem requests help to better study the mother's sexual anatomy: "lens your dappled yeye here" (293.23–294.1). And, finally, in the drunken conversation of the customers in the "Pub" scene (II, 3) occurs a passage with reference to Anna in old age and Cain and Abel in which Anna is identified with the washerwomen at the ford and the river itself: "these wasch woman (dapplehued)" (336.12–13).

As river carrying varied "treasures" to the sea and as sexually tempting woman, ALP has a wide variety of other scattered color associations. As Mrs. Porter she is, appropriately, a "sallowlass" but is also associated with "the white shoulders of Finnuala" (559.33-34)—the name "Finnuala" means "white shoulders" in Irish. At another point she is "the most beautiful of woman of the veilch veilchen veilde" (403.14-15)—*veilchen* are (German) "violets."[15] In the "Night Lessons" section (II, 2), she is "our callback [coalblack] mother Gaudyanna" (294.28-29), and in the ALP section (II, 1), she wears "a period gown of changeable jade" (200.2). At one point she is a "Houri of the coast of emerald" (68.11-12)—a rare nationalist-green association for any of Joyce's women who are generally above such nonsense. At the point of ALP's sexual awakening, as recollected by the washerwomen at the ford (pp. 202-204), she has all the colors of the rainbow including one fully detailed rainbow (R #8, 203.26-29). But ALP's dominant color remains the auburn of her hair, her "singimari saffron strumans of hair" (203.24). In Dolph's scandalous elucidation of the mother's sexual anatomy (II, 2) her orifices as demonstrated in the geometrical diagram are "vectorious readyeyes" (298.14-15) and her "redtangles" of pubic hair are parted to the boys' prying eyes (298.25). The high point of Dolph's investigation is reached when he directs his twin's attention to "the bluishing refluction below" (299.17-18), an image which unites at once ALP's red and blue and her river and woman characteristics. But it is in the figure of Issy, HCE's and ALP's daughter and the dream persona of ALP's youthful sexuality, that the color aspects of the dreamer's deepest sexual tensions are most clearly manifested.

The most notable feature of Issy is that her personality is split in two, Issy herself and her mirror image. But to claim on this basis that she is mad, as Adaline Glasheen does, is surely beside the point.[16] Issy is no madder than anybody else in the dream, and her personality and identity are no less stable than theirs. As Eve, she represents the split that occurred when Adam's rib was torn from him. The male dreamer's awareness of the splitting within him is represented physiologically by Issy's vulva and psychologically by the doubleness of Issy and her mirror image. The existence of one division implies the likelihood of further splitting and Issy, in manifesting all of the sexually-oriented conflicts within the dreamer's psyche, is not only two girls but seven and twenty-nine, all of them continually separating and reuniting as the dream-vision struggles to reconcile the dreamer's conflicts. Colors play a prominent part in those struggles.

It is important in considering Issy to remember that her "other" *is* her mirror image. It is as fruitless, in my judgment, to speculate as to whether Issy is Isolde of Ireland and her mirror image Isolde of Brittany[17] as would be the attempt to separate Browne from Nolan. When, for instance, Issy represents that common if uncomfortable male vision of woman, evident in some of Joyce's letters to Nora, as simultaneously and paradoxically virgin and whore, then Issy and her mirror image are both virgins and both whores. It is worth noting that Glasheen in "Who is Who When Everybody is Somebody Else" does lump all of Issy's myriad identities into one column, not two.[18]

It is scarcely surprising then that Issy is associated with a very broad range of colors. As seven girls she is of course the seven colors of the rainbow. As two and twenty-nine she is frequently various flowers with their varied colors. Thus in a version of the Park incident given in the "Porters' Pub" section (III, 4), the two temptresses are "the daintylines, Elsies from Chelsies, the two legglegels in blooms" (587.26–27). Dandelions are yellow though white at the seed stage; but the echo of the song title, "Two Little Girls in Blue," makes the "legglegels" blue as well. In HCE's self-defensive speech through the mouth of Yawn (III, 3) the pair in the park become the two female figures in Dublin's coat of arms: "At the crest, two young frish, etoiled, flappant, devoiled of their habiliments, vested sable, withdrewers argent" (546.5–7). The flappers or fresh fish are veiled in or devoid of black vests and silver drawers—neither garment in such a color appears in Dublin's coat of arms, or anywhere else in the *Wake*.[19] At her toilette in the "ALP" section (I, 8), Anna panders to HCE by sending "her boudeloire maids to His Affluence, Ciliegia Grande and Kirschie Real, the two chirsines" (207.11–12). "Cherry," in both Italian and German, indicates not only the virginal status of the girls but the very nonvirginal color red. At one point the two are given separate colors, white and brown, as "bawnee Madge Ellis and brownie Mag Dillon" (586.14–15), while at another they are different flowers of virtually identical color, "Hyacinssies with heliotrollops" (603.28). There is even a version of the Park incident in which the girls appear with no overt color associations, "A pair of sycopanties with amygdaleine eyes" (94.16–17), though the display of panties and fig or vulva (sycophant) implies colors. Despite this wide range of colors associated with Issy and her personae, one can find some quite definite patterns of color as well and these are most in evidence at those points at which the personae blend back into a comparatively unitary Issy. Predominant among them is the white/female/sexuality pattern we have already found in *Dubliners*, *A Portrait of the Artist as a Young Man* and *Ulysses*.

White in connection with woman, especially nubile young woman (that is, Issy), is ubiquitous throughout the *Wake*, and any traditional associations of innocence or purity or peace it may bring with it are consistently sabotaged. This is readily seen in the use of the term "Colleen Bawn" in such instances as "colleenbawl" (39.23) or "girleen bawn asthore" (397.5). The entry for "Colleen Bawn" in the *Third Census* runs, in part, as follows:

> *Colleen Bawn* (fair or white girl)—Eily O'Connor, heroine of Boucicault's play, which is based on Griffin's *The Collegians*.... *The Collegians* was made into Benedict's opera *The Lily of Killarney* (1862). Eily, low-born but charming, is secretly married to Hardress Cregan; she is repudiated by him and murdered, at his order, by Danny Mann.[20]

The colloquial Irish term "colleen bawn" (*cailin ban*) was traditionally analogous, to a considerable degree at least, with the *paisdin fionn* or "fair-haired boy" epithet given in the *Wake* to Shaun, that is, a term of approval and endearment. But the knowledge in popular culture of the matters described in Glasheen's entry above has given the phrase associations of melodrama and sexual intrigue very much at odds with the phrase's original connotations of girlish innocence and fairness. The phrase has also been debased in an entirely separate way; it has been used derisively of young women whose professions of nationalistic and Irish Catholic purity and devotion were thought to have become strident and militant. Miss Ivors in "The Dead" might fit this category. It is in this sense that the narrator of "Cyclops" uses the phrase when he says of a Gaelic League musical evening: "and there was a fellow with a Ballyhooly blue ribbon badge spiffing out of him in Irish and a lot of colleen bawns going about with temperance beverages and selling medals and oranges and lemonade and a few old dry buns, gob, flahoolagh entertainment" (*Ulysses*, 12.688–92). We can see this debasement of the phrase being exploited by Joyce in instances such as the narrator's comment in the "Colours Game" (II, 1): "for, shyly bawn and showly nursured, exceedingly nice girls can strike exceedingly bad times unless so richtly chosen's" (252.21–23), where the girlish innocence is underminded by a cynicism ("exceedingly," "richtly") which portrays that innocence as merely another bargaining counter in the marriage marketplace.

Other seemingly innocent whites attached to young women in the *Wake* are similarly subverted. The pedant's distortion of the old nursery rhyme to "see a rightheaded ladywhite don a cockhorse" (121.22–23) introduces scatalogical overtones. A phrase such as "sweet tart of Whiteknees Archway" in the "Night Lessons" section (302.14–15) gives the Virgin's white an unholy sexual tinge with sweetheart, tart, whiteness, white knees, white niece and white knee's archway. In his "Sermon" (III, 2) Jaun deliberately identifies Issy's white as the Virgin's color and then subverts it: "Here she's, is a bell, that's wares in heaven, virginwhite, Undetrigesima, vikissy manonna" (433.3–4). Issy is virginal; indeed she is a madonna; but she is also a belle, with her "undies" on display, and a very "kissy" madonna; and the echo of the Lord's Prayer is blasphemous. And in one of those leering footnotes in the "Night Lessons" section (II, 2) in which Issy displays a cynical prurience she writes: "He's just bug nuts on white mate he hasn't the teath nor the grits to choo and that's what's wrong with Lang Wang Wurm, old worbbling goesbelly" (270.F?). "Mate" is both meat and mate—the woman as object of HCE's frustrated sexual desire is reduced to the depersonalized flesh of pornographic magazines.

The most prominent, but by no means the only, exponent of the white/female/sexuality complex of perceptions in the *Wake* is Issy talking to and about herself and her "other" or mirror image. Here is the conclusion to Issy's answer to Question #10 of the "Quiz" (I, 6):

> Of course I believe you, my own dear doting liest, when you tell me. As I'd live to, O, I'd love to! Liss, liss! I muss whiss! Never that ever or I can remember dearstreaming faces, you may go through me! Never in all my whole white life of my matchless and pair. Or ever for bitter be the frucht of this hour! With my whiteness I thee woo and bind my silk breasths I thee bound! Always, Amory, amor andmore! Till always, thou lovest! Shshshsh! So long as the lucksmith. Laughs! (148.25–32)

Obviously the person Issy addresses is a lover, her mirror image in fact, and the tone is narcissistic and autoerotic. The echoes of the "Hail Mary" ("frucht of this hour") and the marriage service merely accentuate the air of self-arousal, especially in the sentimental caressing tones of the anatomical references: "go through me,"[21] "my whole white life," "my matchless and pair," "my whiteness," "my silk breasths." In her reply to Jaun's sermon (III, 2), Issy speaks of fondling a male lover's penis, and probably also fellatio; the passage includes the phrase "Obealbe myodorers" (459.27). "Obealbe" includes mouth (Irish, *beal*), rounded lips (the "o-") and white (Latin, *albus*). "Myodorers" is my adorers, my odors, my gold or treasures (Irish, *or*) and my tears (Irish, *deora*). But the male figure is merely a stimulus; Issy's love is focused exclusively on herself.

Much more typical of Issy's discourse than the passage just now referred to is this which occurs a few lines earlier in the text: "she's but nice for enticing my friends and she loves your style considering she breaksin me shoes for me when I've arch trouble and she would kiss my white arms for me so gratefully but apart from that she's terribly nice really, my sister " (459.14–18). Here is the female sexual white in a context that despite the variety of personal pronouns and the mention of a sister focuses entirely on Issy's mirror image, that is, Issy herself as her own love object. An even more typical excerpt from Issy's narcissistic speech is this passage from the "Inquisition of Yawn" (III, 3):

> My, you do! Simply adorable! Could I but pass my hands some, my hands through, thine hair.... Chic hands. The way they curve there under nue charmeen cuffol I am more divine like that when I've two of everything up to boyproof knicks. Winning in a way, only my arms are whiter, dear. Blanchemain, idler. Fairhair, frail one. Listen, meme sweety! O be joyfold! Mirror do justice, taper of ivory, heart of the conavent, hoops of gold! (527.15–23)

The echoes of the Litany of the Virgin with its ivory and gold connect with the sexual whites of "whiter," "blanchemain," and "Fairhair" and the reference to Issy's underwear and with the narcissism which marks the speech. It is at moments such as these when Issy and her mirror image achieve a kind of unity—note that Isolde of the White Hands and Isolde of the Fair Hair appear as one—that Issy's speech dramatically blends the white of the Virgin and the white of female sexuality, most nearly reconciles in fact the male visions of woman as virgin and woman as whore.

One further, and classic, example of Issy's articulation of her love affair with herself in terms of the sexual white merits analysis. After Glugg's second failure in the "Colours Game" (II, 1), the girls turn to Chuff, the Shaun-like twin, and offer him a hymn of praise which becomes progressively more seductive and more salacious. Issy, with whom the twenty-nine are collectively identified, is the spokesperson and part of her address runs as follows:

> The mything smile of me, my wholesole assumption, shes nowt mewithout as weam twin herewithin, that I love like myselfish, like smithereens robin-songs, like juneses nutslost, like the blue of the sky if I stoop for to spy's between my whiteyoumightcallimbs. (238.26-30)

The position Issy has adopted, it seems to me, for this particular gaze at her mirror image is that of bending over and looking back between her legs. What she sees, given this position, is her thighs, her underwear, her genital area seen dimly through her underwear, and then her face, thighs and bottom in the mirror. It is a view that bears considerable similarity to both Dolph's diagram of the mother's genitalia in "Night Lessons" (II, 2) and the view of herself that Molly Bloom contemplates as she sits on the chamberpot in "Penelope" (*Ulysses*, 18.1140-48) and that provokes her erotic thoughts including the sexual white. "My wholesole assumption" is on the one hand sexual-anatomical and on the other an identification with the Virgin whose Assumption to heaven, celebrated on August 15, is an important feature of Roman Catholic devotion to the Virgin. "The mything [my thing] smile of me" is genital as well as facial. "She's nowt me without" declares the identity of Issy and mirror image as well as the image seen in the framework of Issy's thighs. The ambivalence of number and pronoun and verb ("weam") and the tendency of the phrases to turn in on themselves reflect the uneasiness of identity. At the same time Issy's ability to project herself into the third person as Christopher Robin does in his song makes possible a kind of reciprocity in her self-love. The "nowt" is also probably the dot at the end of "Ithaca" (*Ulysses*, 17.2332), femaleness finally reduced to orifice, and I consider it quite probable that "juneses nutslost" is the absence of "nuts in May" or male genitalia which would if she were male inhibit her view of "the blue of the sky." The mirror itself is the pond of Narcissus as well as the mirrors of orgiastic rites beloved by writers and portrayers of erotica. "The blue of the sky," as well as being prominent in the literal sense in the viewer's perception, given the viewer's physical position, is also the blue of the Virgin and of Gerty MacDowell. The white is the Virgin's white but is much more pointedly the white of woman's skin, of underwear, of skin glimpsed through underwear. "Whiteyoumightcallimbs" are Issy's white thighs and her "unmentionables" or panties.

The function of woman's underwear in the dream-vision of the *Wake* is not merely to conceal but also to suggest and allow glimpses of the sexual mysteries beneath. Like literary art, women's garments have layers of meaning. Undergarments are the outward and visible sign of the mystery to which they draw attention; they therefore partake of the mystery and are themselves conventionally supposed to be hidden. The paradoxical combination of concealment and exhibitionism, purity and depravity, prurience and prudishness symbolized in the sexual white of *Finnegans Wake* embodies the male dreamer's vision of woman and provides an effective analogue for the chief dream technique by which the *Wake* works, namely, displacement.

Part of the pedant's discussion of the Letter in I, 5 is relevant here. The pedant considers the "quite everydaylooking stamped addressed envelope":

> Admittedly it is an outer husk: its face, in all its featureful perfection of imperfection, is its fortune: it exhibits only the civil or military clothing of whatever passionpallid nudity or plaguepurple nakedness may happen to tuck itself under its flap. Yet to concentrate solely on the literal sense or even the psychological content of any document to the sore neglect of the enveloping facts themselves circumstantiating it is just as hurtful to sound sense (and let it be added to the truest taste) as were some fellow in the act of perhaps getting an intro from another fellow turning out to be a friend in need of his, say, to a lady of the latter's acquaintance, engaged in performing the elaborative antecistral ceremony of upstheres, straighaway to run off and vision her plump and plain in her natural altogether, preferring to close his blinkhard's eyes to the ethiquethical fact that she was, after all, wearing for the space of the time being some definite articles of evolutionary clothing, inharmonious creations, a captious critic might describe them as, or not strictly necessary or a trifle irritating here and there, but for all that suddenly full of local colour and personal perfume and suggestive, too, of so very much more and capable of being stretched, filled out, if need or wish were, of having their surprisingly like coincidental parts separated don't they now, for better survey by the deft hand of an expert, don't you know? Who in his heart doubts either that the facts of feminine clothiering are there all the time or that the feminine fiction, stranger than the facts, is there also at the same time, only a little to the rere? Or that one may be separated from the other? Or that both may then be contemplated simultaneously? Or that each may be taken up and considered in turn apart from the other? (109.8-36)

This is one of the most "open" passages in the entire book. That Joyce is using the metaphor of letter and envelope to describe his Wakean technique of dream displacement seems to me beyond question. That he uses the further metaphor of woman's body and her clothing to elucidate the first metaphor is entirely appropriate. The alternatives of "passionpallid nudity or plaguepurple nakedness" are curious; they refer to both the missive within the envelope and the female body within the clothing. White with nudity is appropriate but why the purple? "Passion ... -purple" may well hint at "purple passages" and may be a Joycean commingling of the approaches Yeats placed in antithesis when he spoke of the "coat/Covered with embroideries" and the "enterprise" of "walking naked."[22] It is worth noting that in the promising qualities of the clothing color comes first, preceding perfume and shape; we can be sure, I believe, that the "local colour" is white. It is noteworthy too that the concluding sentences are all interrogative; the questions of the separate identities of clothes and body, of writing and context, even of Issy and mirror image remain open; the possibility of essential interdependence, even of symbiotic relationship, are real features of the dream-vision.

In the *Wake*, the articulation of the white/woman/sexuality set of associations is by no means confined to Issy, though she is generally the referent for them. Many, many examples can be found scattered through the text but their general tenor fits with the comments I have already made on Issy's sexual whites.[23] There are however four important extensions of the white/female/ sexuality pattern of associations, namely, white with underwear, white with urination, white with male sexual response, and white with red as an antithesis expressing various facets of the dreamer's sexual conflicts. The first of these is conspicuous and important, but since I have already examined it in this chapter I shall merely give the location of a few of the other more striking examples here: 238.23-24, 351.28-30 and 370.5-6.

The white/skin and white/panties sets of images readily extend themselves into the wine/white/wet/urine/female complex of associations, the two earliest notable instances of which appear in the "Museyroom" episode (I, 1). Here are the two passages:

> ...our mounding's mass, now Wallinstone national museum, with, in some greenish distance, the charmful waterloose country and the two quitewhite villagettes who hear show of themselves so gigglesomes minxt the follyages, the prettilees! Penetrators are permitted into the museomound free. (8.1-5)

> This is Willingdone cry. Brum! Brum! Cumbrum! This is jinnies cry. Underwetter! Goat strip Finnlambs! This is jinnies rinning away. (9.26-28)

As has frequently been pointed out this field of Waterloo is the field of all history's battles and the midden-heap of history, and thus also a museum. But as "our mounding's mass" it is the bulk of HCE and as the Wellington monument it is his erect penis. The echo of "mounting" and the mention of "penetrators" also suggest that this may be the *mons veneris*, thus uniting the battlefields of war and sex. The girls urinate ("waterloose," "minxt") among the bushes ("some greenish distance") and deliberately exhibit their goodies ("prettilees") amid the foliage. As "villagettes" the pair are two little villages on the plain of Waterloo and two female inhabitants of those villages. "Quitewhite" is the "signature" of their sexual provocation. The display is both harmful and full of charms to the man who spies on them, a man whose folly and age and pursuit of the girls is evinced in "follyages." This of course is the Incident in the Phoenix Park, the origin of the name of which, *fionn uisce* or "clear water" or "white water" in Irish, is given new relevance by the girls' activities. The girls' urination is not just an accidental occasion for the uncovering of their sexual treasures to the greedy eyes of HCE; the act itself is a deliberate challenge to his maleness. That challenge is more explicit in the second passage. In crying "Brum! Brum! Cumbrum!" HCE-Wellington is rumbling and grumbling (German, *brummen*)[24] and recalling General Cambronne's shout of *merde*. He is under pressure, militarily and sexually. The girls' warcry of "Underwetter!" contains urinating, underwear, wetness and (German) "stormy weather." Their shout of "Goat Strip Finnlambs!" is the German wartime curse on England, *Gott Strafe England*, and also the accusation that the old goat, HCE, is stripping with his lecherous eyes the white or fair lambs, that is the girls themselves, as they are "rinning away," that is running and (German) "flowing." As HCE-Wellingdone first responded to the sight of the jinnies in their "undisides" with an erection ("git the band up," 8.34) he now responds to these more dangerous revelations by masturbating ("branlish," 9.34 [French] *se branler*[25]). But if HCE-Willingdone does brandish his penis at the jinnies, he is careful to do it from a distance as they are running away. Again the notion of challenge to the male security and traditional role is present, a notion made more explicit in the "Prankquean" incident (I, 1).

The pivotal word for the white/sex/urination complex of associations in the "Prankquean" episode is "wit" in its three occurrences of "wit," "witter" and "wittest," one for each of the Prankquean's visits. Patrick McCarthy's analysis of the episode makes these points of especial interest to me here: the increasing wetness of the Prankquean's visits; their increasing whiteness (Dutch, *wit*); and the increasing demand for porter.[26] It may be added that "pulled a rosy one" echoes "to pluck a rose" or "urinate" in English slang.[27] The phrase has further sexual echoes in the notion of deflowering. In any event the connection of white with woman's urinating is quite explicit. The Prankquean's first visit is both a sexual invitation and a sexual challenge or threat which increases in intensity in the subsequent visits as the whiteness, and therefore the blatant sexuality of her provocation, intensifies with each visit. Van Hoother is more and more bedevilled in his attempts to ignore her or give her merely passive recognition. His "dour" (Irish, "tower, tough, stiff") gives him away, becoming at the second visit "wicked" (and wicket) and at the third an *arc de triomphe*, among other things, erection and rainbow. Finally he is provoked into an oblique response when he emerges and defecates (23.4), acts associated in the text with the appearance of a rainbow (R #1), a clap of thunder and, it would appear, the founding of the city and the beginnings of literature.

The Prankquean's riddle contains within it a direct indication of its sexual challenge in the juxtaposition of male porter and female urine in "porterpease." Like Grace O'Malley, her historical prototype, the Prankquean opposes lawless and creative energy to the established order. The repetition of references to rain and raining through the episode emphasizes the creative, life-giving properties of the Prankquean's urination. When she takes the children to "Tourlemonde" (Irish, *Tir na mBan*, "Women's Land") and "Woeman's Land," she actively subverts the father's authority with the upcoming generation. The failure of the male to express sexuality naturally and without guilt leads him through sublimation to the compensating achievements of cities and rainbows and civilization, and leads him in the dream to posit sexuality as an anarchic and threatening energy resident in the woman. McCarthy makes these further observations on the conclusion of the Prankquean episode:

> When he slams the door in her face he is symbolically closing the path to a male-female sexual union which might lead to the conception of a child. The riddle might in fact be rephrased to indicate a desire to "pass the *porte* [door], please," which in turn might imply a desire for sexual union. The Jarl's masturbation ("laying cold hands on himself," "shaking warm hands with himself") indicates his preference for non-conceptual sexual release.[28]

Through the three visits of the Prankquean the progression of color signifies an increasing intensity of her whiteness and wetness. This is the woman's white-sexual attraction and the libation of her white wine/urine as demonstration of woman's creative energies. Up to this point in the dream any woman-whites that appeared to the dreamer were nicely distanced, residing in the comparatively detached ritual of racial memory or history, as in the case of the "jinnies" in the "Museyroom." But the Prankquean can neither be ignored nor merely ogled; she invades his home; the dreamer *must* respond. What marks the "Prankquean" incident is the directness and immediacy of the actions and the response they provoke.

What is happening in the "Prankquean" episode, in my judgment, is the first significant loosening of the dreamer's censoring power as he drifts deeper and deeper into sleep. At this point the deeply hidden complex of his sexual feelings rises into the mainstream of the dream and must be confronted. The personae which represent those feelings begin to have a life of their own and to gain control, and it is in response to them that the first fully detailed rainbow appears, the first real revelation of the dream-vision, despite the desperate efforts of the dreamer's psyche to evade it and to fall back on the recitation of his masculine achievements. It is no accident that the Prankquean comes from the West of Ireland, as did Gretta Conroy (and Nora Barnacle). Gretta's story of Michael Furey with associations of West and rain and snow breached the defenses of Gabriel's self-construct as the Prankquean with her rain and white breaches the defenses of the dreamer.

Although the Prankquean episode does not make an explicit connection between wine and woman's urine, that point is made quite unequivocally in other parts of the book. A passage from the Shem section (I, 7), which I have already had occasion to comment on in chapter 3, is relevant:

> No likedbylike firewater or firstserved firstshot or gulletburn gin or honest brewbarrett beer either. O dear no! Instead the tragic jester sobbed himself wheywhingingly sick of life on some sort of a rhubarbarous maundarin yellagreen funkleblue windigut diodying applejack squeezed from sour grapefruice and, to hear him twixt his sedimental cupslips when he had

gulfed down mmmmuch to mmmmany gourds of it retching off to almost as low withswillers, who always knew notwithstanding when they had had enough ... it came straight from the noble white fat, jo, openwide sat, jo, jo, her why hide that, jo jo jo, the winevat, of the most serene magyansty az archdiochesse, if she is a duck, she's a douches, and when she has a feherbour snot her fault, now is it? artstouchups, funny you're grinning at, fancy you're in her yet, Fanny Urinia. (171.13-28)

White occurs four times in the extract, "white," "why hide," "openwide," "feherbour" (Hungarian) and there's an echo of a fifth white in "winevat." "Feherbour" is (Hungarian) "white skin" and a white wine. "Jo" is both (Hungarian) "nice" or "good" and (Danish) "yes"[29] (and Molly's "yes"). "Fanny Urinia" is "heavenly bottom" and "urine." The story behind this set of images is given by Ellmann.[30] Briefly, Joyce likened his favorite Swiss wine to the urine of an archduchess. In our extract, the image of the white winevat is that of the intimate parts of the archduchess as she urinates; it is also the vision seen by HCE in the Park which is destined to cause him so much trouble.

Within a page of the passage examined above Shem poses "the first riddle of the universe: asking, when is a man not a man?" (170.4-5). Among the scattered answers we find: "still another said when the wine's at witsends, and still another when lovely wooman stoops to conk him" (170.13-14). At the most obvious level of interpretation these two answers say: when he's drunk, and when he's in love. But "witsends" contains white (Dutch), end, wet; when wine passes through the drinker's digestive system, it is, at the end, urine. When woman "stoops to conk" a man in the *Wake* she stoops to urinate, or make "white wine." In both cases the wine can "unman" and thus conquer the male.

As I have said, the identification of sexual white with woman's urine and woman's hegemony, and frequently with hints of white wine, crops up at the most unexpected and scattered points in the *Wake*. Near the end of the "Mime" section (II, 1) speculations are made about the mother and father including this statement: "Punch may be pottleproud but his Judy's a wife's wit better" (255.26). The immediate context has to do with drinking and HCE's management of the pub. Judy of course does traditionally get the better of Punch, but her victory in this case has to do with his pride in his bottle of stout and her wit/white/wet. Her wine is too much for his Guinness. In the "Mamalujo" section (II, 4), "Doelsy" (anagram for "Ysolde") is "delightfully ours, in her doaty ducky little blue and roll his hoop and how she ran, when wit won free, the dimply blissed and awfully bucked" (398.18-21). Wit/white/wet/urine is associated with Issy's freeing and triumph. In his "Sermon" (III, 2), Jaun warns Issy against "Columbian nights entertainments the like of *White limbs they never stop teasing* nor *Minxy was a Manxmaid when Murry wor a Man*" (433.18-20). The association of sexual/white/provocation with urination (Latin, *minxit*) is notable here.

Two further instances of urination and white combining to signify the power, indeed the threat to the male dreamer, of woman's sexual energy merit comment. The gate-bottle incident in I, 3 concludes with the lines:

> The young reine came down desperate and the old liffopotamus started ploring all over the plains, as mud as she cud be, ruinating all the bouchers' schurts and the backers' wischandtugs so that be the chandeleure of the Rejaneyjailey they were all night wasching the walters of, the weltering walters off. Whyte. (64.16–21)

"Reine" contains rain, reign, French "queen" and German "pure one" and refers to Issy. The "old liffopotamus" is of course Anna as river flooding the plain. "Reine" connects with "Rejaneyjailey," Latin "Queen of Heaven," while "liffopotamus" is echoed in the concluding rhythms and sounds which are those of Anna Livia Plurabelle. The flooding is also the tears and urination of mother and daughter culminating in the symbol of their sexual power, the last isolated word, "Whyte."

My final example is taken from a lengthy speech of Butt's (II, 3), which runs in part:

> I did not care three tanker's hoots, ('sham! hem! or chaffit!) for any feelings from my lifeprivates on their reptrograd leanins because I have Their Honours booth my respectable soeurs assistershood off Lyndhurst Terrace, the puttih Misses Celana Dalems, and she in vinting her angurr can belle the troth on her alliance." (351.26–31)

In this tremendously dense web of allusions and associations I must extricate the following for my present purpose: "puttih" is Malayan "white"; "Celana Dalems" is Malayan "panties"; "vinting her angurr" is venting her anger and venting her wine—*angurr* is Malayan "wine,"[31] and "vinting" also has to do with wine. We have in fact that image that most threatens the male dreamer, namely, the woman-women in the Park, exhibiting white bottoms and white panties, making wine and water and war.

To deal with the third extension of the white-female sexuality pattern of associations, namely, white for certain male sexual responses, I must digress briefly from consideration of Issy and other temptress figures. HCE's speeches of self-justification are the richest sources of this male white. In the first "Pub" section he delivers such a speech which slips into guiltridden innuendoes at every turn: "waterside labourers" (363.21), "the wild whips" (Wilde) (363.22–23), "minxmingled hair" (363.26), "hot peas" (363.27), "by whiles of dodging a rere" (Wilde again) (363.29–30), "unlifting upfallen girls" (363.33) and the like. He claims to be misunderstood and speaks of "the rebald danger with they who would bare whiteness against me" (364.1–2). He conflates the temptresses who bared their whiteness against him and thus revealed to the world his guilty desires with the three soldiers and the others who bore witness against him; there is an implication that the three were involved in homosexual exhibitionism of their own. The same tactic appears in Glugg's defense of HCE against the rumors of his indiscretions in the clause "which Bichop Babwith bares to his whitness in his *Just a Fication of Villumses*" (241.35–242.1), though it seems to backfire in this instance. The context reeks with sexual innuendoes and a number of probable and one certain reference to Wilde: "greyed vike cuddlepuller" (241.9)—Lady Campbell is supposed to have referred to the older, bloated Wilde as "a great white slug," here distorted to suggest fellatio, masturbation and Dorian Gray. Lady Campbell's phrase recurs in a stage direction to a long confessional speech of Butt's: "*with a gisture expansive of Mr Lhugewhite Cadderpollard with sunflawered beautonhole pulled up point blanck*" (350.10–11). There is a second "white" here ("blanck") and lots of homosexual undertones such as the "beau" and "ton" (Irish, "buttocks") in "beautonhole." Finally, there is a speech of HCE's, through the mouth of Yawn (III, 3), in which HCE under pressure appears to have become, for a while (pp. 535–36), the ghost of Oscar Wilde speaking in self-defense. The speech has a number of whites and a plethora of Wilde references. Obviously, white with male sexual response and guilty cover-up, and especially with Wilde and homosexuality, is a well established, if limited, pattern of color in the texture of *Finnegans Wake*.

The fourth extension of white/female/sexuality is the red-white sexual clash, the most pervasive, dense, tangled complex of colors in the *Wake*, second in importance only to the primary white/temptress pattern itself. To begin with we must examine more closely the basic color patterns associated with Issy since these and the questions of identity involved with them have caused problems for many students of *Finnegans Wake*.

For a start, there are two Isoldes in the legend of Tristan and Isolde, both of them with white connections. Isolde of Ireland or Isolde of the Fair Hair was betrothed to King Mark of Cornwall but became Tristan's lover when he was escorting her to Mark's court. Isolde of Brittany or Isolde of the White Hands was Tristan's wife who brought about his death. But there have been serious differences of critical opinion regarding Joyce's use of the Tristan-Isolde legend in the *Wake*, especially in the matters of Issy's identity and coloring. Nathan Halper, for instance, has written in a 1975 article:

> Isolt of the fair hair: Isolt of the white hands. (His [H.C.E.'s] wife combines the figures of mother and daughter.) This is related to the contrast of raven and dove. The 'jinnies is a cooin her hand ... the jinnies is a ravin her hair' (8.33). In the story the Fair Hair is gold. But in Joyce's schema her hair is always black (like Molly's in contrast to the blond of Milly).[32]

Obviously, this presents difficulties with regard to Issy's relationship with her mirror image, her relationship to the two Isoldes, the colors associated with her personalities, her overlap with Anna Livia. Much of the confusion is due, I fear, to attempts to separate the characters cleanly from one another, to return each of them to the solitary confinement of the individual personality. But these are the figures of a dream, projections of the dreamer's normally repressed feelings. They are not in the final analysis fully extricable from his cast of mind or from each other. Certainly we can probe their make up and their relationships but we must learn to tolerate their shifting identities. What we cannot attribute to any of them is organic inviolability without doing violence to the paradoxical evidence of the text.

Issy is not dark-haired but has her mother's coloring and so does her "other," her mirror image. Anna has not only Livia Schmitz's auburn hair but the ever-changing colors of the Liffey's waters. Thus Issy's hair, like her mother's, can be designated at any given moment at any point on the range of colors from blond to gold to red. She is introduced in the *dramatis personae* of the "Mime" (II, 1) as "a bewitching blonde" (220.7-8); the four old men spying on the lovers (II, 4) observe that she has "nothing under her hat but red hair and solid ivory" (396.9-10). As she splits into the seven rainbow girls or the twenty-nine leap year girls it is idle to seek her characteristic traits or colors in any one of them rather than another—they simply are not differentiated in that way. And not only is the portrait of Issy colored by the concerns of the dreamer, it is also colored by the observer or narrator of the moment, whether or not we the readers can detect who that observer is or what relation he bears to the dreamer. Then there are the prejudices and blind spots of even the ideal insomniac reader....

Here is Yawn, speaking in his own voice, that is as a projection and version of Shaun's personality, describing Issy:

> —I feel a fine lady ... floating on a stillstream of isisglass ... with gold hair to the bed ... and white arms to the twinklers ... O la la! (486.23-25) [The ellipses are in the original.]

What we have presented to us is an image of the supreme object of Shaun's desire, his sister Issy, with her enticing white skin and golden hair, floating languorously, hinting at pleasures of the bed. But she is also the inviolate virgin—the white and gold are from the Litany of the Virgin and they are the colors of the Church Militant. On the other hand she is at least as much the mirror image as she is Issy herself since she floats in Issy's mirror—"stillstream of isisglass." And the white arms point to an identification with Iseult of the White Hands or Iseult of Brittany, while the golden hair points to Iseult the Fair or Iseult of Ireland.

Issy's addresses to her mirror image typically confuse her self and her "other." Typically also she combines her white with gold, on the one hand making much demurely of the connection with the Virgin and on the other undermining that connection with the crudest salacities.[33] But we must also remember that Issy's gold is prone to shifting towards red and this it tends to do when the sexuality becomes blatant and active. What we get then, most often, is a variety of red-white clashes, combinations and near antitheses. But prior to my consideration of those red-whites I must examine sexual red, separately, in its own right. Essentially, I believe, this red represents the red of the engorged sexual organs, of the skin of a person in the state of sexual excitation, and of the blood and violence associated sadistically with sexuality in some minds, Jaun's for instance as demonstrated in his "Sermon" (III, 2). Or, to put it another way, white symbolizes the sexual provocation while red indicates the physical response to that provocation.

In the "Night Lessons" section (II, 2), one of Issy's footnotes names two pantomimes: "Jests and the Beastalk with a little rude hiding rod" (307.F1). The passage to which the note is appended has to do with co-education of the sexes. The phallic hint of "little rude [red] hiding rod" is so typical of the submerged salacity of Issy's footnotes as to be inescapable for the experienced reader, even without the modification of "Beanstalk" into "Beastalk." HCE may have similar thoughts thrusting to the surface of his mind in the self-justifying speech he makes through the voice of Yawn (III, 3) when he speaks of "littleritt reddinghats" (551.8).

Another of Issy's footnotes in the "Night Lessons" section runs: "Frech devil in red hairing! So that's why you ran away to sea, Mrs Lappy. Leap me, Locklaun, for you have sensed!" (268.F6). The underlying meaning refers to a satanic phallus and Issy's own pubic hair. She also drags in her mother and invites rape from a viking (Irish, *Lochlannach*). It is entirely in keeping with Issy's penchant for casting her more obscene suggestions in religious garments that the invitation to rape is a distortion of the penitent's formula in the sacrament of Penance in the Catholic Church: "Bless me, father, for I have sinned." On two separate occasions (379.16, 440.28) one of the rainbow girls is called Ruby when no color is given to any of the others. And the mourners at Finnegan's *Wake* (I, 1) refer to a companion of Issy's (and therefore an alter ego of Issy's) thus: "But Essie Shanahan has let down her skirts. You remember Essie in our Luna's Convent? They called her Holly Merry her lips were so ruddyberrry and Pia de Purebelle when the redminers riots was on about her" (27.14–17). Note the combination of the Virgin (Holy Mary) and the holly's red berries in "Holly Merry." The reds here seem to signify sexual maturation and sexual attractiveness and probably also the onset of Issy's menses ("Luna's Convent"), that other female libation, another symbol of woman's power.

At the end of Festy King's trial we are told by a witness that two "litigants" were "egged on by their supporters in the shape of betterwomen with bowstrung hair of Carrothageninue ruddiness, waving crimson petties and screaming from Isod's towertop" (87.24–29). The women, waving their red hair and red petticoats, are projections of Issy ("Isod's"), and are undoubtedly egging the men to the only contest Issy is interested in, namely, the competition for her favors. In the pedant's parody of Sir Edward Sullivan (I, 5), a kind of climax of enthusiasm occurs which is given in terms of violent sexual assault dominated by "reds." The passage is rather lengthy so I shall merely list the reds: "redhandedly," "rubric," "rudely," "rubyjets," "Roe's," "bluid," "rouge," "lobster," "rossy," "ruddy" and "Rufus" (122.8–17). Another dramatic concentration of "reds" occurs at the sadistic climax of Jaun's sermon (III, 2):

> I'll have plenary sadisfaction, plays the bishop, for your partial's indulgences if your my rodeo gel.... There's a lot of lecit pleasure coming bangslanging your way, Miss Pinpernelly satin.... For I'll just draw my prancer and give you one splitpuck in the crupper, you understand, that will bring the poppy blush of shame to your peony hindmost till you yelp papapardon and radden your rhodatantarums to the beat of calorrubordolor. (445.9–18)

The reds are: "rodeo" (Latin, "rose"), "Pinpernelly" (scarlet pimpernel), "poppy blush," "peony," "papapardon" (Latin, "poppy"), "radden your rhodatantarums" (redden your rhododendrons) and "calorrubordolor" (Latin, "heat, redness, pain"). The last word is the key one—the image Shaun creates to luxuriate in is Issy's white flesh heated and reddened with beating, shame and sexual arousal.

As with Gerty MacDowell in "Circe" a good deal of blushing and flushing attaches to the appearance of Issy, none of it however attributable to pure modesty. In the "Porter's Pub" scene (III, 4) the sleeping child Issy is portrayed in her own dreams as a future nun "blushing all day" (556.2) and looking "a peach" (556.6). In the lengthy footnote in the form of a letter in "Night Lessons" (II, 2) there are lots of reds, among them this opening sentence: "Come, smooth of my slate, to the beat of my blosh!" (279.F1). "Blosh" is brush, blush, *blas* (Irish, "relish," "desire"). The "beat" in combination with "blush" echoes the sadism of Shaun's "Sermon." In the introduction to that "Sermon" the narrator tells us that "Jaun, after those few prelimbs made out through his eroscope the apparition of his fond sister Izzy for he knowed his love by her waves of splabashing and she showed him proof by her way of blabushing" (431.13–17). Shaun's telescope produces a vision combined of sexual love and looking-desiring ("eroscope"). The preliminaries he begins with consist of "prelimbs," Issy's limbs as a preview of coming attractions. The blush is not one of modesty but the flush of real or feigned sexual arousal, another weapon in Issy's sexual arsenal. A little further on, in the "Sermon" itself, Shaun announces: "A coil of cord, a colleen coy, a blush on a bush turned first man's laughter into wailful moither" (433.28–30). The first man is Adam undergoing the Fall in the Garden of Eden. The "coil" is the serpent; the "colleen" is Eve; and the "blush on a bush" is the apple. However, if we consider that persistent if unofficial Christian tradition that the Original Sin was a sexual transgression and if we read the sentence in that light, then, the "coil" is the penis, the colleen's coyness is sexual provocation, the "blush" is sexual consciousness and arousal and the "bush" is pubic hair. In this case "man's laughter" becoming "wailful moither" is not just man's joy being overcome by death (murder) but man's daughter (Eve, taken from his side) becoming sorrowful mother. But since this is also the incident in the Phoenix Park the "blush" is also the exhibited limbs and underclothes and genitalia of the urinating girls and the aroused response of their watchers. The blush, traditionally the sign of maidenly modesty, has become in the *Wake* a naked signal of sexual provocation, availability and arousal, a symbol of sexual precocity, awareness and guilt, and a weapon in the sexual skirmishing.

Various reds crop up here and there in the *Wake* with hints of association with sexual activity, sexual organs or underclothes. An almost interminable sentence of the pedant's (I, 5) concludes thus: "two and two together, and with a swarm of bisses honeyhunting after, a sign for shyme (O, the pettybonny rouge!) separated modest mouths" (124.26–28). According to McHugh "le Petit Bonnet Rouge" was a name used for the devil.[34] The satanic Shem is obviously present ("shyme"). But, further, the presence of the girls (the pairs), the sound of the French phrase itself and the overtones of "bisses," "honeyhunting," "shyme" and "modest mouths" hint at a sexual connotation, probably the female genitalia. In two instances in the book the word "cherry" occurs in connection with Issy-figures in such a way as to suggest both the red shade associated with "cherry" and the vulgar connotation of "cherry" as hymen and thus virginity and vulva. In the "Museyroom" episode (I, 1) the two temptresses are "Cherry jinnies" (9.13)—a duplication of the "Dear Jenny" to whom Wellington is supposed to have written "Publish and be damned!" The second instance occurs in the confused evidence given in I, 3 regarding HCE's behavior in the Park. An actress who gives her opinion in the matter is described as "looking perhaps even more pewtyflushed in her cherryderry paduasoys, girdles and braces" (58.36–59.1). Here is the blush-flush again, this time in association with feminine beauty, "cherry-" and women's garments.

The Crimean War and the Russian general who is part of it produce another set of sexual reds. In the "Porter's Pub" scene (III, 4), the Four, speaking of the pomp that will attend the king's forthcoming visit to Dublin, mention "the crimosing balkonladies" (569.2). These are the ladies who will watch the royal procession from balconies but the phrase also has Balkans, Crimea, and crimson. The passage in which the phrase appears has strong sexual overtones. Butt (II, 3), speaking of the "urssian gemenal, in his scutt's rudes" (352.1), declares: "I seen his brichashert offensive and his boortholomas vadnhammaggs vise a vise them scharlot runners and how they gave love to him" (352.4–6). "Scharlot" contains the name of Sir James Scarlett, British general in the Crimea, the color "scarlet," and "harlot." "Runners" according to McHugh are brothel touts in Egypt.[35] Being in red ("rudes") is no doubt appropriate for a Russian general but less so is his association with Scott's Road, a brothel area of Shanghai.[36] The passage has other words and phrases with sexual connotations as well. Another passage in the evidence given of HCE's misdeeds (I, 3) has the familiar sexual reds with a variety of sexual references and a probable further mention of General Scarlett:

> A railway barmaid's view (they call her Spilltears Rue) was thus expressed: to sympathisers of the Dole Line, Death Avenue, anent those objects of her pity-prompted ministrance, to wet, man and his syphon. Ehim! It is ever too late to whissle when Phyllis floods her stable. It would be skarlot shame to jailahim in lockup, as was proposed to him by the Seddoms creature what matter what merrytricks went off with his revulveher. (59.36-60.7)

"Rue" is Irish "red." *Meretrix* is Latin "whore." The other sexual references are fairly obvious. What I should like to emphasize however is the pouring or urinating power of the woman which is so prominent here: "Spilltears," "to wet," "floods her stable"—"man and his syphon" are no match for the wetting power of the woman which is related to or identical with the power she holds through her sexuality.

We come now to the last purely red sexual association, one we have already met in *A Portrait of the Artist as a Young Man* and in *Ulysses*, namely, the rose. Rose frequently appears in association with Issy and projections of Issy's personality, almost always with connotations of sexuality, especially of the female genitalia. In Answer #10 of the "Quiz" (I, 6) when Issy considers her sexual attractiveness she speaks of caring for her hands "to make them look so rosetop glowstop nostop" (144.1). In Answer #7 about the "maggies," rose is made symbolic of their sexual stratagems: "as born for lorn in lore of love to live and wive by wile and rile by rule of ruse 'reathed rose and hose hol'd home" (142.35-143.1). "Ruse" and "rose" are virtually synonymous here, and the rose wreathed in ruse is almost certainly the vulva—the rose has of course a long popular history as emblem of not only sexual love and feminine beauty but also the female genitalia. The genital significance of "rose" in the present context is supported by the underwear/genital/secret hints of "hose hol'd home." One of the exhortations given to Issy in Jaun's "Sermon" (III, 2) is ostensibly a version of the First Precept of the Church regarding attendance at Sunday mass: "Never miss your lostsomewhere mass for the couple in Myles you butrose to brideworship" (433.10-11). The statement also exhorts Issy to preserve her virtue till marriage and on the other hand opposes the rites of the mass to the activities of a couple newly married. The "but-" in "butrose" is both colloquial "butt," "bottom," and the Irish *bod*, "penis," indicating once again the genital significance of "rose."

In the ramblings of the four old judges at the trial of Festy King (I, 4) occurs this statement: "Festives and highajinks and jintyaun and her beetyrossy bettydoaty and not to forget now a'duna o'darnel" (94.29-31). "Jintyaun" points to "Shaun" and "gentleman" so that the "her" comes as a surprise to the reader. What has happened, I am confident, is a break or interruption in the sequence of discourse of the Four. "Beetyrossy" contains Betsy Ross, beet-rose, beet-red, tea-rose: "-doaty" is an Anglo-Irish term of diminution and endearment most commonly applied to a very young child. "Beetyrossy bettydoaty" is almost Swift-like "little language." It is also one of those phrases that lead me to suspect that some of Issy's talk to her mirror image is addressed to her own vulva, the center of the sexual power which seems to be the only thing that can touch Issy's feelings.

"The war of the two roses" mentioned four lines further on in connection with the dubious behavior of HCE is certainly the temptations provided him by the display of the two girls in the Park. It is also symbolic, I believe, of the conflicting expectations of maidenly modesty and blatant sexual provocation imposed on girls by the mores of the day and resulting in the kinds of tensions within the personality that are indicated throughout the *Wake* by Issy's splintering into two and seven and twenty-nine.

In Joyce's works the red rose is rarely seen for long in isolation before a white rose joins it. A sharper contrast of red and white appears in *Finnegans Wake* with the introduction of the lily. But again this contrast is not a simple balanced antithesis. Glasheen tends to push lily and rose towards polarity, to see them as fair girl and dark girl, or as good girl and bad girl.[37] To be fair to Glasheen she does not push her attempt to separate these figures to the point of committing herself to a polarity of Colleen Bawn/Isolde of the White Hands/repudiated wife/Lily/white vs. Bohemian Girl/Isolde of the Fair Hair/loved wife/Rose/red, but she points in that direction and at the very least prompts the question as to whether such a polarity identifiable with distinctly separate Issy-figures (e.g., Issy and her mirror image) can be convincingly demonstrated from the text of the *Wake*. I must argue that it cannot, that such cleancut, symmetrical balancing of opposites is at odds with the spirit of *Finnegans Wake* in which the separate elements and personalities are continually being tugged apart and striving towards reunion. Their separation and opposition are continually being unbalanced by the very terms that state that opposition. Thus, when, on the occasion of the naming of HCE (I, 2), a version of the Park incident is given and denied as it is given, the girls in the story are "inseparable sisters, uncontrollable nighttalkers, Skertsiraizde with Donyahzade, who afterwards, when the robberers shot up the socialights, came down into the world as amusers and were staged by Madame Sudlow as Rosa and Lily Miskinguette" (32.7-11). The sisters *are* "inseparable." There is no question of associating Mistinguette, the French dancer, with Lily and not with Rosa, or jokes (Italian, *scherzi*[38]) and raised skirts merely with Rosa and Dunyazad/Donizetti with Lily.

The white of the Lily in the *Wake* is neither virginal nor funereal but the sexual/female white which constitutes the book's most powerful color pattern, and it most often appears with the red of the rose which is equally carnal. On occasion, Lily without rose identifies the temptresses who bedevil HCE. At the opening of I, 4, HCE is seen as a lion in the zoo remembering the water lilies or lotus blossoms of the Nile, "bedreamt him stil and solely of those lililiths undeveiled which had undone him" (75.5-6). Obviously "those lililiths" are the two girls in the Park. "Undeveiled" includes: of the field, veiled, underveiled (underclothed), unveiled, undefiled, undevilled. Among the opinions gathered in I, 3 of HCE's conduct, one report runs: "It was the first woman, they said, souped him, that fatal wellesday, Lili Coninghams, by suggesting him they go in a field. Wroth mod eldfar, ruth red stilstand, wrath wrackt wroth" (58.28-31). The "Lili" who is the cause of his downfall here, though in the singular number, clearly stands for the two girls, and though there is no rose present, mention of the lily is followed by a cluster of reds, "wroth," "redd" and "wroth." There is another pattern of hints here, however, that links the "Lili" with the Orange Ulster cause. The spelling "Lili" points to the Orange song "Lilibullero." Going into the field is not only for illicit sex; it is also the climax of an Orange parade. "Souped" is a reference to the proselytizing soup kitchens of the Famine which offered the starving Catholics food on condition that they renounced their faith in favor of Protestantism.

This Orange connection with Lily as seductress of HCE is not an isolated phenomenon. In I, 3, "the flash brides or bride in their lily boleros one games with at the Nivynubies' finery ball" (66.36-67.1) are almost certainly the girls in the Park—"lily boleros" provides the Orange connection. Following a remarkably clear description of the Park incident in the "Ballad" chapter (I, 2), this passage occurs: "Ofman will toman while led is the lol .... Fikup, for flesh nelly.... If she's a lilyth, pull early! Pauline, allow!" (34.30-33). "Led" is red and "lol" is rose in Volapuk.[39] "Lilyth, pull early! Pauline, allow!" is the opening line of the Orange song, "Lilibullero, Bullen a Law." The rose echoes a word just one line previous to the passage I have quoted, "Rosasharon." It is notable that in the source for "Rose of Sharon," namely the Song of Solomon, one person constitutes both Lily and Rose: "I am the rose of Sharon, and the lily of the valleys" (2:1). In the "Inquisition of Yawn" (III, 3), Issy fantasizes her wedding: "It will all take bloss as oranged at St Audiens rosan chocolate chapelry" (528.5-6). "Lily" is not explicitly mentioned here but the association of "rose" and "orange blossom" implies the presence of "lily."

One other instance of the Orange connections of the lily is worth looking at. At the beginning of the "Ballad" section (I, 2) this phrase occurs: "Iris Trees and Lili O'Rangans" (30.1-2). The pair are clearly the temptresses in the Park. Iris Tree was an English actress and writer whom Joyce knew in Paris. The name also suggests the goddess of the rainbow, Irish, and Irish trees or Irish green. "Lily O'Rangans" sounds on first reading very Irish until we notice that it is also "Lily Orange" or the Orange Lily. This pairing of the two temptresses in terms of Orange and Green is, to the best of my knowledge, unique in the *Wake*. It is of course a natural enough polarity, but it is precisely its clearcut antithetical balance that makes it generally unsuitable for Joyce's purposes—he prefers the waters muddied. The phrase could of course be interpreted as a clash of rainbow and white or even red and white since red as one extreme of the rainbow is sometimes used in the *Wake* to designate the rainbow.[40] It is interesting that, according to Glasheen, John Quinn described Iris Tree as "a fine wench with pink hair."[41] In any event there is a nice irony in the association of Irish green with an English actress in opposition to the Orange lily, precisely the alignment of forces most likely at some point in the future to toll the knell of the Orange cause.

The deepest and most threatening tensions involving sexuality surface in the thought sequence of the dream that is *Finnegans Wake* in terms of red and white, especially and most intensively personified in the lily and the rose. A classic instance of this is evident in the four old men's vision of the sleeping child Issy in the "Porters' Pub" section. She is:

> a gracecup fulled of bitterness. She is dadad's lottiest daughterpearl and brooder's cissiest auntybride. Her shellback thimble-casket mirror only can show her dearest friendeen. To speak well her grace it would ask of Grecian language, of her goodness, that legend golden. Biryina Saindua! Loreas with lillias flocaflake arrosas! Here's newyearspray, the posquiflor, a windaborne and heliotrope; there miriamsweet and amaranth and marygold to crown. And lightest knot unto tiptition. O Charis! O Charissima! A more intriguant bambolina could one not colour up out of Boccuccia's Enameron. Would one but to do apart a lilybit her virginelles and, so, to breath so, therebetween, behold, she had instantt with her handmade as to graps the myth inmid the air. Mother of moth! I will to show herword in flesh. Approach not for ghost sake! It is dormition! She may think, what though little doth she realize, as morning fresheth, it hath happened her, you know what, as they too what two dare not utter. (561.14-30)

As her father's "pearl," Issy is a treasure—and an irritant. Lot's two daughters, as McHugh notes, were impregnated by their father,[42] and this mention of Lot may be the first surfacing in the passage I have quoted of the idea of incest. The "friendeen" or little friend shown to her by her mirror is, I strongly suspect, her vulva. As a "gracecup" she pleases her father with her grace, but there is also "bitterness" in his feelings, no doubt because those very feelings towards Issy could be his *coup de grace*. This is the first allusion to the Virgin and her impregnation in this passage ("Hail Mary, full of grace, the Lord is with thee"). The flowers suggest colors and the twenty-nine girls; prominent among them are the lily and the rose. "Marygold to crown" is another reference to the Virgin Mary, as Queen of Heaven in this case. The distortion of the Lord's Prayer ("and lead us not into temptation") marks the fears of the dreamer of the feelings struggling to the surface of the dream. *Bambola* according to McHugh is Italian "doll dressed as grown-up woman"⁴³ and points to the dreamer's guilt and ambiguity over the immaturity of the object of his desires. The distortion of Boccaccio to "Boccuccia-," Italian "little mouth,"⁴⁴ and of *Decameron* to "Enameron" (*amor*, enamored) further intensify the underlying sexuality. The "virginelles" in one sense at least are Issy's thighs, or possibly, labia, which when parted lead to the contemplation of her vulva. The sleeping Issy is seen by the dreamer here as playing with her genitals as she grasps the myth/moth/miss in her pubic hair or where her pubic hair will grow when she matures. There is another allusion to the Virgin at this point, specifically to the Annunciation ("behold...handmaid"), and a vision of a kind of womanly realization to parallel Christ's incarnation, "herword in flesh." "Dormition," as McHugh notes, is the "falling asleep of the Virgin Mary";⁴⁵ it is also "damnation" and reflects again the terror of the dreamer. Another fear, this time of pregnancy, is present in the final sentence of my quotation, both through a dialect meaning of "freshen" and in the speculation as to the girl's "knowing" when she wakens. This last sentence too categorizes the incestuous urge with homosexuality in its echo of the phrase from Wilde's trial, "a love that dare not speak its name."

The confrontation of the dreamer with urges his waking self "dare not utter" parallels in some ways the boys' probing of the mother's sexual secrets in "Night Lessons" (II, 2), and the point in both is not titillation but maturation through self-knowledge. Here is the dark side of the excitement created for the dreamer by the self-exhibiting of the girls in the Park, the anxiety dream which complements the wish-fulfilment dream. This part of the dream, its final stage before "Recorso" and waking, is probably the most intense part of sleep and dream—it also includes the Honuphrius case and the unconsummated coupling of Mr. and Mrs. Porter. All three incidents represent the dreamer's brutal confrontation with deeply hidden fears and the endurance of them is probably cathartic. It is likely too that the personae of the four old men with their memory lapses, faults of sequence, cranky confusion and general senility are particularly suitable figures for the processing of those most threatening parts of the dream.

Another "Lily" in the *Wake* is Lily Kinsella, Magrath's wife. At first glance she appears to be quite separate from the temptresses, but in fact she is not. Magrath is HCE's arch-enemy and represents a composite of the sons or one son, Shem, in rebellion against the father's authority. In her final soliloquy ALP identifies this lady as "the cad with the pope's [pipe's] wife, Lily Kinsella, who became the wife of Mr Sneakers for her good name" (618.3-5). In the "Honuphrius Case" Lily is Gillia (Italian, "lily"¹⁶), the wife of Magravius (Magrath), and behaves no better than anybody else in the case (572.573). But the most interesting information about Lily Kinsella comes from the washerwomen in the "Anna Livia Plurabelle" section (I, 8):

> What am I rancing now and I'll thank you? Is it a pinny or is it a surplice? Arran, where's your nose? And where's the starch? That's not the vesdre benediction smell. I can tell from here by their *eau do Colo* and the scent of her oder they're Mrs Magrath's.... They've moist come off her. Creases in silk they are, not crampton lawn. Baptiste me, father, for she has sinnned! Through her catchment ring she freed them easy, with her hips' hurrahs for her knees'dontelleries. The only parr with frills in old the plain.... And here is her nubilee letters too. Ellis on quay in scarlet thread. Linked for the world on a flushcaloured field.... You child of Mammon, Kinsella's Lilith! Now who has been tearing the leg of her drawers on her? (204.30-205.12)

The general drift of the passage is fairly obvious, so I shall merely underline a few points relative to my argument. Lily's "drawars" are those of a temptress, silk and lace with frills. They are redolent of her sins and carry the scars of sexual skirmishes. There are reds in evidence, "scarlet," "flushcaloured." "Flushcaloured" is flesh-colored, flesh-heated, flush-colored and heated by the flush of the skin beneath them. What they exhibit in fact is the classic white-and-blush provocation of the temptresses.

A frequently encountered but far from consistent version of the red-white sexuality in the *Wake* is male red vs. woman's white. Thus in the second paragraph of the book there is a shift from the "fair" of the girls to the "wroth" of their relations with Swift-HCE to the reds and rainbows that mark the masculine activities of the sons (3.11–14). In the "Museyroom" episode (I, 1) the contrast is made explicit: "This is jinnies in the bonny bawn [Irish, "white"] blooches. This is lipoleums in the rowdy houses [red hose]" (9.21–22). Since in one important sense the "Museyroom" episode is a version of the incident in the Park, the jinnies are the two urinating girls exposing their white underwear and skin while the lipoleums are the three soldiers in their red uniforms. The same polarity of red and white is explicitly made in a few other versions of the Park incident. In the "Mime" (II, 1), Glugg, defending the father against the rumors of his indiscretions, goes on the attack: "They whiteliveried ragsups, two Whales of the Sea of Deceit, they bloodiblabstard shooters, three Dromedaries of the Sands of Calumdonia" (241.28–30). The girls are in white livery, white underwear that is—"ragsups" applies to their raised skirts and it may also suggest that they are menstruating. The soldiers are redcoats, bloody bastards, lobsters and bloody blabbers. The speaker neatly shifts the hump of HCE's guilt to his antagonists, the girls being whales who entrapped him and the soldiers camels who calumniated him.

Another instance of this polarity appears in a version of the Park incident given by the drunken customers in the first "Pub" scene (II, 3):

> Imagine twee cweamy wosen. Suppwose you get a beautiful thought and cull them sylvias sub silence. Then imaggin a stotterer.... Then ... immengine up to three longly lurking lobstarts. Fair instents the Will Woolsley Wellaslayers. Pet her, pink him, play pranks with them. (337.16–22)

"Twee" is, Dutch, "two." The "cweamy wosen" are creamy or almost white roses. The soldiers are "lobstarts," lobsters and bastards—the red again. But the antithesis is not as clearcut here. "Fair" is at least loosely associated with the soldiers, and "pink" bridges the gap between the red and the white, though its function is very doubtful.

I have claimed that red for male and white for female are very far from being consistently maintained through the book, although red and white are very frequently associated with sexuality. The more salacious points of Jaun's "Sermon" (III, 2) offer examples. At one point he suggests to Issy that "she'd care for a mouthpull of white pudding for the wish is on her rose marine and the lunchlight in her eye" (441.15–17). Jaun is not just talking about lunch; the "mouthpull of white pudding" is fellatio and the rose marine is Issy's lubricious genitalia with her red pubic hair. Here the white is associated with the male and the red with the female. A few lines further on he threatens her putative seducers, two of whom he designates "Rere Uncle Remus, the Baas of Eboracum and Old Father Ulissabon Knickerbocker, the lanky sire of Wolverhampton" (442.8–9). "Eboracum" is York and "lanky sire" is Lancaster, so what we have is the wars of the red rose and the white rose, and both here are male. A little later in the "Sermon" Jaun self-indulgently fantasizes future lovemaking with Issy: "I'd be staggering humanity and loyally rolling you over, my sow-white sponse, in my tons of red clover" (451.19–21). "Roll Me Over in the Clover" is a suggestive popular song. "Sow-white" is also snow-white. "Sponse" is, Latin, "spouse." Although the red and white appear as general accompaniments of the sexual congress here, I believe the most reasonable implications of specific referents for the colors are those I have written about at some length already, namely, the white of provocative and arousing woman's skin and underclothes, and the red of aroused genitalia and active sexual response.

There are two interesting instances of the sexual red-and-white in the "Porter's Pub" episode (III, 4). The couple "in their bed of trial" are "Albatrus Nyanzer with Victa Nyanza... she, our moddereen rue arue rue" (558.26–30). Here he is white (Latin, *alba*) and she is the little red fox (Irish, *madairin rua*). A little earlier in the episode the drunken customers condemn HCE for his conduct in the Park incident and indeed all the sins of man: "by reverendum they found him guilty of ...fornicolopulation with two of his albowcrural correlations... whose colours at standing up... were of a pretty carnation" (557.15–21). The "correlatives," primarily the girls in the Park, are white-legged (Latin, *albo-crural*); their colors are red ("carnation") as a result of their illicit activities. This again is the pattern of white sexual object and red arousal-response.

At that point in the "Colours Game" (II, 1) at which Glugg returns to try his third set of guesses, he stands facing Issy, staring at her, desiring her:

> Highly momourning he see the before him. Melained from nape to kneecap though vied from her girders up. Holy Santalto, cursing saint, sight most deletious to ross up the spyballs like exude of margary! And how him it heaviered that eyerim rust! An they bare falls witless against thee how slight becomes a hidden wound? (247.18-23)

Red ("ross," "-red," "rust,") and white ("vied," "witless") are the colors which dominate the passage. In addition, *rosso* is gold in Amaro, and oxide of mercury is almost gold in color, according to McHugh.[47] Glugg is experiencing mixed emotions of self-pity, despondency and lust, and phrases such as "hidden wound" have at least two meanings, his own shame at his failure and rejection and the hidden genitalia of Issy which he so desperately wants to see. The whites as usual are the hidden sexual treasures of which he may get a fleeting glimpse but more probably conjures up in his imagination. The reds have to do with his response, especially his eyes, although the gold accompanying the red may also hint at Issy's pubic hair.

A little further on in the scene Issy gives Glugg some hints to help his guessing and speaks of: "Long Entry, commanding the approaches to my intimast innermost.... Six thirteens at Blanche de Blanche's of 3 Behind Street and 2 Turnagain Lane.... Radouga, Rab will ye na pick them in their pink of panties" (248.31-36). Here as usual is the sexual white ("Blanche de Blanche's") but instead of red we find pink and rainbow (Russian, *raduga*). Rose and O'Hanlon suggest that Glugg "is dazed and bewildered in his colour-blindness by the multitude of tints, the living kaleidoscope of the whirling, teasing, entrancing girls who dance before him."[48] This plausible suggestion offers an explanation for the pattern of colors. As the girls whirl in the dance the reds and whites of their exposure blend to pink; the revealed underclothes become a rainbow blur; but white remains in evidence not only as a blend of many colors but also as a revelation of more and more of the girl's limbs as their skirts fly higher. A page further on in the scene there is a nice example of the sexual red-rose with some of the connotation I noted in the barmaid's rose in "Sirens": "Twentynines of bloomers gegging een man arose" (249.36-250.1).

The four old men, reminiscing at the end of the Festy King trial (I, 4), see the incident in the Park as "the war of the two roses" (94.35-36). But to the drunken customers in the pub the girls in the Park are "Blashwhite and Blushred of the Aquasancta Liffey Patrol" (380.3-4). First of all, this connects the pair directly with Anna Livia, and they are of course younger, tempting versions of her. "Blashwhite" suggests white or *blanche* York, but also Blanche of Lancaster (mother of Henry IV), thus muddying any distinction between the two girls. McHugh notes in regard to this context: "Heroine of Patrick Kennedy's story *The Twelve Wild Geese* is called Snow-White-and-Rose-Red."[49] If McHugh is correct in seeing this name as being present, that and the identification with ALP constitute a partial reunification of the pair, another piece of evidence to suggest that the red and white duality is more seeming than real, a projection of the dream-vision. The vagueness of "Blash-" and the pinkness of "Blush-" also emphasize the tentative nature of the girls' separation from each other. A version of the Park incident given by the narrator in I, 3 exhibits similarities to the version I have been discussing. Here is the part that refers directly to the girls: "And call all your smokeblushes, Snowwhite and Rosered, if you will have the real cream! Now for a strawberry frolic!" (64.26-28). In this case "smokeblushes," "cream" and "strawberry" blur the sharp distinction of the white and red. They also hint at the tones of lips and cheeks and more.

The ubiquitous red/white/sexuality web of association in the *Wake* exhibits at every turn Joyce's determination to subvert the simple polarities he sets up, thus functioning as an instrument for his insistence on the insufficiency of nicely balanced categories deriving from cliche-ridden, conventional wisdom. In the "Inquisition of Yawn" (III, 3), the Four probe Shaun's subconscious for evidence of his father's misconduct and in jogging his memory they refer to "Thugg, Dirke and Hacker with Rose Lankester and Blanche York" (485.11-12). Obviously the pair of temptresses in the Park are a red rose and a white rose. But the placing of "Rose" in antithesis to "Blanche" emphasizes the color connotations of the word "rose"—roses are red. This in turn compromises the whiteness of "Blanche York" since it too is a rose. What happens in fact is that the symmetrical integrity of the antithesis is violated.[50]

Issy as sex symbol of the *Wake* is a highly colorful figure and has in addition to the sexual red-white patterns of association other patterns of major significance. The most dramatic display of her colors occurs in II, 1, usually known as "The Mime of Mick, Nick and the Maggies" or "The Colours Game." The crucial color in the chapter is Issy's heliotrope which Glugg (Shem) tries but fails to guess. The action of "The Mime" is, in its broad outlines, fairly straightforward and has received considerable attention from critics. Patrick McCarthy's assessment of the chapter in *The Riddles of "Finnegans Wake"* is, to my mind, an effective and convincing elucidation of "The Mime."[51] The reasons McCarthy finds for Shem's failure are his youth, his poor eyesight and his inability to spell. McCarthy adds that Issy does not play fair in the hints she gives. He also points to the frequency with which "heliotrope" is associated with the incident in the Park and concludes: "Heliotrope serves as a dual function: it reveals the strong connection between an apparently innocent children's game and Earwicker's guilty adventure in the Park, and it indicates Issy's preference for Shaun or Chuff, the sun-god who is worshipped by the 'holytroopers.'"[52] Margaret Solomon sees the Mime as

> a prelude of ineffectuality anticipating the type of adult consummation, illustrated earlier in the Prankquean story, which will eventually befall the children.... it [heliotrope] seems at first to be the password for opening the gate for a son-change—in effect, a rebirth—a crossing over into a new cycle of marriage, or fertile sex. The Shem son, however, does not pass, and there is every indication that... the Shaun-type son, would not have passed either.[53]

These two critical viewpoints have this very important common element: they see the Mime as a failure to break out of individual isolation and achieve sexual communication. And the Mime is a paradigm of most attempts by the inhabitants of the dream to achieve satisfactory interpersonal contact. Whether we approach the Mime, as Solomon does, by seeing how the children's game forecasts the failures and frustrations that will mark their adult lives, or whether with McCarthy we perceive it as a set conflict which parallels and hooks into the other set conflicts of the book, especially the Prankquean episode and the incident in the Park, we are forced to the conclusion that the Mime demonstrates the difficulty if not the impossibility for one human being to truly touch another. At least this is the case for most of the characters in the *Wake*. The Mime itself, despite the colorful dancing, is not a cheerful sequence of scenes. As McCarthy points out, Chuff or Shaun, the angelic twin, remains an onlooker throughout the drama. He loses the game too, i.e., he fails to get Issy, because he is too fearful or too unknowing to risk playing the game, or because he feels it might tarnish his respectable image. Glugg fails for reasons that McCarthy has indicated. But Issy fails, too, since she remains in isolation at the end. Issy's failure, I believe, invites further examination.

Issy's hints to Glugg, and her desire that he guess correctly so that they may mate, appear at least temporarily sincere, if we can forget for the moment Issy's totally absorbing narcissism through the rest of the book. Yet the color that he must guess is a highly unlikely one. In fact Issy's only claim to be represented by heliotrope is her tendency to turn *away from* Glugg and towards the angelic Chuff, the son-sun, acme of respectability and public virtue. Thus, heliotrope marks the role that Issy feels compelled to play in the marriage stakes, the role of maidenly modesty and conventional, ladylike decorum. It is in this role that she wishes to be saved from the devilish Shem, "from the wiles of willy wooly woolf!" (223.3), and strives to provoke Chuff's jealous interest. The result of her unease in this pose is that she sends Glugg contradictory signals. The girls have no problem inciting Glugg's interest with their highly erotic and quite unladylike display which includes urination ("Aminxt," 222.32), intimations of arousal on their part ("those first girly stirs," 222.33), and the crude suggestiveness of the "monthage stick in the mel[mel]ode jaw[r]" (music mouth, honeypot, marmalade jar) (223.8). What they fail to do is channel Glugg's lustful energy in the direction of guessing the right color and winning the game. The dazzling display of dancing colors confuses him. Nevertheless, his guesses, or at least the two sets we have the opportunity to hear, are not bad, but the task is hopeless. The game is loaded against Shem. He is bound to lose and as a consequence the girls are bound to be losers too.

"Heliotrope" in the *Wake* has received a modicum of critical attention and when it has been examined the conclusions have varied widely and have, in my judgment, failed to carry conviction. Thus Margaret Solomon's polarity of heliotrope and hyacinth, the former associated with Shaun, heterosexuality and the two girls in the Park, the latter with Shem, homosexuality and the three soldiers, though it makes an interesting exploration, is not entirely convincing and has not really led us anywhere.[53] John Gordon's recent monograph, *Notes on Issy*, advances an ingeniously worked out theory of the antithesis of moonstone and bloodstone (or heliotrope).[54] Briefly, Gordon associates the moonstone or pearl and "its pearly translucence," with "the pre-menstrual Issy, with innocence, whiteness, Snow White, Iseult of the White Hands," and the opal or bloodstone and "its deep green flecked with red" with "the pubescent Issy, with experience, darkness, Rose Red, Iseult of Ireland."[55] Gordon gives very valuable insights into such matters as the relationship of Issy with Pond's Vanishing Cream and with Lucia Joyce's strabismus, but the polarity he sets up is of doubtful validity—essentially, it is too neat and clearcut.

In the *Wake*, the occurrences and probable occurrences of heliotrope and closely related words (such as "sunflower") number about thirty-seven, by my count. Seven of those appear in the "Mime" section; the others are fairly scattered through the text. All seven instances in the "Mime" have to do with the girls' colors and Glugg's guesses; eleven of the others are associated with Issy or the two girls in the Park or woman as object of man's desire.[56] I can find no other pattern of significance. I suggested earlier in this discussion that heliotrope, since it signifies the girls' turning towards Shaun, marks the modest, maidenly role demanded of them by social convention and that this role, because of its contradictions and hypocrisies, contributes to their failure in the game. Further examination of part of the "Mime" lends support to this opinion.

The passage in question occupies most of p. 239, and I shall focus on these two extracts:

> By the hook in your look we're eyed for aye were you begging the questuan with your lutean bowl round Monkmesserag. And whenever you're tingling in your trout we're sure to be tangled in our ticements. It's game, ma chere, be off with your shepherdress on! Upsome cauda! Behose our handmades for the lured! To these nunce we are but yours in ammatures yet well come that day we shall ope to be ores. Then shalt thou see, seeing, the sight. No more hoaxites! Nay more gifting in mennage! A her's fancy for a his friend and then that fellow yours after this follow ours. (239.5–14)

> When every Klitty of a sculderymeid shall hold every yardscullion's right to stimm her uprecht for whimsoever, whether on privates, whather in publics. And when all of us romance catholeens shall have ones for all amanseprated. And the world is maidfree. Methanks. So much for His Meignysthy man! And all his bigyttens. (239.18–23)

This passage comes after Glugg's second failure when the girls in despair have been turning all their charms on Chuff but with little result. In their frustration they begin to envisage a future in which women will be freed from the shackles of societal rules regarding mating behavior. In fact, free love and free choice for women are the burden of their wishes for the future. The spokesman for the girls is Issy and she addresses her mirror image and the other girls—these are really identical. In the former of the two extracts she makes a kind of freethinking Annunciation ("Behold the handmaid of the Lord") and urges her hearers to free action and free love: "Upsome cauda," or up tail, is a parody of the exhortation in the Mass, *Sursum Corda*, or "Lift up your hearts." Instead of being "yours," man's possessions in this case, they hope to be ours and whores. There will be no more weddings (German, *hochzeit*) or giving in marriage—"gifting" is, German, "poison," and marriage distorted to "mennage" makes it a *ménage* and an arrangement designed by and for men. The second extract openly advocates free love and women's suffrage (German, *Stimmrecht*[57]). "Klitty" includes clitoris; "stimm" echoes a German word *stemmen*, for copulation; "whim-" is both whim and the vulgar quim or vulva. "Romance catholeens" are Irish Roman Catholics and romantic Cathleens. Women will be emancipated and separated from man's domination. The world will be free for maids and, possibly, free of the notion of virginity. The message of revolt is radical: the Bible itself will be upturned—"In the beginning..." and all the "begettings." The most interesting word in the passage is "Klitty." In Greek mythology, Clytie, the daughter of Oceanus, pined for love of Apollo and was turned into a heliotrope. The name "Clytie" means "beautiful or shining one"; Apollo of course was the sun god. "Heliotrope" in this context at least sums up all the hypocritical courtship rituals that the girls want to destroy.

Of course, the "Mime" section has colors other than heliotrope. It is in fact the most colorful section of the book and its colors range from "their roseaced glows to their violast lustres" (231.20) and from the satanic black of "the bold bad bleak boy Glugg" (220.13-14) to the angelic white of Chuff, that "fine frank fairhaired fellow of the fairytales" (220.12-13) and Issy's "bewitching blonde" (220.7-8). All of the major patterns and concentrations of color have reference to the girls' display and the response to them. I shall comment briefly on a few examples which I have not discussed in other contexts.

There are five fully detailed rainbows, all of them the dancing girls.[58] The vignette of Lady Marmela Shortbred and Prince La Monade (235.32-236.8) presented by the girls is a suburban-sentimental-Shaunish-Gertyish vision of romantic bliss full of pastel and edible and gooey shades: "cochineal," "caramel," "ivory-mint," "chloses," "glycering," "chocolate," "Cococream," "pink," and "Rose." It is noteworthy that out of this cloying mess and before the end of that same paragraph a stark, obscene "black" surfaces, the kind of raw brutality the sentimentality serves to cover up: "O you longtailed blackman, polk it up behind me!" (236.15-16). Some of this brutally direct color also surfaces in Glugg's thoughts when he dejectedly faces the girls for his third set of guesses: "totter of Blackarss" (251.11), "murkery viceheid"

(251.15–16) and "Gash, they're fair ripecherry!" (251.20). The girls taunt and provoke him, "Twenty-nines of bloomers gegging een man arose" (249.36–250.1), giving him rosy glimpses and an erection. They ask him: "Willest thou rossy banders havind?" (250.3). "Bander" is slang for erection and "rossy" is red and rose as well as Irish, "flirt." In Issy's last-ditch effort to give Glugg a hint of "heliotrope" she pictures "the house of breathings," full of light and color and exotic materials (249.6–20). The word "fairness" appears six times in the passage. The house is, among other things, Issy's own body, the temple at which she worships. At the end of the "Mime" as ALP "collared her pullets," HCE somehow gathers all the colors to himself; he "is hued and cried of each's colour" (256.9–10), and the games are over.

As we have seen, green in *A Portrait* and *Ulysses* is a color with few female-sexual associations, but this is not the case in the *Wake*, and for good reasons John Gordon describes the green-Issy connection:

> Alice Liddell's middle name was "Pleasance." "Pleasance" figures in the *Wake* in two main ways. First the word means "lawn." That helps explain the occurrence of "lawn" in this passage, and in general Issy's connection with leaves, green fruit, bushes—with all green growing things: "Though Wonderlawn's lost us for ever. Alis, alas, she broke the glass! Liddell lokker through the leafery, ours is mistery of pain." (270.19)[59]

Gordon adds, on the same page, that Alice Liddell also appears in the *Wake*, "through frequent use of her initials, APL. 'APL' figures as both an anagram of the mother, ALP, and very often, simply as 'apple.'" A further note of Gordon's is also relevant here:

> 336.21: "It was one of the Grant, old gartener, *qua* golden meddlist, ..." Here and elsewhere HCE's meddling with fruit is connected with his fall. A "medlar" is very similar to an apple. (A later allusion to "medlard apples" [433.35] helps confirm the connection.) This sentence continues by describing HCE's feeling for "the younging fruits, tenderosed like an atalantic's breastswells"—an allusion to Atalanta's golden apples.[60]

Obviously, the association of green with unripe fruit and with Alice Liddell will encompass the youthful Issy and HCE's incestuous longings for her. Obviously too this is an issue that the dream displacement mechanism will attempt to keep well disguised. But it emerges to the surface of the dream thought again and again, as in this instance: "There are 29 sweet reasons why blossomtime's the best. Elders fall for green almonds" (64.35–36). The "29 sweet reasons" are the leap year girls who are multiple manifestations of Issy, and "Elders" points to the biblical story of Susannah and the Elders who spied on her and wished to debauch her. In the dream the signature for this theme is the word "green." In a version of the Park incident being denied by the narrator in I, 2, this parenthetical comment appears: "garthen gaddeth green hwere sokeman brideth girling" (34.27-28). The green here resonates with "garden," "soke-," "bride," "girl," and other phrases from its larger context (such as "rushy hollow," "silkinlaine," "partial exposure," "Rosasharon") to form a loose matrix of fertilization/female/urination images. Another similar collection of images hinting at still suppressed sexual urges appears in the account of the Festy King trial in this line: "wedding on the greene, agirlies, the gretnass of joyboys" (93.36-94.1), the keywords here being Gretna Green, "wedding," "girlies," "-nass" (German, "wet"), "-ass," "joy-" and "-boys." And there is a particularly interesting example of the unripeness/green/incest set of associations in the "Porter's Pub" section (III, 4). The youthful Issy is described as "the darling of my heart, sleeping in her april cot,... with her greengageflavoured candywhistle duetted to the crazyquilt" (556.14-16). Rose and O'Hanlon gloss part of this as: "A whistle of straw by her on the quilt"[61] which, I suppose, is as good an interpretation as another. What interests me however is "greengageflavoured." A greengage is a sweet roundish plum, green to gold in color. In combination with the endearment, the "duetted" (dew-wetted), "april cot" (apricot) and Issy herself, it presents a faint but definite overtone of the incestuous theme.

Green figures prominently in that least guarded of HCE's *apologiae*, the lengthy utterance in his voice that emerges from the mouth of the supine Yawn (III, 3). It seems likely that the "Inquisition of Yawn" is the deepest point of sleep and of the dream and therefore a part most likely to dredge deeply from the subconscious layers of the mind. Here is HCE defending himself against rumors of the incident in the Park:

> On my verawife I never was nor can afford to be guilty of crim crig con of malfeasance trespass against parson with the person of a youthful gigirl frifrif friend chirped Apples, acted by Miss Dashe, and with Any of my cousines in Kissilov's Slutsgartern or Gigglotte's Hill, when I would touch to her dot and feel most greenily of her unripe ones as it should prove most anniece and far too bahad, nireless to say, to my reputation on Babbyl Malket for daughters-in-trade being lightly clad. (532.18-26)

There is scarcely another sentence in the *Wake* that drags up so many of HCE's most deeply buried fears and guilts so thinly disguised, with so many rich euphemisms and with so many suggestive slips. "My verawife" is his very life, but also his true wife, the old love in fact and the last person he wants to become aware of his new feelings. The word "guilty" appears early in the sentence and his guilty stutter reaches such intensity as to almost suppress the highly charged "criminal conduct" and "girl friend." Having got this much out he has a good run at the rest of it but succeeds in embroiling himself more and more. The "youthful girl friend" turns out to be a fictional part acted by a nonentity, a theatrical moustached Miss Dashe, then ALP again ("Any"), then a cousin, and finally his niece. But this latter proves too close to the truth, so he is quickly without a niece (Greek, *anniece*) and "nieceless," and the girl becomes his daughter-in-law—almost. This of course includes the word he has been scrambling to avoid—daughter. He also attempts to transfer the responsibility for the sins that were never committed to the girl(s): they are kissy-love-sluts. But he gives himself away again since the name he has been avoiding is in the phrase—Issy. "Greenily" is "greedily" and the unripe breasts and other curves of the girl; "apples" reinforces the young-fruit analogy: "dot" is dowry and also clitoris and indeed all other real or imagined erogenous zones. The mention of erogenous zones and the giggles-gigolo-giglot in "Gigglotte's" point to a very root feature of HCE's incestuous urges: the fear of the aging man that he can no longer arouse a woman's sexual interest.

Shaun's "Sermon" (III, 2) provides several fine examples of the green/incest/Issy set of associations. Not only is Shaun's desire for Issy incestuous since he is her brother, but we must also remember that Shaun, in roles such as that of the preacher of the sermon, is virtually usurping the father's place or, at least, trying out the paternal mantle which he hopes to inherit. As he warns Issy to avoid sexual temptations during his absence and as he wallows in the erotic images which he so lovingly proscribes, one of his prohibitions runs: "And is that any place to be smuggling his madam's apples up? Deceitful jade. Gee wedge! Begor, I like the way they're half cooked" (436.6–8). "Jade" is a playful or deceitful woman as well as the semiprecious green stone. The green connection with young plants and fruits is reinforced by "apples," and the sexual innuendo is sounded by the female ("madam's") distortion of the male anatomical feature, the Adam's apple, and the vaguely suggestive tone of the action and the speaker's response to it. These connections are made again in statements such as: "Deal with Nature the great greengrocer and pay regularly the monthlies" (437.16–17). This superfluous advice of Shaun's to Issy to be regular in her monthly periods is not so much a warning against pregnancy as it is Shaun's habit of utilizing every opportunity to indulge his obsession with things sexual or at least, as here, intimately feminine.

At another point in his "Sermon" Shaun advises Issy: "Keep cool your fresh chastity which is far better far. Sooner than part with that vestalite emerald of the first importance,... which you treasure up so closely where extremes meet" (440.31–35). Virginity as Shaun conceives it is a purely physical matter, an asset to be used for barter only in the most favorable sexual market. But the cumulative effect of "fresh," "cool," "emerald," also connects Issy's sexual attractiveness with youth and growing plants. Perhaps the most revealing statement of the green/Issy/incest association to be found in the "Sermon" is this:

> Recollect the yella perals that all too often beset green gerils, Rhidorhoda and Daradora, once they gethobbyhorsical, playing breeches parts for Bessy Sudlow in fleshcolored pantos instead of earthing down in the coalhole trying to boil the big gun's dinner. (434.6–10)

"Yella perals" are yellow pearls or a stream of urine, which brings us back to the Park incident. The green or innocent or nubile girls are two roses (Greek, *rhoda*; the second name is merely a distortion of the first). Roses remind us of the Prankquean, of the slang phrase for urination, "to pluck a rose," and of the rosy display consequent on that action. The "fleshcolored pantos" are not just pantomimes but panties. Shaun is just as adroit as his father in transferring the responsibility for the Park incident onto the provokingly green girls, who really ought to be home performing their domestic duties.

One final connection of sexuality/green/incest has a certain minor importance since it provides an association that on at least three occasions triggers patterns of thoughts on the part of the dreamer that are disturbed and vaguely sexual and probably conceal the incest theme.[62] In I, 1, Jute encourages Mutt to excavate the mudmound of history, "Starting off with a big boaboa and three-legged calvers and ivargraine jadesses with a message in their mouths" (19.22–24). Naturally, the first thing that will emerge in this dig is sure to be the incident in the Park: the big father (Italian, *babbo*), the three soldiers and the two "jadesses." "Ivargraine" is "evergreen" and also contains, *ivar*, Hungarian, "sex."[63] As Glasheen points out, the Evergreen Touring Company of Liverpool toured the British Isles in the early years of the century with Wills's play, *A Royal Divorce*.[64] The name of the company's manager, W. W. Kelly, adds another green association to his play about Napoleon's marital strife. The name of the play and its echoes of green are associated in the dreamer's mind with the incident in the Park and his own urges to break his marriage vows. The second instance of this set of associations occurs at a point where the narrator is quashing rumors of sexual indiscretions on the part of HCE and the title of the play *A Royal Divorce* is mentioned with "Semperkelly's immergreen tourers" and a conflation of HCE and Napoleon (32.29–33.10). The third instance occurs at the beginning of the Mime and is much less explicit (221.19–20). Nevertheless the greens of W. W. Kelly and his company do provide a further strand in the web of girls/display/Issy/incest/green associations.

Issy and her multiple manifestations as rainbow girls and flower girls are, in the literal sense, highly colorful. This is very apparent in the names under which they appear and in their own conversation. The two girls in the Park are "Myramy Huey and Colores Archer" (63.12–13), which combines a myriad of hues with the colors of the rainbow arch. In her response to Shaun's sermon, Issy says: "Flee a girl, says it is her colour" (458.32–33). The sentence is obscure but "flee" is a very slight rearrangement of letters away from "feel" which brings to mind Bloom's speculations on the blind youth's sensations in touching a woman's hair and skin: "Feeling of white" (*Ulysses*, 8.1131).

Two separate sentences from Issy's answer #10 of "The Quiz" (I, 6) give interesting evidence of her thoughts about color in relation to her person. The first is this: "But hold hard till I've got my latchkey vote and I'll teach him when to wear what woman callours" (146.14-16). Here "callours" combines call ours, call hers, callers, calor (heat) with colors, in a militant statement against an unwelcome old suitor. Color is a very central part of the female self she is defending. The second sentence appears to reminisce about a (probably imaginary) love encounter:

> Now open, pet, your lips, pepette, like I used my sweet parted lipsabuss with Dan Holohan of facetious memory taught me after the flannel dance, with the proof of love, up Smock Alley the first night he smelled pouder and I coloured beneath my fan, *pipetta mia*, when you learned me the linguo to melt. (147.29-34)

This is one of those occasions on which I believe it likely that the mirror image Issy is addressing is her vulva. "Poudor" is powder and, Latin, "shame." But Issy's modesty is a sham and we may be sure that the source of her coloring is sexual arousal.

But it is in their association with the rainbow that Issy and her surrogate manifestations most dramatically display their colorfulness. John Gordon claims that "rainbows characteristically accompany Issy's advent."[65] Certainly she has strong and numerous connections with rainbows, and so does her mother, particularly when ALP is seen as young and nubile, at which times the distinction between her and Issy gets blurred. Issy and her seven manifestations directly constitute eight of the twenty-eight formally detailed rainbows in the book.[66] But there are many other connections of Issy and the girls with rainbows in the *Wake*. We are told that each of the girls in Rainbow #2 "had her rainbow huemoures" (102.26-27), that is seven humors/amours/hues. On one occasion one of the pair of temptresses in the Park is "Iris," goddess of the rainbow (30.1). HCE piously condemns ladies' stripping as "iridescent huecry" (68.20) and the narrator in I, 1 identifies womankind as "dugters of Nan" (19.29-30). "Dug" in the sense of mammalian udder was also used of a woman's breast or nipple, and, as McHugh points out, the phrase echoes the name given to a pair of adjacent rounded hills situated in Kerry, "the Paps of Ana."[67] But *duga* is "rainbow" in the Slavic tongues.[68] In the "Inquisition of Yawn" (III, 3) the Four speak of Issy as "soft aglo iris of the vals" (528.23) which makes her the iris or glowing rainbow rather than the Lily of the Valley. In the "Porter's Pub" section (III, 4) the sleeping Issy is described not by comparison to the rainbow but with a concentration of colors and shades sufficient to challenge the rainbow: "blushing," "Ivory," "boyblue's," "black," "orange," "pearl," "greengageflavoured," "primarose," "mauves" and "whitethorn" (556.1-22). In the "Shem" section (I, 7) constable Sigurdsen is quoted to the effect that he has seen Shem "reeling ... on his way from a protoprostitute (he would always have a (stp!) little pigeoness somewhure with his arch girl, Arcoiris ...)" (186.25-28).

Finally, there is the dawn scene just before the "Recorso":

> They know him, the covenanter, by rote at least, for a chameleon at last, in his true falseheaven colours from ultraviolent to subred tissues. That's his last tryon to march through the grand tryomphal arch. His reignbolt's shot. Never again! (590.7–10)

The failure primarily referred to here is the attempt at copulation of the Porter couple and the ignominious conclusion of that attempt in the remark, "You never wet the tea!" (585.31). The rainbows associated with HCE are defeated; he has penetrated as far as he can towards the center of the female mystery and towards the understanding of himself through the rainbow vision of the dream. Bright day in which he must play out his roles of father, publican and citizen is at hand. "The grand tryomphal arch" in this reading is a female rainbow, physiologically the pubic arch of Anna, psychologically the omphalos or center of the mother's creative and life-organizing power as river, rain-maker and urinator.

What I find emerging in these sexual and woman-oriented rainbow associations is a set of female-rainbow connections in opposition to the conventional and traditional male-Noah-covenant system. I have already discussed in this chapter the rich concentration of colors and rainbows present in the washerwomen's speculations about Anna's youthful sexual experiences. This is, of course, the youthful Anna who blends with her daughter, Issy. The actors in the drama are Anna with "the reignbeau's heavenarches arronged orranged her" (203.27), and "a local heremite, Michael Arklow was his riverend name" (203.18–19). There is a sharp contrast between Anna's queenly "-s heavenarches," "undergoading" the hermit, and Michael's subdued "Arklow." "-Arches" also suggests Greek *archos*, "chief" or "pre-eminent" as in archdeacon or archduchess. In the Apocalypse, Michael is the archangel who defeated Satan but in the *Wake*, Issy perceives that "Arck could no more salve his agnols [lambs, angels] from the wiles of willy wooly woolf!" (223.2–3). In the washerwomen's discussion Anna's sexual initiation is at one point identified with the incident in the Park: "Was it waterlows year, after Grattan or Flood, or when maids were in Arc or when three stood hosting?" (202.16–18). "Waterlows" and "Flood" remind us of the girls urinating and the presence of "in Arc" makes the connection of rainbow with the stream of urine likely. "Arc" also hints at Joan of Arc, that historical figure who is in her own right a symbol of woman's independence, will and strength.

Finally, with regard to woman and rainbow there is a further line of connection I must discuss. This involves the association of rainbow with peace and the punning on peace and piss. In the "Shem" chapter (I, 7) there is a version of Hosty's ballad in which this line occurs: *"Not yet his Arcobaleine forespoken Peacepeace upon Oath"* (175.12). "Arcobaleine" is Italian, "rainbow,"[69] and "Peacepeace" on earth is what Noah's rainbow promised. But the sentence undermines its most obvious meaning in that it contains an underlying suggestion that the masculine covenant of God with Noah will be foresworn and that woman's "pee-pee" or "piss-piss" will be implicated in that collapse. In the "Inquisition of Yawn" (III, 3), a discussion of the Park incident contains this exchange:

> —Concaving now convexly to the semidemihemispheres and, from the female angle, music minnestirring, were the subligate sisters, P. and Q., Clopatrick's cherierapest, *mutatis mutandis*, in pretty much the same pickle, the peach of all piedom, the quest of all quicks?
> —Peequeen ourselves, the prettiest pickles of unmatchemable mute antes I ever bopeeped at, seesaw shallsee, since the town go went gonning on Pranksome Quaine.
> —Silks apeel and sulks alusty? (508.21-29)

There is no mention of rainbow here and only two vague color words ("cherie-," "peach") but it does contain two elements relevant to my discussion. Firstly, the Prankquean is clearly identified with the girls in the Park and their display, and secondly, she is the "Peequeen" or urination queen. A few lines further on the two girls are indicated in this question: "Both were white in black arpists at cloever spilling, knickt?" (508.33). McHugh tells us that *klaverspil* is Danish, "piano playing," and suggests that "white in black" refers to the keys of the piano as well as to Black Arts.[70] But "arpists" is harpists and artists with the emphasis on the "piss" sound, and "spilling" is urinating. We may recall that McCarthy suggests as one of Glugg's causes of failure his inability to spell and spill, and indeed in a footnote in "Night Lessons" Issy describes Glugg as "not aebel to speel eelyotripes" (303.F1). The power of the woman to urinate, to make rain and river, is the symbol of her generative and regenerative power and constitutes its own rainbow in contrast with which Noah's rainbow of masculine covenant is an ambiguous and impotent sign.

Black with white is a color combination that Joyce uses a number of times in the *Wake* in connection with Issy and her sexually provocative manifestations, but never with the kind of clearcut antithesis that those paired colors conventionally suggest. In the drunken talk of the customers in the pub in "Mamalujo" (II, 4) there is reference to "blackwatchwomen, all in white" (379.33), and in the "Inquisition of Yawn" (III, 3) the voice of HCE mentions "a mouthless niggeress, Blanchette Brewster" (537.23-24). In neither case is there any ground for identification with any of the *Wake*'s women. A footnote of Issy's in "Night Lessons" uses the phrase "Black and White Wenchcraft" (269.F4), and in a passage I quoted in the last paragraph there appears the phrase "white in black arpists" (508.33) for the girls in the Park. Both of these phrases associate "the Black Arts" with the female sexual white but this is not an association further developed. The only really prominent black-white pattern with the temptresses is, as one might suspect, that of raven and dove.

In I, 1, there is a neat polarity of doves with the two girls in the Park and ravens with the three soldiers: "Our pigeons pair are flewn for northcliffs. The three of crows have flapped it southenly, kraaking" (10.36-11.1). But such a neat polar identification is extremely rare. A comment of the Four in the "Porter's Pub" section (III, 4) appears to associate raven with HCE and dove with ALP: "Hold the raabers for the kunning his plethoron. Let leash the dooves to the cooin her coynth" (579.14–16). But on other occasions HCE is both raven and dove. Thus the Norwegian Captain is referred to in this phrase: "coocoo him didulceydovely to his old cawcaws" (327.35–36). And when the Norwegian Captain marries and settles down in Dublin he is both the domesticated viking and the homing pigeon: "Cawcaught. Coocaged." (329.13). Despite scattered instances of this sort, the most persistent association is that of raven-dove or dove alone with Issy and the pair of temptresses into whom she splits. In the "Museyroom" "the jinnies," as they make war and water on Willingdone, "is a cooin her hand and the jinnies is a ravin her hair" (8.33–34). Issy speaks of her mirror image: "me and meother ravin, my coosine of mine" (238.25). At one point in Jaun's sermon Issy interrupts, "flushing but flashing from her dove and dart eyes" (457.27–28). Here there is dove but no raven, but the "white" connotations of dove are virtually overwhelmed by the echo of "dark" in "dart," the Irish "black" in "dove" and the implied light and dark contrast in "flushing and flashing."

The dove/girl is often a prostitute. Shem is said to "always have a (stp!) little pigeoness somewhure" (186.27-28), and the "cool-pigeons" (29.10–11) in I, 1 are stool pigeons and doves who are Finn MacCumhaill's but whose professional activities and display in the Park are reflected in the anatomical term *cul* (French and Irish). According to McHugh, "soiled dove" is slang for prostitute,[71] and that phrase occurs twice and strikingly in the *Wake*. The first instance describes HCE "loving so lightly dovessoild the candidacy" (336.30). "Candidacy" has a Latin meaning of being clothed in white. The other instance is a part of the bizarre description in I, 3: "one dilalah, Lupita Lorette, shortly after in a fit of the unexpectednesses drank carbolic with all her dear placid life before her and paled off while the other soiled dove that's her sister-in-love, Luperca Latouche, finding one day... that she stripped teasily for binocular man" (67.33–68.2). What we have in fact is that old "binocular" vision of woman as virgin and whore, or, as Bloom puts it: "I'm all clean come and dirty me" (*Ulysses*, 13.797).

There is one other curious connection of dove and raven with sexuality which involves not, directly at least, Issy or the pair in the Park but certain ladies of literature and Aubrey Beardsley. The Beardsley passage or passages occur on pp. 356–58 with a further isolated reference on p. 365. At 357.15–17 we find: "*Culpo de Dido!* Ars we say in the classies. *Kunstful*, we others said. What ravening shadow! What dovely line!" This is echoed at 365.23–24: "By where dauvening shedders down whose rovely lanes." In addition, a sentence in parenthesis, "when I doot my sliding panel and I hear cawcaw" at 357.20, is balanced a page further on with another sentence in parenthesis: "when I ope my shylight window and I see coocoo" (358.1). "What rovining shudder! what deadly loom!" also appears in parenthesis at 358.4–5. The speaker throughout is HCE defending himself against the malicious accusations of the customers in the pub. He also refers to himself as "colombophile and corvinophobe alike" (358.12–13), that is, as dove-lover and raven-hater. Aubrey Beardsley is actually named at 357.2–3: "Mr Aubeyron Birdslay." It seems fairly clear that what HCE has on his mind—it's getting late in the pub and he is probably not quite sober—is an occasion or a number of occasions recently when he sat on the toilet and perused for autoerotic stimulus a book illustrated by Beardsley.

In a 1980 article, "The Illustrator in the *Wake:* Aubrey Beardsley," H. Burrell examines "the descriptions in 356.19–358.16 which might be called the Beardsley passage," and he makes a convincing case that the book in question is *The Lysistrata of Aristophanes, Now First Wholly Translated into English* (by Samuel Smith.), published by Leonard Smithers "for private distribution" in 1896 and illustrated by Beardsley.[72] The following extract from Burrell will serve to demonstrate both the flavor of "the Beardsley passage" and the way in which dove-raven fits in:

> In the "Toilet of Lampito" "....allthose everwhalmed upon that preposterous blank seat" (365.35) include the masturbating cupid powdering Lampito's derriere...while Lysistrata bends over and lets forth a blast from her breech..., "what ravening shadow! What dovely line!" (357.16) is to be seen in the dark female pubic areas....
> In the frontispiece Lysistrata is caressing with an olive-branch a realistic lingam, "a general golf stature" (357.31)...[73]

Little needs to be added to Burrell's account. The juxtaposition of phallus and olive branch and the presence of the dove of peace in the *Lysistrata* illustrations, and the portrayal of the female genital areas in shadings of black and white are certainly sufficient to bring to HCE's mind the dove and raven which are already present with sexual connotations in the dream.

Despite the fact that in *Finnegans Wake* the daughter Issy and her surrogate figures become the focus of the dreamer's deepest sexual urges and conflicts, there is also in the background a calmer, mature model of sexual relationship, focused on ALP. This does not really come into the foreground until ALP's final monologue but it, and the colors associated with it, are adumbrated earlier in the book. This does not generally appear in HCE's speeches, which are usually defensive, given under pressure and inclined to braggadocio. In such cases masculine achievement, especially conquest, is his prime line of defense, even when speaking of ALP, and red is his color: "He would redden her with his vestas" (536.18); "And I cast my tenspan joys on her, arsched overtupped, from bank of call to echobank, by dint of strongbow" (547.30–31). As the copulating Mr. Porter, HCE (and his watchers) "become quite crimstone in the face!" (570.34). But even HCE, when he forgets himself, sometimes sounds the note of the final soliloquy. An aside in one of his self-defensive speeches alludes to his virtuous married status and uses the phrase: "my goldrush gainst her silvernetts" (366.11). The phrase has of course an aggressive quality —the goal-rush against the net in some energetic ballgame— but it also has the gold and silver of the mature sexual relationship presented in Anna's final soliloquy. In the very first section of the book the mourners at Finn's or Finnegan's wake console the central figure of the ceremony by speaking of his widow: "If you only were there to explain the meaning, best of men, and talk to her nice of guldenselver. The lips would moisten once again" (28.10–12). This may not be the most promising sentiment with which to try calming the reluctant corpse, but they persist and in so doing include another color, blue, from ALP's last speech: "There'll be bluebells blowing in salty sepulchres the night she signs her final tear. Zee end. But that's a world of ways away" (28.27–29). And in the "Mamafesta" (I, 5), ALP foreshadows her closing address with *"My Golden One and My Selver Wedding"* (104.9).

A few sentences from the opening paragraphs of ALP's final monologue will serve to exemplify its tone and its colors:

> Soft morning, city! Lsp! I am leafy speaking. Lpf! Folty and folty all the nights have falled on to long my hair. Not a sound, falling. Lispn! No wind no word. Only a leaf, just a leaf and then leaves.... It is for me goolden wending.... I am leafy, your goolden, so you called me, may me life, yea your goolden, silve me solve, exsogerraider! (619.20–30)

ALP is "leafy," not only because she is Liffey, or Livia with its blue-grey connotation, but also because the leafy trees are reflected in her waters and as those leaves fall they drift on the surface of the river down to the sea at Dublin. "Leafy" also signifies the green of nature, of the generation and growth associated in the *Wake* with woman and river and urination. There is also an echo here of the statement by the ghost of Stephen's mother in "Circe": "I was once the beautiful May Goulding. I am dead" (*Ulysses*, 15.4173–74). So the green has connotations of death and drowning as well as birth and growth. ALP is facing death and dissolution as well as rebirth in her imminent mating with the green waves of Dublin Bay. "Golden" and the repetition of "folty," with its echoes of fall colors and its connotations of hair (in Irish), point to Anna's auburn hair. As she rambles on in an old woman's way she fondly recalls her hair and the admiration given her "copper" and "Auburn" locks (617.34, 36). Among the memories and images that cross her mind are raven-and-dove with Yeats's swans. She repeats the "leafy" motif: "Once it happened, so it may again. Why I'm all these years within years in soffran, allbeleaved" (625.29–30). "Soffran" is "suffering," "sovereign" and the "saffron" of ALP's hair. "Allbeleaved" includes: covered in leaves, all-believed, all-bereaved, all-beloved, and white-or Finn-loved.

The last hundred lines or so of ALP's monologue (approximately pp. 626–28) mark the merging of the Liffey waters with the tidal influx of the Irish Sea between Island Bridge and Howth. Her thoughts as her river identity wanes swing back and forth from the past to the future—her present is disappearing. The colors are first the local specifics of the past: "Who'll search for *Find Me Colors* now on the hillydroops of Vikloefells? But I read in Tobecontinued's tale that while blubles blows there'll still be sealskers" (626.17–19). Finn MacCumhaill, the color guessing game of the "Mime" and the bluebells of Anna's youth on the Wicklow Hills mark the past. So do the invasions of "bark and tan" and "fan me coolly" (626.22–23). The "blubles" recollect the bluebells and the bubbles of the swirling Liffey waters and the bugles of invaders as river has met sea at Dublin Bay since the dawn of history. Her last color word is "Finn" in the phrase "Finn, again!," bringing the book swinging back to her husband and its title: *Finnegans Wake*.

5

From Their Roseaced Glows to Their Violast Lustres: The Colors of the *Wake*

The colors of the *Wake* form convoluted patterns which can with patience be traced and related to the major themes and techniques of the work and can thus, in the main, be accounted for. Yet some patterns remain inscrutable—*Finnegans Wake* does not readily yield up its secrets. Such a tantalizing color pattern is "Hwang Ho" or Yellow River. Adaline Glasheen locates forty-six appearances of "Hwang Ho" in the *Wake*—my count is thirty-two—but admits it is "a motif I can't in general account for."[1] She connects it with Cordelia and with metamorphosis, but I must confess that I cannot, from my examination of the occurrences of "Hwang Ho," see either connection. In fact I can as yet find no significant pattern whatever in the occurrences in the *Wake* of "Hwang Ho." And not once does Joyce make any color play with Yellow River of the sort that one might expect, e.g., Chinese/yellow, yellow/auburn/Liffey, yellow/stream/urine, yellow/peril/pearls. For this reader at least, Hwang Ho remains enigmatic and isolate.

To indicate the dominant color patterns of *Finnegans Wake* and to form the basis for the concluding observations of this study I have devised the following chart:

1. WHITE
   (a) *sexuality-temptress*, provocation, woman's exposed skin—woman's underwear, revealing/concealing, the dream-method—Lily, Lily Magrath, Lilith, Lilibullero—Colleen Bawn, Issy and mirror image, two girls in Park, clean/dirty, Virgin/Whore—wit, wetting, urination, provocation, wine, woman's energy and challenge, Prankquean.
   (b) *Finn/HCE*, Dublin (Eblana), the Pale, Fingal, Finnegan, fall, Phoenix, resurrection—white head/hat/horse, William of Orange, Wellington, Hill of Howth, Wilde, homosexuality, male exhibitionism, fall, questions of identity.

(c) *fight*, slaughter (Fingal), Irish tricolor, Orange vs. Green, Phoenix Park murders, Sinn Fein, splitting within psyche, Mark Twain.
(d) *day*, conventional vision, pragmatic Christianity, Patrick, tyranny.

2. RED
   (a) *HCE/Adam*, Dublin (Georgia), Ulster, British imperialist invader, St. Patrick, Rory O'Connor—shame, guilt, (red-handed), drunkenness (red face)—victim (hunted red fox)—earwig, incestuous desires—salmon, invader, Wellington, Wellington monument, *Wellingtonia Sequoia*, phallus, shame, Russian general, fall.
   (b) *flush/blush*, sexual arousal, engorged genitalia, Russian general and harlots, sadism, orgasm—rose, girls, genitalia, virginity (cherry), menstruation, sexual ruses.

3. WHITE-RED
   (a) *HCE*, soul/body, flesh/blood, birth/death, hypostatic union, male/female, sexual union, artistic creation.
   (b) *Lily/Rose*, woman, genitalia/skin, the girls in the Park, the Prankquean, threat/temptation.

4. BLACK and WHITE-BLACK
   (a) *HCE/DUBLIN*, doubling or splitting, Sullivans, Doyles, Ireland (dark rosaleen), Shem/Shaun—Mr. Porter, pint of Guinness, Genesis, male potency.
   (b) *Shem*, Satan, printer's ink, writer's ink, truth, excrement and art—Blake/Byron/Joyce/eye patch/blindness, persecution.

5. DOVE-RAVEN
   (a) *HCE/Noah*, loyalty/treachery, peace/violence, love/hate, missionary/invader-Viking, Alpha/Omega, subversion of balance—Issy/mirror image, two girls in Park, all pairs, prostitutes/Beardsley's pornography.

6. WHITE-GOLD
   (a) *Shaun*, St. Kevin, Irish Catholicism, public piety, liturgy, Irish tricolor, public patriotism, chauvinism, tyranny—the litany of the Virgin, Issy.
   (b) *HCE/Hill of Howth*, patriarchal phallic papal authority.

7. GREEN
   (a) *Unripe fruit*, Issy, incest, growing things, youth, virginity, temptation, Alice Pleasance Liddell, ALP, apple, *A Royal Divorce*.
   (b) *Ireland*, nationalism, blindness, eye, illusion, tricolor, death, Catholic obscurantism, all national flags, pretensions and rivalries.
   (c) *HCE/dying god*, nature, spring, resurrection, growth.

8. AUBURN
   (a) *Anna's hair*, "The Deserted Village," reddish Liffey waters—tea, brown, muddy, flood, Kate—Fulvia/*fluvia*, fiery, Issy, gold, the Virgin.

9. DAPPLED
   (a) *river/Anna*, light/shade, apple, Eden, temptation, Issy, incest, fall.

10. BROWN
    (a) *HCE under pressure*, bear/fox, cigar, Browne and Nolan, splitting of personality, multiple personalities.

11. BLUE
    (a) *Anna Livia* (final monologue), night, memory, sadness, leafy green, love/life, HCE.
    (b) *Intransigence/aggression*, Ulster protestantism, fascism—male sexual predacity, Tristan, Boylan.

12. VIOLET
    (a) *Violent*, violate, rape, Tristan, invade, Ulsterviolence, blindness (limit of human spectrum).

13. HELIOTROPE
    (a) *Issy*, attraction to Shaun/son/sun, hypocritical bourgeois maidenly role for woman.

14. GREY
    (a) *HCE* (as middle-aged patriarch), James Joyce (as pater familias)—Dorian Gray, Oscar Wilde, Shem, Joyce as artist sacrificed for art, the grey donkey.

15. RAINBOW
    (a) *HCE/Noah*, God's promise, peace, patriarchal power, king, male dignity—arc/ark, broken circle, broken promise, pot of gold, illusion, lie, fall, defeat, alcohol, alternative futures.
    (b) *Seven Girls*, HCE's deepest sexual desires, Shem/Joyce's students—Prankquean, urination, pubic arch, peace/piss, arc of stream of urine/river, wine, challenge to male authority, arousal/frightening of male, male civilizing reaction, Joan of Arc.
    (c) *Seven Garments*, violent father figure, royalty, druid, general, male dignity, *arc de triomphe*—anger, aggression, invasion, Strongbow, rape, war—reveal/conceal, emergence, exposure, exhibitionism.
    (d) *Druid/Bishop Berkeley*, dream-vision, artistic vision, Wakean vision, Shem/Joyce, self-perception, nationalism/superstition/self-delusion/self-destruction.

The above chart attempts to outline in two dimensions, as it were, a tangle of associational patterns that are at least three-dimensional. Despite the numerous overlappings in the chart, it resembles, in relation to the actual patterns of connection, a fairly neatly arranged and labelled board of electrical terminals, behind which exists a massive tangle of criss-crossing, joining, separating wires. In each series or set of series in the chart the color or color combination presented in *capitals* at the beginning is not presented as a starting point but a common color thread. Generally speaking, at least in the major, more elaborate series, one could start at any point and continue tracing the series circularly or out into other series. In addition many intermediate terms could be inserted between the terms as I have given them. Nevertheless the chart does I believe trace the major structural patterns of association in the *Wake* to which colors contribute a significant part and to which the successful reader must become attuned and sensitive. The order in which I have listed the sets of series reflects roughly their significance, pervasiveness, and degree of elaboration. Obviously, the placing of the "Rainbow" set of series at the end is an exception—it is itself exceptional.

The various series of associations I have outlined in the chart show fairly clearly, I believe, the colors entwining themselves with the major themes and methods of the book and forming thereby a significant feature of the technique by which the crucial nubs of the *Wake*'s perceptions are gradually brought to the reader's conscious awareness. Series 1(a) displays the chief associational patterns and thematic implications of what I have called "the sexual white." The key feature in the series is the ambivalence of the dreamer's vision of woman and his response to woman. He sees her as clean and dirty, Virgin and Whore, object of desire and portent of doom. This tells us little about woman but a great deal about the dreamer. He can neither reconcile the contradictions nor abide them with equanimity but must ceaselessly struggle between admitting them and denying them. He endlessly debates the issues through his various dream voices: "Jaun's Sermon" (III, 2) posits virginity as a negotiable commodity that Issy or any woman discards or reclaims as the situation suggests, rather like a garment—or an envelope (433.3). Jaun also conflates the ivory of the Litany of the Virgin with orgiastic sadism (437.28-33) and the four old men mix up the Virgin with lace panties and perversion (238.23-24).[2] At another point the Four associate the sexual white with "reunited selfdom" (394.35-395.1). What all of the juxtapositions display primarily are the dreamer's unresolved sexual conflicts and secondarily and more emphatically his struggles with self-perception. When in the "Mime" (II, 1) Glugg (Shem) in frustration is striving to break through the conventional white to see the seven colors of dream-vision (247.31) he is in fact working out on the sexual level the conflict of alternative visions of reality acted out in terms of philosophy and religion by the Druid and the Saint in the "Recorso" (611.612). The sexual whites also demonstrate in their wet/urine associations the drowning-flooding imagery of the woman's challenge to male supremacy as it impinges on the dreamer's consciousness and hark back to Stephen's drowning images in the early chapters of *Ulysses*. In their underwear associations the sexual whites function as a paradigm for the revealing-concealing tug-of-war of the "dream-work" and the *Wake*'s strategies for getting at the truth. These uses of the sexual whites are a natural development of the similar whites in *Ulysses* and *A Portrait* and *Dubliners*. How these earlier sexual whites have changed in the *Wake* is in their more deliberate use as a prominent feature of the communicative technique and in their increased emphasis on woman's energy and power, on her ability and intention to overthrow patriarchal authority and the systems which support it. In the Wakean dreamer's mind woman emerges as the man's rival for the center of life's stage; his attitudes towards her become more ambiguous and convoluted and drive him back into questioning himself.

Series 1(b) in my chart traces the whites linking HCE and those personae cognate with him, and provides a clear correlative to series 1(a)—Joyce is boring into the mountain from two sides. Both the topographical and human projections of HCE appear selected to lend him weight, solidity, stability, importance. But they degenerate into the music hall catch-cry, "Take off that white hat!," the confusion of white hat and white head, of Wellington's white horse and white arse. The result is a destabilizing of the dreamer's sense of security and identity compounded by the confrontation with his own latent homosexual tendencies. The frequently repeated question addressed to HCE and ending in "my fair (or white) sir" or "my dark sir" epitomizes this challenge to his stability of identity.

In series 1(c) political and nationalistic fervor and the wars and killings they lead to provide another paradigm for the struggles within the psyche of the dreamer. Through all three series the color white is an important triggering mechanism for the emergence into the dreamer's awareness of the most deeply buried conflicts, the confrontation with which threatens to tear him apart and yet is absolutely necessary for his struggle to achieve reconciliation and wholeness.

Series 1(d) surfaces overtly only once but its existence is unmistakable on that occasion, namely the Druid-Saint debate in which Patrick's white garb (and black and white approach) seem clearly to represent the conventional, approved vision of imminent daylight in opposition to the druidic, artistic, Wakean perception of things. The pattern may also connect with Shaun's whites and with other white-rainbow clashes, but I have been unable to establish a connection. It remains therefore a comparatively isolated pattern, though obviously of importance in the major scene in which it appears.

Although occurrences of the color red are slightly less numerous in *Finnegans Wake* than those of black-dark I consider the patterns of association involving the former color more significant and far-reaching. The lengthy and convoluted series 2(a) could be subdivided but only by breaking up what are essentially the components of HCE as man, that is, as representative of the adult male human (*aner* in classical Greek) as opposed to his role as representative of humankind (*anthropos*). What stands out in the series is, firstly, HCE's kinship with Adam and great male doers, and, secondly, the complete overshadowing of his claims of achievement by his feelings of guilt, shame and failure and his sense of inevitable doom. This Wakean portrait of twentieth century man is a bleak one, painting him as hunted rather than hunter and frightened of impotence while guilt-ridden at the image of the phallus. In this context the red Boylan of "Circe" and "Penelope" appears an unreal anachronism. Series 2(b) outlines a pattern which reduces to physical and organic determinacy the sexuality so paradoxically rendered by the sexual whites. Here indeed is sexuality in Boylan's terms and a depressingly limiting vision it is.

The two white-red series are mutually (and paradoxically) exclusive and complementary and they bear similar relationships to the separate red and white series. The red-whites which attend HCE all have unifying and reconciling effects. They constitute the most hopeful image pattern of wholeness *Finnegans Wake* provides. Even the sexually suggestive Munster answer to the fourth question of the "Quiz" (I, 6) presents in its pairing of "mouth's flower rose" and "silvry speech" a rare lyricism and near-tenderness (140.21–27). For once sexual union is seen in terms of fulfilment rather than threat and rather vaguely behind the image of sexual union is the image of the artist begetting and bringing to birth his literary creations. On the other hand the group of images listed under 3(b), the more specifically woman's reds-whites, are both crude and threatening to the dreamer. The lily and the rose are the pair of ladies who most overtly lead HCE towards a fall and his guilt-ridden thoughts sense their threat everywhere, even in a seemingly innocent news item in the "Evening World": "Opportunity fair with the China floods and we hear those rosy rumours" (28.23–24). The Prankquean, with her red changing to white and her increasing wetness, is the most potent personification of the female pairs and the most dramatic challenge to the dreamer's frantic efforts to preserve the status quo. And yet she too is an ambiguous figure. By uniting in her own person the female pairs and red and white she is a unifying or reconciling figure—in her name she unites *p* and *q* or the *p-k* split in Celtic languages and culture.

The patterns of association of black and of white-black (4[a] and 4[b]) are so enmeshed together that attempts to outline them separately result in almost exact duplications of series. It makes more sense therefore to leave them together. Series 4(b) outlines the satanic blacks associated with Shem and his writing. They indicate the sordid nature of the raw materials from which the artist must create beauty and the abuse he must tolerate from society if he remains honest and faithful to his task. Combined with dark (Irish, "blind"), black becomes the eye troubles and black eye patch of James Joyce suffering for his art. Shem's blacks also point to the artist's weaknesses in common with his fellow man—he only differs in his attempts at perceiving and rendering the truth. When white joins black in association with Shem's writing we have an image of black ink on the white page, of the reconciliation of the sacred and profane, of the fixing, however tentatively, on a portion of truth.

Series 4(a) presents the black-whites which mark the conflicts and splits within HCE's psyche. These are geographic and occur also in the names of his personae. They culminate in the pint of Guinness, black with a creamy head, frequently distorted in the text to link with Genesis, symbol of male creative and procreative powers.

Series 5 outlines the most dramatic instance of black-white patterns of association, that of raven and dove. Raven and dove are associated in the *Wake* with almost every binary element of importance—they are all pairs and they are all pairs interchangeably. The chief function of raven-dove, as I have pointed out with regard to specific instances of their occurrences, is the simultaneous proposition and disequilibrium of the balanced antithesis. The violation of the antithesis is effected primarily by the Irish meaning of *dubh* which is almost an exact homonym for the English dove and is then extended by all the tricks of word distortion, puns and allusions that Joyce is capable of. The Wakean vision insists that the conflicts within the personality are experientially real, yet they are all creations of and are contained within the individual sensibility. All the projections of guilt, all the delegations of blame and all the quests for certainty are finally circular. The only certainty the reader of the *Wake* has is the "certainty" described by the pedant in I, 5:

> [T]he affair is a thing once for all done and there you are somewhere and finished in a certain time, be it a day or a year or even supposing, it should eventually turn out to be a serial number of goodness alone knows how many days or years. (118.7-11)

In contemplating what he thought was the duality of raven-dove, the reader finds himself moving on the circumference of a circle, the merry-go-round of *Finnegans Wake*.

Shaun as fairhaired boy and idol of the populace (6[a]) is wrapped in the flags of religion and patriotism—the papal white and gold and the Irish tricolor. That earlier Shaun-figure, Malachi Mulligan, is also given white and gold in the opening pages of "Telemachus." Uniting church and country is that Shaun-projection, St. Kevin of green Glendalough, with the shadow of Kevin Barry, the student-revolutionary who became a national martyr during the Troubles, faintly in the background. In one sense Shaun is still merely trying out for these roles he covets. Papal and patriarchal and phallic authority belongs to the father who displays it as gorse-, heather- and snow-crowned Howth Head.

Most of the other series I have listed are fairly straightforward and, in the light of my earlier discussion of them, self-explanatory. Before considering the Rainbow series I shall make a few comments on series 7(a), the green of unripe fruit. This series outlines the yearning for rejuvenation of the aging father made manifest in his penchant for green growing things and most especially in his incestuous desires for that unripe fruit, his daughter Issy. The only demonstrable connection I can find between this and other series is through apple/ALP/Eden to series 9 (dappled). But there are, for this reader at least, faint echoes of other connections: Stephen's obsession with the green/white/mother/drowning/guilt complex of images; the green of "Mother Ireland"; the fact that Issy's distinctive color is the sexual white; the prominence of leafy greens in Anna's final monologue.

The most prominent and significant series of color associations in *Finnegans Wake* are those connected with the rainbow, series 15(a) to 15(d) in my chart. In fact the rainbow series demonstrate effectively the working of colors in the creation of the larger meanings of the book. The rainbow functions as a largescale model of "*leitmotiv*" or "motif-agglomeration" in Clive Hart's terms. Hart in his book is concerned only with verbal motifs, not with repetitions of colors or images or even ideas, but his description of the verbal motifs nevertheless has considerable relevance for the functioning of color patterns:

> A series of motifs, however slender, creates a skeletal grid-pattern which, provided it has some truly functional relationship to the book's themes, helps the reader to organise his responses in phase with those themes. Indeed this ordering and unifying function of the *leitmotiv* is probably its greatest strength.[3]

Hart goes on to describe what he sees as "three main planes" in the text of *Finnegans Wake:* "In the foreground is the manifest content...; in the middle-ground is a mass of highly symbolic, but often puzzling, material...; in the background are the motif-controlled grids or frames of reference against which the symbols can function."[4] Despite the necessary simplification of Hart's "planes," it is a useful diagram for looking at the workings of the language of the *Wake*. Colors necessarily work on all three planes but their patterns of association belong more properly to the background or "frames of reference." The rainbow provides the most important of the color-related "frames of reference."

Series 15(a) outlines the pattern of rainbow associations that borrows most heavily from the Genesis account of the first rainbow as the sign of God's covenant with Noah that there would be peace between God and man and no more floods. The rainbows in this series are therefore primarily symbols of patriarchal dignity and power and they occur in connection with appropriate personae of HCE, e.g., the Russian general (R #21; 339.28–29), Balkelly as royal Druid (R #27; 611.6–7), and High King Leary himself (R #28; 611.35–612.15). In the first "Pub" chapter (II, 3) the customers remark of HCE: "Arrorsure, he's the mannore of Arrahland oversense he horrhorrd his name in thuthunder" (378.6–7), thus attributing to their host identity with Old Testament patriarchs who sat down to bargain personally with God. But the rainbow signifies fall as surely as it signifies covenant; in this sense it is a false promise, a lie that drags with it illusions and such certain signs of future fall as alcohol. What the rainbow really promises is a future, a very doubtful future in which the only certainty is that the father will have fallen and been replaced by a new generation.

Series 15(b) outlines the female-sexual rainbow associations which in effect present an alternative woman's rainbow to challenge the traditional hegemony of man. Woman's strength seems to lie in her sexuality, man's weakness in his, at least as far as the dreamer's fears are concerned. The first dramatic personification of this challenge is the Prankquean who, like her historical counterpart, Grace O'Malley, usurps the aggressive male role. The name Anna also means grace (in Hebrew). The fall of man that woman brings about may be a *felix culpa*, redemptive and productive of grace even if the dreamer's overwhelming fears blind him to the possibility. The last figure I have named in this series is Joan of Arc, Joan of the Rainbow, the mythical-historical virgin who, at the head of a male army, challenged to its very foundations the patriarchal authority of the Church and State.

It is only with some violence that I have extricated series 15(c) (Seven Garments) from 15(a) and 15(b). I could just as easily have run 15(a) or 15(b) into 15(c). Nevertheless there is a significant pattern involving seven garments that merits isolating for discussion at least. As I pointed out in chapter 3 the seven garments of HCE are associated with those personae of his who are proud, authoritative figures, the very types I cited in my discussion above of series 15(a). The seven garments are thus also symbols of male, patriarchal dignity. But they go further and, as in the Prankquean episode, mark the HCE-personae in anger and aggression. The crucial figure in this rainbow pattern is Strongbow and the crucial acts are invasion, rape and war. The last refuge of the frustrated male appears to be violence against woman, a violence disguised as an act of civilizing. When HCE boasts in the "Inquisition of Yawn" (III, 3) of his city-building achievements one of his statements runs: "And I cast my tenspan joys on her, arsched overtupped, from bank of call to echobank, by dint of strongbow" (547.30–31). This is HCE's building of Dublin's bridges and quays, but it is also the taming of the woman by sexual aggression—arse, arse over tip, tup, dint, strongbow. But much of this is bluster. The rainbow garments like all garments in the *Wake* reveal more than they conceal and what they especially reveal is HCE emerging from his pub into the Phoenix Park to meet his destiny.

Series 15(d) in my chart has to do with vision and perception. These rainbow associations attend Balkelly, Shem and Joyce himself. Shaun of course rejects rainbows and dream-vision just as he rejects Shem's blackness; yet it is a word of Shaun's, "irismaimed," that best sums up the ramifications of this series. Shaun is speaking of his brother:

> My shemblable! my freer! I call you my halfbrother because you in your soberer otiumic, moments remind me deeply of my natural saywhen brothel in feed, hop and jollity, S. H. Devitt, that benighted irismaimed, who is tearly belaboured by Sydney and Alibany. (489.28–32)

As "irismaimed," Shem is Irishman and blinded (like Joyce) by the demands of his rainbow vision—Iris is goddess of the rainbow. He is "benighted" because, for Shaun, rainbow- or dream-vision is merely dangerous blundering about in the dark. But many an Irishman was transported to Australia and not a few were subsequently knighted and honored with high public office. Here also is the figure of the artist, Joyce, laboring in exile through "tearly" difficulties and receiving honors abroad before he gets the slightest recognition from his native land. And yet in spite of Shaun's rejection of Shem there is, in the distortion of "United Irishman," evidence of a subliminal recognition that only through mutual acceptance rather than denial can integration into wholeness of the dreamer's psyche be realized.

The sign of the rainbow is, like every other sign in *Finnegans Wake*, radically ambiguous. Rainbow in Irish is *tuar ceatha* or shower-sign. The Irish word and its English transliteration occur at 490.28–30 where Joyce has fun conflating "shower-sign" with "sure sign." Anyone familiar with the vagaries of Irish weather knows that there are no sure signs, least of all rainbows. And a built-in irony in the tradition of the rainbow as sign of God's promise that there will be no more floods is the fact that we only see a rainbow in nature when it is already raining. Despite the ambiguity the central function of the rainbow in *Finnegans Wake* is, I believe, fairly clear: at those points in the dream when sleep is deepest, the daytime censor is most lulled, and the most deeply repressed conflicts and guilts of the dreamer float to the surface of the dream thought, then rainbows are most in evidence and the rainbow vision of the dream is at its most penetrating. Thus rainbows are especially in attendance on these issues: the nightmare of Irish history, especially in its invasions; the rituals and strictures of the Church; alcohol; the personality conflicts signified by the Shem-Shaun split; the dread of aging and of being replaced by a new generation; the simultaneous enticement and threat of woman; the agonies of literary creation, that is, of probing those psychic wounds. The rainbows in the

Wake are therefore natural descendants of the color concentrations attendant on the Christmas dinner, the bird-girl epiphany and the creation of the villanelle in *A Portrait of the Artist* and events of like intensity in *Ulysses*, especially the hallucinatory visions in "Circe."

In my investigation of Joyce's use of colors in *Finnegans Wake* I have examined some outside color systems, particularly the colors of national flags, Church liturgy and alchemy. None of them turned out to be of much use for elucidating color patterns in the *Wake*, though Joyce clearly borrowed from all three in writing his book. The reason lies in Joyce's method of composition. For most of his sources he merely made lists of words and phrases and rarely seems to have revisited his source but merely inserted items from his lists in his writing as the task at hand seemed to require. As a result these items as they appear in the published work are distanced from the sources in which they were originally embedded. However, because of the publication in 1980 of Barbara DiBernard's study of alchemy in *Finnegans Wake*,[5] I believe I must give that topic some further consideration.

DiBernard's study is a useful book for all students of *Finnegans Wake*. It ferrets out the presence of alchemical material in areas of the *Wake* in which they have heretofore been undetected. It makes many perceptive connections and interpretations along the way. It clarifies especially the use of the alchemical process in the *Wake* as a metaphor for the creative process of the artist and shows how this emphasizes the sham or fake aspect of artistic creation. And it demonstrates an alchemical link in the *Wake* between artistic creation and sexual intercourse, a link in which incest is prominent. Nevertheless her claim that "Joyce finds in alchemy a kind of ur-myth which fits his desire to express the most basic themes and cycles of human life"[6] is surely exaggerated. She writes:

> Alchemy serves not only as a metaphor for the artistic process, but also as a source or analogue for many of the major themes of the *Wake*, including incest, colors, forgery, death and rebirth, the dream form, the use of excrement, the Golden Age, number symbolism, the macrocosm-microcosm theory, and the reconciliation of opposites.[7]

Such a claim must founder on the fact of Joyce's habit of hoarding scraps that came his way. From the myriad sources which could have given Joyce material for such "themes" it would be very difficult to separate the claims of the alchemical tradition, although DiBernard clearly establishes that alchemy did make some contribution. In short, DiBernard's discussion of alchemical colors in the *Wake* told me little of how Joyce was actually employing colors.

I began this book with a comment of Clive Hart's on a passage from *A Portrait of the Artist as a Young Man*. Here again is the passage:

> The phrase and the day and the scene harmonised in a chord. Words. Was it their colours? He allowed them to glow and fade, hue after hue: sunrise gold, the russet and green of apple orchards, azure of waves, the greyfringed fleece of clouds. No, it was not their colours: it was the poise and balance of the period itself. Did he then love the rhythmic rise and fall of words better than their associations of legend and colour? Or was it that, being as weak of sight as he was shy of mind, he drew less pleasure from the reflection of the glowing sensible world through the prism of a language manycoloured and richly storied than from the contemplation of an inner world of individual emotions mirrored perfectly in a lucid supple periodic prose? (pp. 166–67).

Now that I have examined Joyce's use of colors through the major works, this statement of Stephen's seems to me in retrospect to display an uncanny intuition as to the directions Joyce's evolving goals and artistic methods would take in the years ahead. With its not quite balancing of the alternatives and yet with the conclusion left in interrogative form the statement itself adumbrates the ways in which Joyce in *Finnegans Wake* holds meanings in suspension. In one sense he does abandon "the glowing sensible world" for "the inner world of individual emotions" when he focuses in the *Wake* on the conflicts within the individual soul. But in the broader sense he has the best of both worlds since in the *Wake* he uses "the prism of a language manycoloured and richly storied" to go out and capture the phenomena that catch his attention in "the glowing sensible world"—international strife, patriotic jingoism, mountain and river, the battle between the sexes—and forges them into a complex of metaphors with which to get at the "inner world of individual emotions." Colorfulness, in both literal and figurative senses, is a significant part of the technique by which Joyce fashions his "most kaleidoscopic book."

In the "Recorso," as the dreamer-hero-reader-writer rises reluctantly towards wakefulness and Yawndom, "When the messanger of the risen sun, (see other oriel) shall give to every seeable a hue and to every hearable a cry and to each spectacle his spot and to each happening her houram" (609.19–22), he must prepare to deal with the tyranny of daytime fact. But he is strengthened by having confronted in the dream some of the most unsettling questions, as when Glugg in "The Mime" (II, 1) is in disgrace and frustration "all over which girls as he don't know whose hue" (227.24–25). The phrases scattered through the book that play with the word "hue" frequently echo the children's rime "St. Ives." A lengthy parody of it occurs in the washerwomen's scandalous gossip of HCE and ALP: "Hadn't he seven dams to wive him? And every dam had her seven crutches. And every crutch had its seven hues. And each hue had a differing cry" (215.15–17). The original rime, or a well known version of it, runs:

> As I was going to Saint Ives
> I met a man with seven wives;
> Each wife had seven sacks;

> Each sack had seven cats;
> Each cat had seven kits.
> Kits, cats, sacks, wives,
> How many were going to St. Ives?

The less alert responder, if accurate with his mental arithmetic, might come up with the answer 2,801. But despite all the rainbow-sevens the correct answer is: one. The paramount awareness of individual identity imprisons man in isolation. Armed with the wisdom of dream-vision he must emerge to confront the threats of the phenomenal world and only then can he return to truly encounter "the hueful panepiphanal world" of himself. That journey is enacted, not as an event but as a possibility, in *Finnegans Wake*.

Notes

Chapter 1

1. In this study all references to *A Portrait of the Artist as a Young Man* apply to the Viking Critical Library edition, ed. Chester G. Anderson (New York: Viking Press, 1968).

2. All references to *Ulysses* are to: *Ulysses: A Critical and Synoptic Edition*, ed. Hans Walter Gabler (New York: Garland, 1984). Thus a reference to *Ulysses* in this study located as 3.470–80, means Episode 3, lines 470 to 480 in the Gabler edition. All references to *Finnegans Wake* apply to the Compass Books edition (author's corrections incorporated) (New York: Viking Press, 1959). A reference given as 334.6 means p. 334, line 6.

3. Clive Hart, *Structure and Motif in* Finnegans Wake (Evanston, Ill.: Northwestern University Press, 1962), pp. 151–52. Hart's reference is to the London 1948 edition of *A Portrait;* his p. 190 becomes pp. 166–67 in my edition.

4. *Letters of James Joyce,* vol. 1, ed. Stuart Gilbert (London: Faber and Faber, 1957), p. 269.

5. Clive Hart's *A Concordance to* Finnegans Wake, Corrected ed. (Mamoroneck, N.Y.: Paul P. Appel, 1974) has been of use to me in counting color references in *Finnegans Wake*. However, I have had to make the determination in each instance as to what constitutes a color reference in the unique language of the *Wake*. See also Note 9 below.

6. In this study all references to *Dubliners* apply to the Viking Critical Library edition, ed. Robert Scholes and A. Walton Litz (New York: Viking Press, 1969).

7. The black panther is mentioned at 1.57, 1.62, 14.1025, 14.1033 and 15.4930. Boylan's tan shoes appear at 8.1168, 10.307, 10.1241, 11.761 and 11.977.

8. Robert Scholes, "'Counterparts' and the Method of *Dubliners*," in Clive Hart ed. *James Joyce's* Dubliners: *Critical Essays* (London: Faber and Faber, 1969), rpt. in the Viking Critical edition of *Dubliners*, p. 382.

9. I have consulted Gary Lane's *A Word Index to James Joyce's* Dubliners (New York: Haskell House, 1972), in counting the color references, and I have also examined the color charts in B. Fliot Wigginston's article "*Dubliners* in Order," *James Joyce Quarterly*, 7, No. 4 (Summer 1970), pp. 294–314. However the statistics of color references I give in this study are essentially my own. Frequently, I have had to make a determination as to whether a particular word in a particular context appeared likely to carry color denotation or connotation. Examples of such words are fair, flush, pale, rose, light and the like. The *Word Index* does not, of course, make such judgments, while Wigginston counts only specifically

denotative color words, ignoring what he calls "the tonations, shades and shadows." Nevertheless the patterns Wigginston finds and his conclusions (as far as they go) are not seriously at odds with mine.

10. Thomas F. Smith, "Colour and Light in 'The Dead,'" *James Joyce Quarterly*, 2, No. 4 (Summer 1965), p. 306.

11. Ibid., p. 307.

12. A. Walton Litz, "'Two Gallants,'" in Clive Hart, ed. *James Joyce's* Dubliners, rpt. in the Viking Critical edition of *Dubliners*, p. 370.

13. Breon Mitchell, "*A Portrait* and the *Bildungsroman* Tradition," in Thomas F. Staley and Bernard Benstock, ed. *Approaches to Joyce's* Portrait: *Ten Essays* (N.P.: University of Pittsburgh Press, 1976), p. 71.

14. In counting color references in *A Portrait* I have consulted Leslie Hancock's *Word Index to James Joyce's* Portrait of the Artist (Carbondale and Edwardsville: Southern Illinois University Press, 1967). But my comments on my use of the *Word Index* for *Dubliners*, in Note 9 above, have equal validity here.

15. Hugh Kenner, *Dublin's Joyce* (Bloomington: Indiana University Press, 1966), rpt. in part in the Viking Critical edition of *A Portrait* as Hugh Kenner, "The *Portrait* in Perspective," p. 425.

16. Richard Ellmann, *James Joyce*, new and revised ed. (New York: Oxford University Press, 1983), pp. 296-97.

17. William York Tindall, *The Literary Symbol* (New York: Columbia University Press, 1955), rpt. in part in the Viking Critical edition of *A Portrait*, pp. 383-84.

18. By my count, "grey" occurs forty-two times in *A Portrait*, i.e., more frequently than any color except white/fair, black/dark and red/rose.

19. Tindall, in the Viking Critical *Portrait*, p. 381.

20. Page 12 has thirty-one color words.

21. Tindall, in the Viking Critical *Portrait*, p. 387.

22. "Red" in connection with "rose" is a special case and is quite unlike the run of reds throughout *A Portrait*.

23. Frank O'Connor, *The Mirror in the Roadway* (New York: Alfred A. Knopf, 1956), rpt. in part as "Joyce and Dissociated Metaphor" in the Viking Critical edition of *A Portrait*, p. 373.

24. Harry Levin, *James Joyce: A Critical Introduction* (Norfolk, Conn.: New Directions, 1960), rpt. in part as "The Artist" in the Viking Critical edition of *A Portrait*, p. 407.

25. Robert Scholes, "Stephen Dedalus, Poet or Aesthete?" *PMLA*, 79 (Sept. 1964), rpt. in the Viking Critical edition of *A Portrait*, pp. 470-71.

26. Patrick White, "The Key in *Ulysses*," *James Joyce Quarterly*, 9, No. 1 (Fall 1971), p. 13.

27. Hugh Kenner, *Ulysses* (London: George Allen and Unwin, 1980), p. 16.

28. Ibid., p. 17.

29. Joseph Allen Boone, "A New Approach to Bloom as 'Womanly Man': The Mixed Middling's Progress in *Ulysses*," *James Joyce Quarterly*, 20, No. 1 (Fall 1982), pp. 69-70.

30. Brook Thomas, "The Artistic Touch of the Hidden Hand," *James Joyce Quarterly*, 15, No. 1 (Fall 1977), p. 37.

31. Richard M. Kain, "The Significance of Stephen's Meeting Bloom," *James Joyce Quarterly*, 10, No. 1 (Fall 1972), p. 155.

32. Richard Ellmann, Ulysses *on the Liffey*, corrected ed. (New York: Oxford University Press, 1973), Appendix.

33. The three are "gold," "Chrysostomos" and "gilded" (1.170). In counting color references in *Ulysses* I have made some use of Miles L. Hanley's *Word Index to James Joyce's* Ulysses (Madison: University of Wisconsin Press, 1962). That use however has been limited by Hanley's decision to give "page and line reference for those words occurring 25 times or less, for proper names, and for words connected with the various themes of the book" (p. iv). The counts given here are essentially of my own determination.

34. Elliott Coleman, "Heliotropical Noughttime: Light and Color in *Finnegans Wake*," *Texas Quarterly*, 4, No. 4 (Winter 1961), pp. 162–77.

35. Suzette Henke, *Joyce's Moraculous Sindbook: A Study of* Ulysses (Columbus: Ohio State University Press, 1978), pp. 63–64.

36. White/pale/fair/ivory and black/dark each occur about 280 times in *Ulysses*. Red occurs about 243 times and the other colors are a long way behind.

37. Mulligan's primrose waistcoast appears at 1.550, 3.312, 9.489, 10.1065, 14.813 and 14.1212.

38. Grey, with its 78 occurrences in *Ulysses*, comes next in frequency to black, white, red, green, yellow and blue.

39. Marilyn French, *The Book as World: James Joyce's* Ulysses (Cambridge, Mass.: Harvard University Press, 1976), p. 40.

40. Ibid., pp. 130–31.

41. Ibid., pp. 137–38.

42. Suzette Henke, *Joyce's Moraculous Sindbook*, pp. 130–33.

43. Hely's men appear at 8.123–26, 10.310–11, 10.377–79, 10.1236–38 and in the person of Denis Breen in "Circe," 15.479–85.

Chapter 2

1. Michael Groden, Ulysses *in Progress* (Princeton: Princeton University Press, 1977), p. 13.

2. Ibid., p. 17.

3. Ibid., p. 21. The book Groden quotes from is: Arnold Goldman, *The Joyce Paradox: Form and Freedom in His Fiction* (London: Routledge and Kegan Paul, 1966).

4. Ibid., p. 18.

5. Ibid., p. 20. Stuart Gilbert, *James Joyce's* Ulysses: *A Study* (1930; rpt. New York: Vintage, 1952). S. L. Goldberg, *The Classical Temper: A Study of James Joyce's* Ulysses (London: Chatto and Windus, 1961).

6. Joseph Campbell and Henry Morton Robinson, *A Skeleton Key to* Finnegans Wake" (1944; 2nd ed. New York: Viking, 1961), p. 3. The word the cover blurb gives as "redemption" is "resurrection" in this and the Faber and Faber editions of *A Skeleton Key*.

7. Margot Norris, *The Decentered Universe of* Finnegans Wake: *A Structuralist Analysis* (Baltimore: Johns Hopkins University Press, 1976), pp. 1–2.
8. Ibid., p. 2.
9. She implies as much on p. 2.
10. Adaline Glasheen, *Third Census of* Finnegans Wake: *An Index of the Characters and Their Roles* (Berkeley: University of California Press, 1977), p. 137.
11. Ronald Bates, "The Feast is a Flyday," *James Joyce Quarterly*, 2, No. 3 (Spring 1965), pp. 174–87.
12. Danis Rose and John O'Hanlon, *Understanding* Finnegans Wake: *A Guide to the Narrative of James Joyce's Masterpiece* (New York: Garland, 1982).
13. Patrick A. McCarthy, *The Riddles of* Finnegans Wake (Cranbury, N.J.: Associated University Presses, 1980).
14. Margaret C. Solomon, *Eternal Geomater: The Sexual Universe of* Finnegans Wake (Carbondale and Edwardsville: Southern Illinois University Press, 1969).
15. See the bibliography.
16. Of *Ulysses* Joseph Frank writes: "Joyce cannot be read—he can only be reread. A knowledge of the whole is essential to an understanding of any part." Joseph Frank, *The Widening Gyre: Crisis and Mastery in Modern Literature* (Bloomington: Indiana University Press, 1963), p. 19.
17. Donnchadh O Corrain, "Finn or Finn Mac Cumaill," *Ireland: A Cultural Encyclopaedia*, gen. ed. Brian de Breffny (New York: Facts on File Inc., 1983), p. 88.
18. John Paul Riquelme, *Teller and Tale in Joyce's Fiction: Oscillating Perspectives* (Baltimore: Johns Hopkins University Press, 1983), p. 32.
19. Sigmund Freud, *The Interpretation of Dreams*, trans. A. A. Brill (New York: Carlton House, n.d.), p. 189. The title of Freud's book appears in *Finnegans Wake* at 338.29–30.
20. Ibid., p. 234.
21. Ibid., p. 230.
22. Ibid., p. 71.
23. Ibid., p. 86.
24. Rose and O'Hanlon, *Understanding* Finnegans Wake, p. xvii.
25. Norris, *The Decentered Universe of* Finnegans Wake, p. 108.
26. Ibid., p. 24.
27. Ibid., p. 15.
28. Roland McHugh, *The* Finnegans Wake *Experience* (Dublin: Irish Academic Press, 1981), p. 95.
29. Hugh Kenner, *Dublin's Joyce* (Boston: Beacon Press, 1956), p. 304; quoted in Norris, *The Decentered Universe of* Finnegans Wake, pp. 124–25.
30. Norris, *The Decentered Universe of* Finnegans Wake, p. 8.
31. David G. Wright, *Characters of Joyce* (Totowa, N.J.: Barnes and Noble, 1983), p. 106.

32. McCarthy, *The Riddles of* Finnegans Wake, p. 28.
33. Norris, *The Decentered Universe of* Finnegans Wake, p. 28.
34. Solomon, *Eternal Geomater*, p. 60.
35. McCarthy, *The Riddles of* Finnegans Wake, p. 59.
36. Groden, Ulysses *in Progress*.
37. Brook Thomas, "Formal Re-creation: Re-reading and Re-joycing the Re-rightings of *Ulysses*," in Bernard Benstock, ed., *The Seventh of Joyce*, (Bloomington: Indiana University Press, 1982), p. 5.
38. Ibid., p. 9. The *Ulysses* reference is 3.27-28 in my edition.
39. Riquelme, *Teller and Tale in Joyce's Fiction*, pp. 2-3.
40. Ibid., pp. 3-4.
41. Manfred Putz, "The Identity of the Reader in *Finnegans Wake*," *James Joyce Quarterly*, 11, No. 4 (Summer 1974), pp. 387-88.
42. Ibid., p. 389.
43. The most detailed analysis is Glasheen's series of five articles: Adaline Glasheen, "The Opening Paragraphs," *A Wake Newslitter*, NS 2, No. 2 (April 1965), pp. 3-8; "The Opening Paragraphs (contd.)," *A Wake Newslitter*, NS 2, No. 3 (June 1965), pp. 21-25; "The Opening Paragraphs (contd.)," *A Wake Newslitter*, NS 2, No. 4 (August 1965), pp. 24-27; "The Opening Paragraphs (contd.)," *A Wake Newslitter*, NS 2, No. 6 (December 1965), pp. 17-22; "The Opening Paragraphs (concluded)," *A Wake Newslitter*, NS 3, No. 1 (February 1966), pp. 6-14. Joyce's "key" is given in the first of these articles.
44. E.L. Epstein, "James Joyce and the Body," in E.L. Epstein, ed., *A Starchamber Quiry*, (London: Methuen, 1982), p. 83.
45. Kimberley Devlin, "Self and Other in *Finnegans Wake:* A Framework for Analyzing Versions of Shem and Shaun," *James Joyce Quarterly*, 21, No. 1 (Fall 1983), pp. 31-50.
46. Ibid., p. 34.
47. Ibid., pp. 35-36.
48. Ibid., pp. 38-39.
49. Matthew 7:5.
50. Bernard Benstock, *Joyce-Again's Wake: An Analysis of* Finnegans Wake (Seattle: University of Washington Press, 1965), pp. 224-25.
51. Also at 72.34, 469.21 and 553.26-27.
52. Patrick S. Dinneen, ed. *An Irish English Dictionary*. 2nd. ed. (Dublin: Educational Company of Ireland Ltd., 1927), p. 436.
53. In addition to Joyce himself and Campbell and Robinson, the following critics are among those who have examined this scene and its significance: Bernard Benstock, *Joyce-Again's Wake*, p. 258; Margaret Solomon, *Eternal Geomater*, pp. 123-25; William York Tindall, *A Reader's Guide to* Finnegans Wake, pp. 320-21; Michael Begnal in Begnal and Eckley, *Narrator and Character in* Finnegans Wake, pp. 106-8; M. J. Sidwell, "A Daintical Pair of Accomplasses," in Bates and Pollock, ed., *Litters from Aloft*, pp. 54-55; Margot Norris, *The*

Decentered Universe of Finnegans Wake, pp. 87–91; and Grace Eckley, "Looking Forward to a Brightening Day," in Begnal and Senn, *A Conceptual Guide to* Finnegans Wake, pp. 224–25.

54. Joseph Campbell and Henry Morton Robinson, *A Skeleton Key to* Finnegans Wake. 2nd ed. (New York: Viking, 1961), p. 348.
55. William York Tindall, *A Reader's Guide to* Finnegans Wake (New York: Farrar, Straus and Giroux, 1969), pp. 320–21.
56. Paul Anghinetti, "Berkeley's Influence on Joyce," *James Joyce Quarterly*, 19, No. 3 (Spring 1982), p. 316.
57. Roland McHugh, *Annotations to* Finnegans Wake (London: Routledge and Kegan Paul, 1980), p. 612.
58. A.D. 432 is the popularly accepted date of Patrick's mission to Ireland.
59. McHugh, *Annotations*, p. 448.
60. *James Joyce in Padua*, ed., trans., and intro. Louis Berrone (New York: Random House, 1977), p. 20.
61. Fritz Senn, "Weaving, unweaving," in E.L. Epstein, ed., *A Starchamber Quiry* (London: Methuen, 1982), p. 45.
62. John Gordon, *Notes on Issy*, A Wake Newslitter Monograph No. 7 (Colchester: A Wake Newslitter Press, 1982), p. 10.

Chapter 3

1. These occur at 35.9, 71.17, 76.32, 78.7, 328.9–10, 332.22, 443.36, 511.10, 542.3, 564.23 and 567.25.
2. Roland McHugh, *Annotations to* Finnegans Wake (London: Routledge and Kegan Paul, 1980), p. 511.
3. HCE's greens occur at 5.6, 7.30, 58.6–7, 74.2–3, 88.2, 117.7, 131.21 and 378.11.
4. See McHugh, *Annotations*, p. 72: "Green Man Rise-O: game in which child concealed under coats suddenly jumps up and chases others."
5. Ibid., p. 58.
6. *Toll* is "mad" in German; Joyce was nicknamed "the mad hatter"; Delgany is in County Wicklow—Parnell represented a Wicklow riding.
7. See the discussion of this ancient name for Dublin in Brendan O'Hehir, *A Gaelic Lexicon for* Finnegans Wake (Berkeley: University of California Press, 1967), p. 40.
8. The five are 111.26–30, 137.6–7, 334.16–17, 388.16–17 and 510.30.
9. One version is given in McHugh, *Annotations*, p. 10: "Wellington asked if he were Irish: 'If a gentleman happens to be born in a stable, it does not follow that he should be called a horse.'"
10. See Adaline Glasheen, *Third Census of* Finnegans Wake: *An Index of the Characters and their Roles* (Berkeley: University of California Press, 1977), pp. 302–3.
11. See McHugh, *Annotations*, p. 32.
12. 32.23, 320.8, 322.1, 322.5, 536.14, 538.34–35, 584.15, 607.3, 614.14 and 623.9.

Notes for Chapter 3   185

13. At 320.8, 322.1 and 322.5.
14. 536.14 and 538.34–35 (Arthur Ransom wrote *Oscar Wilde*).
15. Wilde's full name was Oscar Fingall O'Flahertie Wills Wilde.
16. Glasheen, *Third Census*, p. 292.
17. Ibid., p. 274.
18. Ibid., p. 78.
19. This passage is famed for being the earliest known part of the *Wake* that Joyce wrote.
20. Stuart Gilbert, ed., *Letters of James Joyce* (London: Faber and Faber, 1957), pp. 247–48.
21. Glasheen, *Third Census*, p. 211.
22. Ibid., p. 258.
23. *A Wake Newslitter*, NS 14, No. 6 (December 1977), p. 100.
24. Glasheen, *Third Census*, p. 161.
25. 17.24–25, 132.5 and 449.21.
26. Glasheen, *Third Census*, p. 99.
27. This paradoxical vision is discussed in David A. White, *The Grand Continuum: Reflections on Joyce and Metaphysics* (Pittsburgh: University of Pittsburgh Press, 1983) under the headings: "Motion and Rest," "Identity and Difference," "Space and Time," "The Wheel of History" and "Cause and Effect."
28. McHugh, *Annotations*, p. 310.
29. Ibid., p. 241.
30. Wilhelm Fuger, "Ravens and Doves," *A Wake Newslitter*, NS 14, No. 5 (December 1977), pp. 91–95. The passage quoted is on p. 94.
31. McHugh, *Annotations*, p. 72.
32. Ibid., p. 72.
33. Ibid., p. 496.
34. Ibid., p. 512.
35. Roland McHugh, "Rainbows," *A Wake Newslitter*, NS 15, No. 5 (October 1978), pp. 76–77.
36. Glasheen, *Third Census*, p. 259.
37. Gilbert, ed., *Letters of James Joyce*, pp. 247–48.
38. Adaline Glasheen, "The Opening Paragraphs," *A Wake Newslitter*, NS 2, No. 2 (April 1965), pp. 3–8; "The Opening Paragraphs (contd.)," *A Wake Newslitter*, NS 2, No. 3 (June 1965), pp. 21–25; "The Opening Paragraphs (contd.)," *A Wake Newslitter*, NS 2, No. 4 (August 1965), pp. 24–27; "The Opening Paragraphs (contd.)," *A Wake Newslitter*, NS 2, No. 6 (December 1965), pp. 17–22; "The Opening Paragraphs (concluded)," *A Wake Newslitter*, NS 3, No. 1 (February 1966), pp. 6–14. Joyce's "key" is given in the first of these articles.
39. Glasheen, "The Opening Paragraphs (contd.)," *A Wake Newslitter*, NS 2, No. 4 (August 1965), p. 24.

Notes for Chapter 3

40. Ibid., p. 25.
41. Glasheen, "The Opening Paragraphs (contd.)," *A Wake Newslitter*, NS 2, No. 6 (December 1965), p. 8.
42. Ibid., p. 21.
43. Glasheen, "The Opening Paragraphs (concluded)," *A Wake Newslitter*, NS 3, No. 1 (February 1966), p. 7.
44. Since it is likely that most Wakeans identify the rainbows as they occur in the text according to McHugh's list, I shall in discussing the rainbows give McHugh's identification in each case thus: (R #1). McHugh's list appears in *A Wake Newslitter*, NS 15, No. 5 (October 1978), pp. 76–77.
45. Glasheen, "The Opening Paragraphs (contd.)," *A Wake Newslitter*, NS 2, No. 6 (December 1965), p. 21.
46. In *Annotations*, p. 529, McHugh notes: "Zeppelins were made at Friedrichshafen, Germany."
47. Ibid., p. 468.
48. Ibid., p. 182.
49. Glasheen, *Third Census*, p. 259.
50. McHugh, *Annotations*, p. 215.
51. This is McHugh's R #24. The nine choirs of angels constitute a doubtful rainbow, not only because there are nine rather than seven, but also because there does not appear to be a single identifiable color reference among them. On the other hand the mention of spectrum, prism, white light and daytime strongly suggests the presence of a rainbow.
52. McHugh, *Annotations*, p. 409.
53. Ibid., p. 178.
54. Ibid., p. 229.
55. Ibid., p. 179.
56. Ibid., p. 180.
57. Glasheen, *Third Census*, p. lxxviii.
58. McHugh, *Annotations*, p. 384.
59. Glasheen's "Synopsis" in the *Third Census* (p. xl) notes simply: "9. A picture of the Seven Rainbow Girls whose answer is 'A collideorscape.'" But Patrick McCarthy in his *The Riddles of* Finnegans Wake (Cranbury, N.J.: Associated University Press, 1980) analyzes Questions #9 most convincingly as a statement of Joyce's techniques in composing the *Wake* (see McCarthy, pp. 71–72).
60. H. W. Fowler and F. G. Fowler, ed., *The Concise Oxford Dictionary of Current English*, 5th ed. (Oxford: Oxford University Press, 1964), p. 660.

Chapter 4

1. Margot Norris, "Anna Livia Plurabelle: The Dream Woman," in Suzette Henke and Elaine Unkeless, ed., *Women in Joyce* (Urbana: University of Illinois Press, 1982), p. 211.
2. Suzette Henke, "Stephen Dedalus and Women: A Portrait of the Artist as a Young Misogynist," in Henke and Unkeless, ed., *Women in Joyce*, p. 82.
3. Clive Hart, *Structure and Motif in* Finnegans Wake (Evanston, Ill.: Northwestern University Press, 1962), p. 153.
4. At least 13.27 ("desarted"), 265.6–7 ("Sweetsome"), 552.22 ("sweet") and 617.36 ("Swees").
5. Richard Ellmann, *James Joyce*, new and rev. ed. (New York: Oxford University Press, 1982), p. 561.
6. Letter to Harriet Weaver of March 7, 1924, in Stuart Gilbert, ed., *Letters of James Joyce*, vol. 1 (London: Faber and Faber, 1957), p. 213, quoted in Richard Ellmann, *James Joyce*, new and rev. ed., pp. 563–64.
7. Richard Ellmann, *James Joyce*, new and rev. ed., p. 603.
8. Margot Norris, "Anna Livia Plurabelle: The Dream Woman," in Henke and Unkeless, ed., *Women in Joyce*, pp. 200–201.
9. Ibid., p. 202.
10. Ibid., p. 200.
11. Ibid., p. 202.
12. John Gordon, *Notes on Issy*, A Wake Newslitter Monograph no. 7 (Colchester: A Wake Newslitter Press, 1982), p. 1.
13. Ibid., p. 2.
14. In *Understanding* Finnegans Wake: *A Guide to the Narrative of James Joyce's Masterpiece* (New York: Garland, 1982), p. 25, Danis Rose and John O'Hanlon make this point: "A.L.P. is associated with apples and H.C.E. with oranges: hence his interment at 3.23 involves oranges being laid 'to rust upon the green.' When the hen pecking at the midden in I.5 uncovers fragments of orange peel, it is therefore uncovering bits of H.C.E.'s corpse." The association of HCE with orange is readily demonstrable from the text. But this is never, as far as I can judge, placed in balance with ALP's apple. Therefore I have not given space to the discussion of such an antithesis in this study.
15. Roland McHugh, *Annotations to* Finnegans Wake (London: Routledge and Kegan Paul, 1980), p. 403.
16. Adaline Glasheen, *Third Census of* Finnegans Wake: *An Index of the Characters and Their Roles* (Berkeley: University of California Press, 1977), p. 138.
17. E.g., Glasheen in *Third Census*, p. 137.
18. Ibid., pp. lxxii–lxxxiv.
19. The coat of arms is reproduced in black and white in Rose and O'Hanlon, *Understanding* Finnegans Wake, p. 77.
20. Glasheen, *Third Census*, p. 59.
21. Cf. "Circe," 15.3789.

22. W. B. Yeats, "A Coat," *The Collected Poems of W. B. Yeats* (London: MacMillan, 1955), p. 142.
23. "Jaun's Sermon" (III, 2) at 433.3, 433.18–19, 437.28–33; "The Inquisition of Yawn" (III, 3) at 486.23–25; "Mamalujo" (II, 4) at 394.35–395.1; and "The Mime" (II, 1) at 247.18–34, provide some of the more striking examples.
24. McHugh, *Annotations*, p. 9.
25. Ibid.
26. Patrick A. McCarthy, *The Riddles of* Finnegans Wake (Cranbury, N.J.: Associated University Presses, Inc., 1980), pp. 116–17.
27. McHugh, *Annotations*, p. 21.
28. McCarthy, *The Riddles of* Finnegans Wake, p. 110.
29. McHugh, *Annotations*, p. 171.
30. Ellmann, *James Joyce*, new and rev. ed., p. 455.
31. McHugh, *Annotations*, p. 351.
32. Nathan Halper, "Of the Stuttering Hand," *A Wake Newslitter*, NS 12, No. 1 (February 1975), p. 8.
33. 527.15–30 provides a good example.
34. McHugh, *Annotations*, p. 124.
35. Ibid., p. 352.
36. Ibid.
37. Glasheen, *Third Census*, pp. 60, 248.
38. McHugh, *Annotations*, p. 32.
39. Ibid., p. 34.
40. E.g., 3.13–14.
41. Glasheen, *Third Census*, p. 289.
42. McHugh, *Annotations*, p. 561.
43. Ibid.
44. Ibid.
45. Ibid.
46. Ibid., p. 572.
47. Ibid., p. 247.
48. Rose and O'Hanlon, *Understanding* Finnegans Wake, p. 141.
49. McHugh, *Annotations,* p. 380.
50. Pink, the blending of red and white, forms only one distinct pattern in the *Wake*, namely, with genitalia, underwear and especially condom (e.g., 567.6–9, 570.24–25). It usually occurs in the leering comments of the Four and does not connect with the sexual red-white.

Notes for Chapter 5   189

51. McCarthy, *The Riddles of* Finnegans Wake, pp. 136–39.
52. Ibid., p. 144.
53. Margaret C. Solomon, *Eternal Geomater: The Sexual Universe of* Finnegans Wake (Carbondale and Edwardsville: Southern Illinois University Press, 1969), pp. 30–32.
54. John Gordon, *Notes on Issy*, pp. 8–12.
55. Ibid., p. 9.
56. The seven instances in the "Mime" are at 223.11, 223.28(3), 235.5, 237.1 and 249.16–17. The other eleven are at 266.L1, 280.24, 284.23, 303.F1, 408.35, 461.9, 470.7, 533.2, 561.20–21, 603.28 and 610.36.
57. McHugh, *Annotations*, p. 239.
58. These are: R #10 (223.6–7), R #11 (226.30–32), R #12 (227.16-18), R #13 (238.10–11) and R #14 (247.34–248.2).
59. Gordon, *Notes on Issy*, p. 1.
60. Ibid., p. 2.
61. Rose and O'Hanlon, *Understanding* Finnegans Wake, p. 267.
62. The occasions occur at: 19.23, 32.29–30 and 221.19–20.
63. This (*ivar* = sex) is one those identifications pencilled in the margin of my text in my own handwriting the source of which I have been unable to verify. It is not in McHugh's *Annotations*. But it is correct.
64. Glasheen, *Third Census*, p. 154.
65. Gordon, *Notes on Issy*, p. 16.
66. They are Rainbows #2, 7, 10, 11, 12, 13, 14 and 26.
67. McHugh, *Annotations*, p. 19.
68. See my note #63 above.
69. McHugh, *Annotations*, p. 175.
70. Ibid., p. 508.
71. Ibid., p. 336.
72. H. Burrell, "The Illustrator in the *Wake*: Aubrey Beardsley," *A Wake Newslitter*, NS 17, No. 6 (December 1980), pp. 95–98.
73. Ibid., p. 97.

Chapter 5

1. Adaline Glasheen, *Third Census of* Finnegans Wake (Berkeley: University of California Press, 1977), pp. 117–18.
2. See John Gordon's explication of this passage in his *Notes on Issy* (Colchester: A Wake Newslitter Press, 1982), p. 10.

3. Clive Hart, *Structure and Motif in* Finnegans Wake (Evanston, Ill.: Northwestern University Press, 1962), p. 171.
4. Ibid., p. 172.
5. Barbara DiBernard, *Alchemy and* Finnegans Wake (Albany: State University of New York Press, 1980).
6. Ibid., p. 59.
7. Ibid., p. 10.

Bibliography

Primary Sources by James Joyce

A First Draft-Version of Finnegans Wake. Ed. David Hayman. Austin: University of Texas Press, 1963.
A Portrait of the Artist as a Young Man. Viking Critical Library. Text, Criticism and Notes. Ed. Chester G. Anderson. New York: Viking, 1968.
Dubliners. Viking Critical Library. Text, Criticism and Notes. Ed. Robert Scholes and A. Walton Litz. New York: Viking, 1969.
Finnegans Wake. Compass Books ed. New York: Viking, 1959.
James Joyce in Padua. Ed., trans. and intro. Louis Berrone. New York: Random House, 1977.
James Joyce: The Critical Writings. Ed. Ellsworth Mason and Richard Ellmann. New York: Viking, 1964.
Letters of James Joyce. Vol 1. Ed. Stuart Gilbert. London: Faber and Faber, 1957; Vol 2 and 3. Ed. Richard Ellmann. New York: Viking, 1966.
The James Joyce Archive. Photoprint ed. Gen. ed. Michael Groden. New York: Garland, 1977-79. Part 7: *Finnegans Wake:* Notebooks (16 volumes) and Part 8: *Finnegans Wake:* Draft, Typescripts and Proofs (20 volumes). Ed. David Hayman and Danis Rose.
Ulysses: A Critical and Synoptic Edition. Ed. Hans Walter Gabler. 3 vols. New York: Garland, 1984.

Secondary Sources

Books

Atherton, James S. *The Books at the Wake: A Study of Literary Allusions in James Joyce's* Finnegans Wake. London: Faber and Faber, 1959.
Bates, Ronald and Pollock, Harry J., ed. *Litters From Aloft.* Papers Delivered at the Second Canadian James Joyce Seminar, McMaster University. Tulsa Monograph Series, No. 13. Tulsa: University of Tulsa Press, 1971.
Beckett, Samuel, et al. *Our Exagmination Round his Factification for Incamination of Work in Progress.* London: Faber and Faber, 1929.
Begnal, Michael H. and Eckley, Grace. *Narrator and Character in* Finnegans Wake. Lewisburg, Pa.: Bucknell University Press, 1975.
Begnal, Michael H. and Senn, Fritz, ed. *A Conceptual Guide to* Finnegans Wake. University Park, Pa.: Pennsylvania State University Press, 1974.
Benstock, Bernard. *James Joyce: The Undiscover'd Country.* Dublin: Gill and MacMillan, 1977.

Bibliography

———. *Joyce-Again's Wake: An Analysis of* Finnegans Wake. Seattle: University of Washington Press, 1965.

———, ed. *Critical Essays on James Joyce.* Critical Essays on Modern British Literature Series. Boston: G.K. Hall, 1985.

———, ed. *The Seventh of Joyce.* Bloomington: Indiana University Press, 1982.

Benstock, Bernard and Bushrui, Suheil Badi, ed. *James Joyce: An International Perspective: Centenary Essays in Honour of the Late Sir Desmond Cochrane.* Irish Literary Studies 10. Gerrards Cross, Bucks.: Colin Symthe, 1982.

Boldereff, Francis M. *Hermes to His Son Thoth: Being Joyce's Use of Giordano Bruno in* Finnegans Wake. Woodward, Pa.: Classic Non-Fiction Library, 1968.

Bonheim, Helmut. *A Lexicon of the German in* Finnegans Wake. Berkeley: University of California Press, 1967.

Bowen, Zack and Carens, James F., eds. *A Companion to Joyce Studies.* Westport, Conn.: Greenwood Press, 1984.

Boyle, Robert, S. J. *James Joyce's Pauline Vision: A Catholic Exposition.* Carbondale: Southern Illinois University Press, 1978.

Campbell, Joseph and Robinson, Henry Morton. *A Skeleton Key to* Finnegans Wake. Compass Books ed. New York: Viking, 1961.

Cheng, Vincent John. *Shakespeare and Joyce: A Study of* Finnegans Wake. University Park: Pennsylvania State University Press, 1984.

Christiani, Dounia Bunis. *Scandinavian Elements of* Finnegans Wake. Evanston: Northwestern University Press, 1965.

Cope, Jackson I. *Joyce's Cities: Archaeologies of the Soul.* Baltimore, Md.: Johns Hopkins University Press, 1981.

Curtis, Edmund. *A History of Ireland.* London: Methuen, University Paperbacks, 1961.

Dalton, Jack P. and Hart, Clive, ed. *Twelve and a Tilly: Essays on the Occasion of the 25th Anniversary of* Finnegans Wake. London: Faber and Faber, 1966.

De Bhaldraithe, Tomas, ed. *English-Irish Dictionary.* Dublin: Stationery Office, 1959.

de Breffny, Brian, gen. ed. *Ireland: A Cultural Encyclopaedia.* New York: Facts On File Inc., 1983.

DiBernard, Barbara. *Alchemy and* Finnegans Wake. Albany: State University of New York Press, 1980.

Dinneen, Rev. Patrick S., ed. *An Irish-English Dictionary.* 2nd ed. Dublin: Educational Company of Ireland, 1927.

Eckley, Grace. *Children's Lore in* Finnegans Wake. Syracuse: Syracuse University Press, 1985.

Ellmann, Richard. *James Joyce.* 2nd ed. New York: Oxford University Press, 1982.

———. *Ulysses on the Liffey.* New York: Oxford University Press, 1972; rpt. with corrections, 1973.

Epstein, Edmund L., ed. *A Starchamber Quiry: A James Joyce Centennial Volume, 1882-1982.* London: Methuen, 1982.

Fitch, Noel Riley. *Sylvia Beach and the Lost Generation: A History of Literary Paris in the Twenties and Thirties.* New York: W. W. Norton, 1983.

Fowler, H. W. and Fowler, F. G., ed. *The Concise Oxford Dictionary of Current English.* 5th ed. Oxford: Oxford University Press, 1964.

Frank, Joseph. *The Widening Gyre: Crisis and Mastery in Modern Literature.* Bloomington: Indiana University Press, 1963.

French, Marilyn. *The Book as World: James Joyce's* Ulysses. Cambridge, Mass.: Harvard University Press, 1976.

Freud, Sigmund. *The Interpretation of Dreams.* Trans. A. A. Brill. New York: Carlton House, n.d.

Garvin, John. *James Joyce's Disunited Kingdom and the Irish Dimension.* Dublin: Gill and MacMillan, 1976.
Gilbert, Stuart. *James Joyce's* Ulysses: *A Study.* 1930. rpt. New York: Vintage Books, 1952.
Glasheen, Adaline. *Third Census of* Finnegans Wake: *An Index of the Characters and Their Roles.* Berkeley: University of California Press, 1977.
Goldberg, S. L. *The Classical Temper: A Study of James Joyce's* Ulysses. London: Chatto and Windus, 1961.
Goldman, Arnold. *The Joyce Paradox: Form and Freedom in His Fiction.* London: Routledge and Kegan Paul, 1966.
Goldsmith, Oliver. *Poems and Plays.* Intro. Austin Dobson. Everyman's Library, No. 415. London: J.M. Dent, 1910.
_____. *The Vicar of Wakefield: A Tale Supposed to Be Written by Himself.* Ed. Arthur Friedman. London: Oxford University Press, 1974.
Gordon, John. *Notes on Issy.* A Wake Newslitter Monograph No. 7. Colchester: A Wake Newslitter Press, 1982.
Groden, Michael. Ulysses *in Progress.* Princeton: Princeton University Press, 1977.
Hancock, Leslie. *Word Index to James Joyce's* Portrait of the Artist. Carbondale and Edwardsville: Southern Illinois University Press, 1967.
Hanley, Miles L. *Word Index to James Joyce's* Ulysses. Madison: University of Wisconsin Press, 1962.
Hart, Clive. *A Concordance to* Finnegans Wake. Corrected ed. Mamoroneck, N. Y.: Paul P. Appel, 1974.
_____. *Structure and Motif in* Finnegans Wake. Evanston: Northwestern University Press, 1962.
_____, ed. *James Joyce's* Dubliners: *Critical Essays.* London: Faber and Faber, 1969.
Hart, Clive and Hayman, David, ed. *James Joyce's* Ulysses. Berkeley: University of California Press, 1974.
Henke, Suzette. *Joyce's Moraculous Sindbook: A Study of* Ulysses. Columbus: Ohio State University Press, 1978.
Henke, Suzette and Unkeless, Elaine, ed. *Women in Joyce.* Urbana: University of Illinois Press, 1982.
Hodgart, Matthew J. C. and Worthington, Mabel P. *Song in the Works of James Joyce.* New York: Columbia University Press, 1959.
Hogan, Robert, editor-in-chief. *Dictionary of Irish Literature.* Westport, Conn.: Greenwood Press, 1979.
Kenner, Hugh. *A Colder Eye: The Modern Irish Writers.* New York: Alfred A. Knopf, 1983.
_____. *Dublin's Joyce.* Bloomington: Indiana University Press, 1966.
_____. *Joyce's Voices.* Berkeley: University of California Press, 1978.
_____. Ulysses. Unwin Critical Library Series. London: George Allen and Unwin, 1980.
Lane, Gary, ed. *A Word Index to James Joyce's* Dubliners. New York: Haskell House, 1972.
Levin, Harry. *James Joyce: A Critical Introduction.* 2nd ed. Norfolk, Conn.: New Directions Publications, 1960.
Litz, A. Walton. *Art of Jame Joyce: Method and Design in* Ulysses *and* Finnegans Wake. London: Oxford University Press, 1961.
_____. *James Joyce.* Twayne's English Authors. New York: Twayne, 1966.
Lyons, F. S. L. *Ireland since the Famine.* 2nd ed. N.P.: Collins/Fontana, 1973.
Magalaner, Marvin, ed. *A James Joyce Miscellany.* 2nd Series. Carbondale: Southern Illinois University Press, 1959.
Manganiello, Dominic. *Joyce's Politics.* London: Routledge and Kegan Paul, 1980.
MacCabe, Colin. *James Joyce and the Revolution of the Word.* London: MacMillan, 1979.

———, ed. *James Joyce: New Perspectives.* Sussex: Harvester Press; Bloomington: Indiana University Press, 1982.
McCarthy, Patrick A. *The Riddles of* Finnegans Wake. Cranbury, N.J.: Associated University Presses, 1980.
McCormack, W. J. and Stead, Alistair, ed. *James Joyce and Modern Literature.* London: Routledge and Kegan Paul, 1982.
McHugh, Roland. *Annotations to* Finnegans Wake. London: Routledge and Kegan Paul, 1980.
———. *The* Finnegans Wake *Experience.* Dublin: Irish Academic Press, 1981.
———. *The Sigla of* Finnegans Wake. Austin: University of Texas Press, 1976.
Mink, Louis O. *A* Finnegans Wake *Gazetteer.* Bloomington: Indiana University Press, 1978.
Noon, William T., S. J. *Joyce and Aquinas.* New Haven: Yale University Press, 1957.
Norris, Margot. *The Decentered Universe of* Finnegans Wake: *A Structuralist Analysis.* Baltimore: Johns Hopkins University Press, 1976.
O'Connor, Frank. *The Mirror in the Roadway.* New York: Alfred A. Knopf, 1956.
O'Hehir, Brendan. *A Gaelic Lexicon for* Finnegans Wake. Berkeley: University of California Press, 1967.
O'Hehir, Brendan and Dillon, John M. *A Classical Lexicon for* Finnegans Wake. Berkeley: University of California Press, 1977.
Peterson, Richard F., Cohn, Alan M. and Epstein, Edmund L., ed. *Work in Progress: Joyce Centenary Essays.* Carbondale and Edwardsville: Southern Illinois University Press, 1983.
Potts, Willard, ed. *Portraits of the Artist in Exile: Recollections of James Joyce by Europeans.* Seattle: University of Washington Press, 1979.
Power, Arthur. *Conversations with James Joyce.* Ed. Clive Hart. London: Millington, 1974.
Riquelme, John Paul. *Teller and Tale in Joyce's Fiction: Oscillating Perspectives.* Baltimore: Johns Hopkins University Press, 1983.
Rose, Danis and O'Hanlon, John. *Understanding* Finnegans Wake: *A Guide to the Narrative of James Joyce's Masterpiece.* New York: Garland, 1982.
Scott, Bonny Kime. *Joyce and Feminism.* Bloomington: Indiana University Press, 1984.
Senn, Fritz, ed. *New Light on Joyce from the Dublin Symposium.* Bloomington: Indiana University Press, 1972.
Solomon, Margaret C. *Eternal Geomater: The Sexual Universe of* Finnegans Wake. Carbondale and Edwardsville: Southern Illinois University Press, 1969.
Staley, Thomas F., ed. *James Joyce Today: Essays on the Major Works.* Bloomington: Indiana University Press, 1966.
Staley, Thomas F. and Benstock, Bernard, ed. *Approaches to Joyce's* Portrait: *Ten Essays.* N.P.: University of Pittsburgh Press, 1976.
Tindall, William York. *The Literary Symbol.* New York: Columbia University Press, 1955.
———. *A Reader's Guide to* Finnegans Wake. New York: Farrar, Straus and Giroux, 1969.
———. *A Reader's Guide to James Joyce.* New York: Farrar, Straus and Giroux, 1959.
Tommola, Jorma and Virtanen, Tuija, ed. *Working Papers in English Studies, No. 6.* Turku, Finland: Department of English, University of Turku, 1985.
White, David A. *The Grand Continuum: Reflections on Joyce and Metaphysics.* Pittsburgh: University of Pittsburgh Press, 1983.
Wright, David G. *Characters of Joyce.* Totowa, N.J.: Barnes and Noble, 1983.
Yeats, W. B. *The Collected Poems.* London: Macmillan, 1955.

Articles

Anghinetti, Paul. "Berkeley's Influence on Joyce." *James Joyce Quarterly,* 19, No. 3 (Spring 1982), pp. 315–29.
Atherton, James S. "The Identity of the Sleeper." *A Wake Newslitter,* NS 4, No. 5 (October 1967), pp. 83–85.

Aubert, Jacques. "Notes on the French Element in *Finnegans Wake.*" *James Joyce Quarterly*, 5, No. 2 (Winter 1968), pp. 110–24.

Bates, Ronald. "The Feast is a Flyday." *James Joyce Quarterly*, 2, No. 3 (Spring 1965), pp. 174–87.

Beebe, Maurice. "*Ulysses* and the Age of Modernism." *James Joyce Quarterly* 10, No. 1 (Fall 1972), pp. 172–88.

Begnal, Michael H. "The Fables of *Finnegans Wake.*" *James Joyce Quarterly*, 6, No. 4 (Summer 1969), pp. 357–67.

———. "The Language of *Finnegans Wake.*" In *A Companion to Joyce Studies*. Ed. Zack Bowen and James F. Carens. Westport, Conn.: Greenwood Press, 1984, pp. 633–46.

———. "The Mourners at the *Wake*: The Family and Friends of HCE." *Western Humanities Review*, 24, No. 4 (Autumn 1970), pp. 383–93.

———. "The Narrator of *Finnegans Wake.*" *Eire/Ireland*, 4, No. 3 (Autumn 1969), pp. 38–49.

———. "The Prankquean in *Finnegans Wake.*" *James Joyce Quarterly*, 1, No. 3 (Spring 1964), pp. 14–18.

———. "Who Speaks When I Dream? Who Dreams When I Speak? A Narrational Approach to *Finnegans Wake.*" In *Litters From Aloft*. Papers delivered at the Second Canadian James Joyce Seminar, McMaster University. Tulsa Monograph Series, No. 13, Tulsa: Tulsa University Press, 1971, pp. 74–90.

Beja, Morris. "Dividual Chaoses: Case Histories of Multiple Personality and *Finnegans Wake.*" *James Joyce Quarterly*, 14, No. 3 (Spring 1977), pp. 241–50.

———. "The Joyce of Sex: Sexual Relationships in *Ulysses.*" In *The Seventh of Joyce*. Ed. Bernard Benstock. Bloomington: Indiana University Press, 1982, pp. 255–66.

———. "The Wooden Sword: Threatener and Threatened in the Fiction of James Joyce." *James Joyce Quarterly*, 2, No. 1 (Fall 1964), pp. 33–41.

Bekker, Pieter. "Reading *Finnegans Wake.*" In *James Joyce and Modern Literature*. Ed. W. J. McCormack and Alistair Stead. London: Routledge and Kegan Paul, 1982, pp. 185–201.

Benstock, Bernard. "Arabesques: Third Position of Concord." *James Joyce Quarterly*, 5, No. 1 (Fall 1967), pp. 30–39.

———. "A Covey of Clerics in Joyce and O'Casey." *James Joyce Quarterly*, 2, No. 1 (Fall 1964), pp. 18–32.

———. "James Joyce and the Women of the Western World." In *Litters From Aloft*. Papers delivered at the Second Canadian James Joyce Seminar, McMaster University. Tulsa Monograph Series No. 13. Tulsa: Tulsa University Press, 1971, pp. 91–108.

———. "A Light from Some Other World: Symbolic Structure in *A Portrait of the Artist.*" In *Approaches to Joyce's* Portrait: *Ten Essays*. Ed. Thomas F. Staley and Bernard Benstock. N.P.: University of Pittsburgh Press, 1976, pp. 185–212.

———. "L. Boom as Dreamer in *Finnegans Wake.*" *PMLA*, 82, No. 1 (March 1967), pp. 91–97.

———. "The Quiddity of Shem and the Whatness of Shaun." *James Joyce Quarterly*, 1, No. 1 (Fall 1963), pp. 26–33.

———. "'The Sisters' and the Critics." *James Joyce Quarterly*, 4, No. 1 (Fall 1966), pp. 32–35.

———. "The State of the *Wake.*" *James Joyce Quarterly*, 14, No. 3 (Spring 1977), pp. 237–40.

———. "*Ulysses* Without Dublin." *James Joyce Quarterly*, 10, No. 1 (Fall 1972), pp. 118–31.

Benstock, Shari Bernard. "The Genuine Christine: Psychodynamics of Issy." In *Women in Joyce*. Ed. Suzette Henke and Elaine Unkeless. Urbana: University of Illinois Press, 1982, pp. 169–96.

———. "Nightletters: Woman's Writing in the *Wake.*" In *Critical Essays on James Joyce*. Ed. Bernard Benstock. Boston: G. K. Hall, 1985, pp. 221–23.

———. "The Printed Letters in *Ulysses.*" *James Joyce Quarterly*, 19, No. 4 (Summer 1982), pp. 415–27.

———. "Sexuality and Survival in *Finnegans Wake.*" In *The Seventh of Joyce*. Ed. Bernard Benstock. Bloomington: Indiana University Press, 1982, pp. 247–54.

Benstock, Shari and Benstock, Bernard. "The Benstock Principle." In *The Seventh of Joyce*. Ed. Bernard Benstock. Bloomington: Indiana University Press, 1982, pp. 10–21.
_____. "The Joycean Method of Cataloguing." *James Joyce Quarterly*, 17, No. 1 (Fall 1979), pp. 49–60.
_____. "*Ulysses*: Narrative Movement and Place." In *Work in Progress: Joyce Centenary Essays*. Ed. Richard F. Peterson, et al. Carbondale and Edwardsville: Southern Illinois University Press, 1983, pp. 30–46.
Bierman, Robert. "Structural Elements in 'The Dead.'" *James Joyce Quarterly*, 4, No. 1 (Fall 1966), pp. 42–45.
Boone, Joseph Allen. "A New Approach to Bloom as 'Womanly Man': The Mixed Middling's Progress in *Ulysses*." *James Joyce Quarterly*, 20, No. 1 (Fall 1982), pp. 67–85.
Bowen, Zack R. "Epiphanies, Stephen's Diary, and the Narrative Perspective of *A Portrait of the Artist as a Young Man*." *James Joyce Quarterly*, 16, No. 4 (Summer 1979), pp. 485–88.
Boyle, Robert S. J. "A Miracle in Black Ink: A Glance at Joyce's Use of the Eucharistic Image." *James Joyce Quarterly*, 10, No. 1 (Fall 1972), pp. 147–60.
_____. "'Two Gallants' and 'Ivy Day in the Committee Room.'" *James Joyce Quarterly*, 1, No. 1 (Fall 1963), pp. 3–9.
Brandabur, Edward. "'The Sisters.'" In *Dubliners*. Viking Critical Library ed. New York: Viking, 1969, pp. 333–43.
Brivic, Sheldon. "The Father in Joyce." In *The Seventh of Joyce*. Ed. Bernard Benstock. Bloomington: Indiana University Press, 1982, pp. 74–80.
_____. "Joycean Psychology." In *Work in Progress: Joyce Centenary Essays*. Ed. Richard F. Peterson et al. Carbondale and Edwardsville: Southern Illinois University Press, 1983, pp. 106–16.
Burrell, Harry. "The Prankquean Riddle." *A Wake Newslitter*, NS 13, No. 4 (August 1976), pp. 66–68.
_____. "The Illustrator in the *Wake*: Aubrey Beardsley." *A Wake Newslitter*, NS 17, No. 6 (December 1980), pp. 95–98.
Byrd, Don. "Joyce's Epiphanies." *The Sewanee Review* (Summer 1946); rpt. *A Portrait of the Artist as a Young Man*. Viking Critical Library ed. New York: Viking, 1968, pp. 358–70.
Card, James Van Dyck. "Roses and Camellias, White and Red." *James Joyce Quarterly*, 23, No. 1 (Fall 1985), pp. 82–83.
_____. "The Ups and Downs, Ins and Outs of Molly Bloom: Patterns of Words in 'Penelope.'" *James Joyce Quarterly*, 19, No. 2 (Winter 1982), pp. 127–39.
Carens, James F. "*A Portrait of the Artist as a Young Man*." In *A Companion to Joyce Studies*. Ed. Zack Bowen and James F. Carens, Westport, Conn.: Greenwood Press, 1984, pp. 255–359.
Coleman, Elliott. "Heliotropical Noughttime: Light and Color in *Finnegans Wake*." *Texas Quarterly*, 4, No. 4 (Winter 1961), pp. 162–77.
Collins, Ben L. "Joyce's 'Araby' and the 'Extended Simile.'" *James Joyce Quarterly*, 4, No. 2 (Winter 1967), pp. 84–90.
Corrington, John William. "Isolation as Motif in 'A Painful Case.'" *James Joyce Quarterly*, 3, No. 3 (Spring 1966), pp. 182–91.
Cumpiano, Marion W. "The Flowerpot on the Pole: A Motif Approach to *Finnegans Wake*." *James Joyce Quarterly*, 21, No. 1 (Fall 1983), pp. 61–68.
_____. "The Salmon and Its Leaps in *Finnegans Wake*." *James Joyce Quarterly*, 14, No. 3 (Spring 1977), pp. 255–73.
Cunningham, Frank R. "Joyce's 'Grace': Gracelessness in a Lost Paradise." *James Joyce Quarterly*, 6, No. 3 (Spring 1969), pp. 219–23.
Dalton, Jack P. "Habemus Dominationis" [sic]. *James Joyce Quarterly*, 1, No. 2 (Winter 1964), pp. 10–14.

Deane, Shamus. "Joyce and Nationalism." In *James Joyce: New Perspectives*. Ed. Colin MacCabe. Sussex: Harvester Press; Bloomington: Indiana University Press, 1982, pp. 168–83.
Devlin, Kimberley. "Self and Other in *Finnegans Wake*: A Framework for Analyzing Versions of Shem and Shaun." *James Joyce Quarterly*, 21, No. 1 (Fall 1983), pp. 31–50.
DiBernard, Barbara. "Technique in *Finnegans Wake*." In *A Companion to Joyce Studies*. Ed. Zack Bowen and James F. Carens. Westport, Conn.: Greenwood Press, 1984, pp. 647–85.
Dick, Susan. "Tom Kernan and the Retrospective Arrangement." *James Joyce Quarterly*, 18, No. 2 (Winter 1981), pp. 147–59.
Dohmen, William F. "'Chilly Spaces': Wyndham Lewis as Ondt." *James Joyce Quarterly*, 11, No. 4 (Summer 1974), pp. 368–86.
Duncan, Edward. "James Joyce and the Primitive Celtic Church." *Alphabet*, No. 7 (December 1963), pp. 17–38.
Easson, Angus. "Parody as Comment in James Joyce's 'Clay.'" *James Joyce Quarterly*, 7, No. 2 (Winter 1970), pp. 75–81.
Eckley, Grace. "Looking Forward to a Brightening Day." In *A Conceptual Guide to* Finnegans Wake. Ed. Michael H. Begnal and Fritz Senn. University Park: Pennsylvania State University Press, 1974, pp. 211–36.
———. "The Wellington Career in *Finnegans Wake*." *Eire/Ireland*, 12, No. 3 (Fomhar, 1977), pp. 23–40.
Epstein, Edmund L. "Chance, Doubt, Coincidence and the Prankquean Riddle." *A Wake Newslitter*, NS 6, No. 1 (February 1969), pp. 3–7.
———. "Hidden Imagery in James Joyce's 'Two Gallants.'" *James Joyce Quarterly*, 7, No. 4 (Summer 1970), pp. 369–70.
———. "James Joyce and the Body." In *A Starchamber Quiry: A James Joyce Centennial Volume, 1882–1982*. Ed. E. L. Epstein. London: Methuen, 1982, pp. 73–106.
———. "James Joyce and Language." In *Work in Progress: Joyce Centenary Essays*. Ed. Richard F. Peterson et al. Carbondale and Edwardsville: Southern Illinois University Press, 1983, pp. 58–69.
———. "Joyce and Judaism." In *The Seventh of Joyce*. Ed. Bernard Benstock. Bloomington: Indiana University Press, 1982, pp. 221–24.
Fargnoli, A. Nicholas. "A-taufing in the *Wake*: Joyce's Baptismal Motif." *James Joyce Quarterly*, 20, No. 3 (Spring 1983), pp. 298–305.
Feeley, John. "Joyce's 'The Dead' and the Browning Quotation." *James Joyce Quarterly*, 20, No. 1 (Fall 1982), pp. 87–96.
Ferrer, Daniel. "The Freudful Couchmare of Λd: Joyce's Notes on Freud and the Composition of Chapter XVI of *Finnegans Wake*." *James Joyce Quarterly*, 22, No. 4 (Summer 1985), pp. 367–82.
Feshbach, Sidney. "Death in 'An Encounter.'" James Joyce Quarterly, 2, No. 2 (Winter 1965), pp. 82–89.
———. "'Fallen on His Feet in Buenos Ayres' (*D* 39): Frank in 'Eveline.'" *James Joyce Quarterly*, 20, No. 2 (Winter 1983), pp. 223–27.
———. "A Slow and Dark Birth: A Study of the Organization of *A Portrait of the Artist as a Young Man*." *James Joyce Quarterly*, 4, No. 4 (Summer 1967), pp. 289–300.
Fischer, Therese. "From Reliable to Unreliable Narrator: Rhetorical Changes in Joyce's 'The Sisters.'" *James Joyce Quarterly*, 9, No. 1 (Fall 1971), pp. 85–92.
Ford, Jane. "James Joyce and Those (K)nights of 'Ruful Continence.'" In *The Seventh of Joyce*. Ed. Bernard Benstock. Bloomington: Indiana University Press, 1982, pp. 242–46.
Fredkin, Grace. "S in *Finnegans Wake*." *James Joyce Quarterly*, 23, No. 2 (Winter 1986), pp. 189–99.
Freimarck, John. "'Araby': A Quest for Meaning." *James Joyce Quarterly*, 7, No. 4 (Summer 1970), pp. 366–68.

French, Marilyn. "Joyce and Language." *James Joyce Quarterly*, 19, No. 3 (Spring 1982), pp. 239-55.

Fuger, Wilhelm. "'Episthemadethemology' (*Finnegans Wake* 374.17): ALP's Letter and the Tradition of Interpolated Letters." *James Joyce Quarterly*, 19, No. 4 (Summer 1982), pp. 405-13.

———. "More on Doves and Draves (363.07)." *A Wake Newslitter*, NS 15, No. 3 (June 1978), pp. 44-47.

———. "Ravens and Doves." *A Wake Newslitter*, NS 14, No. 6 (December 1977), pp. 91-95.

Glasheen, Adaline. "The Opening Paragraphs." *A Wake Newslitter*, NS 2, No. 2 (April 1965), pp. 3-8.

———. "The Opening Paragraphs (contd.)." *A Wake Newslitter*, NS 2, No. 3 (June 1965), pp. 21-25.

———. "The Opening Paragraphs (contd.)." *A Wake Newslitter*, NS 2, No. 4 (August 1965), pp. 24-27.

———. "The Opening Paragraphs (contd.)." *A Wake Newslitter*, NS 2, No. 6 (December 1965), pp. 17-22.

———. "The Opening Paragraphs (concluded)." *A Wake Newslitter*, NS 3, No. 1 (February 1966), pp. 6-14.

Golden, Sean. "Parsing Rhetorics: The Cad as Prolegomena to the Readings of *Finnegans Wake*." In *The Seventh of Joyce*. Ed. Bernard Benstock. Bloomington: Indiana University Press, 1982, pp. 173-77.

Gordon, John. "The Secret of Boylan's Bottom Drawer." *James Joyce Quarterly*, 18, No. 4 (Summer 1981), pp. 450-58.

Grayson, Thomas W. "James Joyce and Stephen Dedalus: The Theory of Aesthetics." *James Joyce Quarterly*, 4, No. 4 (Summer 1967), pp. 310-19.

Halper, Nathan. "The Narrative Thread in the Cad Episode." In *The Seventh of Joyce*. Ed. Bernard Benstock. Bloomington: Indiana University Press, 1982, pp. 171-72.

———. "Of the Stuttering Hand." *A Wake Newslitter*, NS 12, Oo. 1 (February 1985), pp. 7-9.

Hampson, R. G. "Joyce's Bed-Trick: A Note on Indeterminacy in *Ulysses*." *James Joyce Quarterly*, 17, No. 4 (Summer 1980), pp. 445-48.

Handwerk, Gary. "What Really Goes before the Fall? Narrative Dynamics in *Finnegans Wake* III. 4." *James Joyce Quarterly*, 20, No. 3 (Spring 1983), pp. 307-84.

Hayman, David. "Farcical Themes and Forms in *Finnegans Wake*." *James Joyce Quarterly*, 11, No. 4 (Summer 1974), pp. 323-42.

Henke, Suzette. "Gerty MacDowell: Joyce's Sentimental Heroine." In *Women in Joyce*. Ed. Suzette Henke and Elaine Unkeless. Urbana: University of Illinois Press, 1982, pp. 132-49.

———. "James Joyce and Women: The Matriarchal Muse." In *Work in Progress: Joyce Centenary Essays*. Ed. Richard F. Peterson et al. Carbondale and Edwardsville: Southern Illinois University Press, 1983, pp. 117-31.

———. "Stephen Dedalus and Women: A Portrait of the Artist as a Young Misogynist." In *Women in Joyce*. Ed. Suzette Henke and Elaine Unkeless. Urbana: University of Illinois Press, 1982, pp. 82-107.

Henseler, Donna L. "'Harpsdichord,' The Formal Principle of HCE, ALP and the Cad." *James Joyce Quarterly*, 4, No. 1 (Fall 1968), pp. 53-68.

Kain, Richard M. "The Significance of Stephen's Meeting Bloom." *James Joyce Quarterly*, 10, No. 1 (Fall 1972), pp. 146-60.

Kenner, Hugh. "The Cubist *Portrait*." In *Approaches to Joyce's* Portrait: *Ten Essays*. Ed. Thomas F. Staley and Bernard Benstock. N.P.: University of Pittsburgh Press, 1976, pp. 171-84.

Kiberd, Declan. "The Vulgarity of Heroics: Joyce's *Ulysses*." In *James Joyce: An International Perspective: Centenary Essays in Honour of the Late Sir Desmond Cochrane*. Irish Literary Studies 10. Ed. Bernard Benstock and Suheil Bushrui. Gerrards Cross, Bucks.: Colin Smythe, 1982, pp. 156–68.

Kimball, Jean. "Family Romance and Hero Myth: A Psychoanalytic Context for the Paternity Theme in *Ulysses*." *James Joyce Quarterly*, 20, No. 2 (Winter 1983), pp. 161–73.

———. "Freud, Leonardo and Joyce: The Dimensions of a Childhood Memory." In *The Seventh of Joyce*. Ed. Bernard Benstock. Bloomington: Indiana University Press, 1982, pp. 57–80.

Knuth, Leo. "A Bathymetric Reading of Joyce's *Ulysses*, Chapter X." *James Joyce Quarterly*, 9, No. 4 (Summer 1972), pp. 405–22.

———. "*Finnegans Wake*: A Product of the Twenties." *James Joyce Quarterly*, 11, No. 4 (Summer 1974), pp. 323–42.

———. "Shem's Riddle of the Universe." *A Wake Newslitter*, NS 9, No. 5 (October 1972), pp. 79–89.

Kopper, Edward A., Jr. "Bloom and Earwicker: The Comic Pilgrims." *Modern British Literature*, 1, No. 1 (1976), pp. 84–88.

———. "Notes on Grace O'Malley and the *Wake*." *James Joyce Quarterly*, 5, No. 1 (Fall 1967), pp. 68–70.

Lachtman, Howard. "The Magic-Lattern Business: James Joyce's Ecclesiastical Satire in *Dubliners*." *James Joyce Quarterly*, 7, No. 2 (Winter 1970), pp. 82–92.

Lanser, Susan Sniader. "Stephen's Diary: The Hero Unveiled." *James Joyce Quarterly*, 16, No. 4 (Summer 1969), pp.417–23.

Lernout, Geert. "Dutch in *Finnegans Wake*." *James Joyce Quarterly*, 23, No. 1 (Fall 1985), pp. 45–66.

Levin, Lawrence L. "The Sirens Episode as Music: Joyce's Experiment in Prose Polyphony." *James Joyce Quarterly*, 3, No. 1 (Fall 1965), pp. 12–24.

Levine, Jennifer. "Rejoycings in *Tel Quel*." *James Joyce Quarterly*, 16, Nos. 1–2 (Fall 1978 - Winter 1979), pp. 17–216.

Levitt, Morton P. "A Hero for Our Time: Leopold Bloom and the Myth of *Ulysses*." *James Joyce Quarterly*, 10, No. 1 (Fall 1972), pp. 132–46.

———. "Shalt be Accurst? The Martyr in James Joyce." *James Joyce Quarterly*, 5, No. 4 (Summer 1968), pp. 285–96.

Litz, A. Walton. "'Two Gallants.'" In *James Joyce's* Dubliners: *Critical Essays*. Ed. Clive Hart. London: Faber and Faber, 1969. Rpt. Viking Critical Library *Dubliners*. New York: Viking, 1969, pp. 368–78.

MacArthur, Ian. "Sexuality in *Finnegans Wake*." *A Wake Newslitter*, NS 15, No. 1 (February 1978), pp. 3–16.

———. "Structure and Motif in Jaun." *A Wake Newslitter*, NS 15, No. 5 (October 1978), pp. 76–77.

MacKillop, James. "'Beurla on It': Yeats, Joyce and the Irish Language." *Eire/Ireland*, 15, No. 1 (Spring 1980), pp. 138–48.

Matthews, F.X. "Festy King in *Finnegans Wake*." *James Joyce Quarterly*, 6, No. 2 (Winter 1968), pp. 154–57.

McCarthy, Patrick A. "Our Wee Free State: *Finnegans Wake* and Irish Independence." *Modern British Literature*, 2, No. 1 (Spring 1977), pp. 75–80.

———. "The Structures and Meanings of *Finnegans Wake*." In *A Companion to Joyce Studies*. Ed. Zack Bowen and James F. Carens. Westport, Conn.: Greenwood Press, 1984, pp. 559–632.

———. "'A Warping Process': Reading *Finnegans Wake*." In *Work in Progress: Joyce Centenary Essays*. Ed. Richard F. Peterson et al. Carbondale and Edwardsville: Southern Illinois University Press, 1983, pp. 47–57.

McCormack, W.J. "Nightmares of History: James Joyce and the Phenomenon of Anglo-Irish Literature." In *James Joyce and Modern Literature*. Ed. W. J. McCormack and Alistair Stead. London: Routledge and Kegan Paul, 1982, pp. 185–201.

McHugh, Roland. "Drawers." *A Wake Newslitter*, NS, Occasional Papers, No. 7 (March 1983), p. 5.

———. "Rainbows." *A Wake Newslitter*, NS 15, No. 5 (October 1978), pp. 76–77.

Mitchell, Breon. "*A Portrait* and the *Bildungsroman* Tradition." In *Approaches to Joyce's Portrait: Ten Essays*. Ed. Thomas F. Staley and Bernard Benstock. N.P.: University of Pittsburgh Press, 1976, pp. 61–76.

Morley, Patricia A. "Fish Symbolism in Chapter Seven of *Finnegans Wake:* The Hidden Defense of Shem the Penman." *James Joyce Quarterly*, 6, No. 3 (Spring 1969), pp. 267–70.

Morse, J. Mitchell. "Burrus, Caseous and Nicholas of Cusa." *Modern Language Notes*, 75, No. 4 (April 1960), pp. 326–34.

———. "Phoenicians and Phoenixes." *A Wake Newslitter*, NS 14, No. 6 (December 1977), p. 100.

Naremore, James. "Consciousness and Society in *A Portrait of the Artist*. In *Approaches to Joyce's Portrait: Ten Essays*. Ed. Thomas F. Staley and Bernard Benstock. N.P.: University of Pittsburgh Press, 1976, pp. 113–34.

———. "Style As Meaning in *A Portrait of the Artist*." *James Joyce Quarterly*, 4, No. 4 (Summer 1967), pp. 331–42.

Nilsen, Kenneth. "Down Among the Dead: Elements of Irish Language and Mythology in James Joyce's *Dubliners*." *Canadian Journal of Irish Studies*, 12, No. 1 (June 1986), pp. 23–34.

Norris, Margot. "Anna Livia Plurabelle: The Dream Woman." In *Women in Joyce*. Ed. Suzette Henke and Elaine Unkeless. Urbana: University of Illinois Press, 1982, pp. 197–213.

O'Brien, Darcy. "Some Psychological Determinants of Joyce's View of Love and Sex." In *New Light on Joyce from the Dublin Symposium*. Ed. Fritz Senn. Bloomington: Indiana University Press, 1972, pp. 15–27.

———. "The Twins That Tick Homo Vulgaris: A Study of Shem and Shaun." *Modern Fiction Studies*, 12, No. 1 (Summer 1966), pp. 183–99.

O'Connor, Frank. "Joyce and Dissociated Metaphor." From his *The Mirror in the Roadway*. Alfred A. Knopf, 1955. Rpt. in Viking Critical Library *A Portrait of the Artist as a Young Man*. Ed. Chester G. Anderson. New York: Viking, 1968, pp. 371–77.

O'Dwyer, Riana. "Ireland's long vicefreegal existence': A Context for *Finnegans Wake* 34–36." In *The Seventh of Joyce*. Ed. Bernard Benstock. Bloomington: Indiana University Press, 1982, pp. 178–81.

O'Hehir, Brendan. "Anna Livia Plurabelle's Gaelic Ancestry." *James Joyce Quarterly*, 2, No. 3 (Spring 1965), pp. 158–66.

O'Shea, Michael J. "Catholic Liturgy in Joyce's *Ulysses*." *James Joyce Quarterly*, 21, No. 2 (Winter 1984), pp. 123–35.

Peltonen, Kristiina. "Colours and Colour Symbolism in James Joyce's *Dubliners*, *A Portrait of the Artist as a Young Man* and *Ulysses*. In *Working Papers in English Studies*, No. 6. Ed. Jorma Tommola and Tuija Vertanen. Turku Finland: Department of English, University of Turku, 1985, pp. 107–18.

Peterson, Richard F. "Stephen and the Narrative of *A Portrait of the Artist as a Young Man*." In *Work in Progress: Joyce Centenary Essays*. Ed. Richard F. Peterson, et al. Carbondale and Edwardsville: Southern Illinois University Press, 1983, pp. 15–29.

Putz, Manfred. "The Identity of the Reader in *Finnegans Wake*." *James Joyce Quarterly*, 11, No. 4 (Summer 1974), pp. 387–93.

Ranald, Margaret Loftus. "Stephen Dedalus' Vocation and The Irony of Religious Ritual." *James Joyce Quarterly*, 2, No. 2 (Winter 1965), pp. 97–102.

Raynaud, Claudine. "Woman, the Letter Writer; Man, the Writing Master." *James Joyce Quarterly*, 23, No. 3 (Spring 1986), pp. 299-324.

Restuccia, Frances L. "Not Foreknowledge, Simply Knowledge: Secular Typology in *Ulysses*." *James Joyce Quarterly*, 20, No. 4 (Summer 1983), pp. 429-42.

Richards, Thomas Karr. "Provisional Fixity in James Joyce's 'Proteus.'" *James Joyce Quarterly*, 20, No. 4 (Summer 1983), pp. 385-98.

Ridgeway, Ann. "Two Authors in Search of a Reader." *James Joyce Quarterly*, 1, No. 4 (Summer 1964), pp. 41-51.

Riquelme, John Paul. "Enjoying Invisibility: The Myth of Joyce's Impersonal Narrator." In *The Seventh of Joyce*. Ed. Bernard Benstock. Bloomington: Indiana University Press, 1982, pp. 22-24.

Robinson, Marian. "Woman Will Water the Wild World Over." *A Wake Newslitter*, NS 15, No. 2 (April 1978), pp. 19-23.

Russell, Stanley C. "A Baedeker to Bloom." *James Joyce Quarterly*, 3, No. 4 (Summer 1966), pp. 226-35.

Saldivar, Ramon. "Bloom's Metaphors and the Language of Flowers." *James Joyce Quarterly*, 20, No. 4 (Summer 1983), pp. 399-420.

Schneidau, Herbert. "One Eye and Two Levels: On Joyce's 'Cyclops.'" *James Joyce Quarterly*, 16, Nos. 1-2 (Fall 1978 - Winter 1979), pp. 95-103.

Scholes, Robert. "'Counterparts' and the Method of *Dubliners*." In *James Joyce's* Dubliners: *Critical Essays*. Ed. Clive Hart. London: Faber and Faber, 1969. Rpt. in Viking Critical Library *Dubliners*. New York: Viking, 1969, pp. 379-87.

_____. "Stephen Dedalus, Poet or Esthete?" *PMLA*, 89 (Sept. 1964), pp. 484-89. Rpt. in Viking Critical Library *A Portrait of the Artist as a Young Man*. Ed. Chester G. Anderson. New York: Viking, 1968, pp. 468-80.

_____. "*Ulysses*: A Structuralist Perspective." *James Joyce Quarterly*, 10, No. 1 (Fall 1972), pp. 161-71.

Schwab, Gabriele. "Mollyloquy." In *The Seventh of Joyce*. Ed. Bernard Benstock. Bloomington: Indiana University Press, 1982, pp. 81-85.

Senn, Fritz. "Book of Many Turns." *James Joyce Quarterly*, 10, No. 1 (Fall 1972), pp. 29-46.

_____. "Dogmad or Doubliboused?" *James Joyce Quarterly*, 17, No. 3 (Spring 1980), pp. 237-61.

_____. "Weaving, Unweaving." In *A Starchamber Quiry: A James Joyce Centennial Volume, 1882-1982*. Ed. E. L. Epstein. London: Methuen, 1982, pp. 45-70.

Sharpless, F. Parvin. "Irony in Joyce's *Portrait:* The Stasis of Pity." *James Joyce Quarterly*, 4, No. 4 (Summer 1967), pp. 320-30.

Sidwell, M.J. "A Daintical Pair of Accomplasses: Joyce and Yeats." In *Litters from Aloft*. Papers delivered at the Second Canadian James Joyce Seminar, McMaster University. Ed. Ronald Bates and Harry J. Pollock. Tulsa Monograph Series No. 13. Tulsa: University of Tulsa Press, 1971, p. 15-25.

Smith, Thomas F. "Colour and Light in 'The Dead.'" *James Joyce Quarterly*, 2, No. 4 (Summer 1965), pp. 304-7.

Sosnoski, James J. "Reading Acts and Reading Warrants: Some Implications for Readers Responding to Joyce's Portrait of Stephen." *James Joyce Quarterly*, 16, Nos. 1-2 (Fall 1978 - Winter 1979), pp. 43-63.

Splitter, Randolph. "The Sane and Joyful Spirit." *James Joyce Quarterly*, 13, No. 3 (Spring 1976), pp. 350-65.

Staley, Thomas F. "Strings in the Labyrinth: Sixty Years with Joyce's *Portrait*." In *Approaches to Joyce's* Portrait: *Ten Essays*. Ed. Thomas F. Staley and Bernard Benstock. N.P.: University of Pittsburgh Press, 1976, pp. 3-23.

Steinberg, Erwin R. "The Bird-Girl in *A Portrait* as Synthesis: The Sacred Assimilated to the Profane." *James Joyce Quarterly*, 17, No. 2 (Winter 1980), pp. 149-63.

Stern, Frederick C. "Pyrrhus, Fenians and Bloom." *James Joyce Quarterly*, 5, No. 3 (Spring 1968), pp. 211-28.

Stone, Harry. "'Araby' and the Writings of James Joyce." *Antioch Review*, (Fall 1965). Rpt. in Viking Critical Library *Dubliners*. Ed. Robert Scholes and A. Walton Litz. New York: Viking, 1969, pp. 344-67.

Swartzlanden, Susan. "Multiple Meaning and Misunderstanding: The Mistrial of Festy King." *James Joyce Quarterly*, 23, No. 4 (Summer 1986), pp. 465-76.

Thomas, Brook. "The Artistic Touch of the Hidden Hand." *James Joyce Quarterly*, 15, No. 1 (Fall 1977), pp. 36-42.

———. "Formal Re-creation: Re-reading and Re-joycing the Re-rightings of *Ulysses*." In *The Seventh of Joyce*. Ed. Bernard Benstock. Bloomington: Indiana University Press, 1982, pp. 5-9.

———. "Not a Reading *of*, but the Act of Reading *Ulysses*." *James Joyce Quarterly*, 16, Nos. 1-2 (Fall 1978 - Winter 1979), pp. 81-93.

Tindall, William York. "The Literary Symbol." From his *The Literary Symbol*. New York: Columbia University Press, 1955. Rpt. in Viking Critical Library *A Portrait of the Artist as a Young Man*. Ed. Chester G. Anderson. New York: Viking, 1968, pp. 378-87.

Tymoczko, Maria. "Symbolic Structures in *Ulysses* from Early Irish Literature." *James Joyce Quarterly*, 21, No. 3 (Spring 1984), pp. 215-30.

Unkeless, Elaine. "The Conventional Molly Bloom." In *Women in Joyce*. Ed. Suzette Henke and Elaine Unkeless. Urbana: University of Illinois Press, 1982, pp. 150-68.

Wallace, James D. "Noodynaady's Actual Ingrate Tootle." *James Joyce Quarterly*, 14, No. 3 (Spring 1977), pp. 290-99.

Walton, Franklin. "Wilde at the *Wake*." *James Joyce Quarterly*, 14, No. 3 (Spring 1977), pp. 300-312.

Walzl, Florence L. "*Dubliners*: Women in Irish Society." In *Women in Joyce*. Ed. Suzette Henke and Elaine Unkeless. Urbana: University of Illinois Press, 1982, pp. 31-56.

———. "Gabriel and Michael: The Conclusion of 'The Dead.'" *James Joyce Quarterly*, 4, No. 1 (Fall 1966), pp. 17-31.

———. "Symbolism in Joyce's 'Two Gallants.'" *James Joyce Quarterly*, 2, No. 2 (Winter 1965), pp. 73-81.

Weir, Lorraine. "The Choreography of Gesture: Marcel Jousse and *Finnegans Wake*." *James Joyce Quarterly*, 14, No. 3 (Spring 1977), pp. 315-25.

White, Patrick. "The Key in *Ulysses*." *James Joyce Quarterly*, 9, No. 1 (Fall 1971), pp. 10-25.

Wigginston, B. Eliot. "*Dubliners* in Order." *James Joyce Quarterly*, 7, No. 4 (Summer 1970), pp. 297-314.

Index

Ambiguity, 3, 4, 5, 9, 10, 46, 50–51, 58–59, 63, 93–94, 95, 103, 110; beginning/ending, 10, 95, 104; black/white, 69–70; chameleon, 89; dark/black, 11, 14, 23, 110; dove/raven, 94, 95, 123, 162, 171; dream/reality, 98, 105, 109–10, 115, 118, 168, 176; Dublin, Ire./Dublin, Ga., 60, 88, 89, 122; greys, 16–17; heroine in *Finnegans Wake*, 163; illustrated by color patterns, 23, 109; life/death, 38; man's attitude toward woman, 119–21; man/woman, 61; mirror images, 125, 128, 129, 136–37, 152, 157, 160; names, 81–82; native/invader, 71–73, 76, 90; personality, 80; polarities of consciousness, 21; psyche/self, 117–18, 169; rainbow, 96–99, 173–74; reader/writer, 58–59; realities, 3; self/other, 61–62; sexuality, 33, 36, 44, 91, 102; snow/death, 7; society/nature, 23; virginity/sexuality, 14, 22, 168; whites, 9, 10, 82–83; woman as art creation/sexual being, 19, 168
Anghinetti, Paul, 73–74
Artist: creative potential, 24; destiny/drowning, 24, 28; dreamer, 74; genius, 23; growth, 22; Joyce as, 174; transforming mission, 15. *See also* Birth process
Auburn: heroine of *Finnegans Wake*, 120, 122, 125
Author: dreamer, 55; intentions, 54; presence, 10; relationship with narrator, 58–59; relationship with posited reader, 58, 59; relationship with protagonist, 10, 11

Beardsley, Aubrey, 160–61
Benstock, Bernard, 67–68
Birth process, 12; artistic, 14, 22, 57; of soul, 13, 22, 23. *See also* Artist
Black, 4, 11, 106, 107; blindness, 2, 63, 106, 110; and dark, 11, 14, 23, 110; Dublin, 60, 76, 83–84; heroine in *Finnegans Wake*, 125. *See also* White/black

Blue, 6; heroine of *Finnegans Wake*, 120, 162; hunt, 79; male color, 79, 114; sexuality, 39; Ulster Protestantism, 66, Virgin, 129
Boone, Joseph Allen, 24
Brown, 4, 6, 12; contradiction, 4–5; father, 81; heroine in *Finnegans Wake*, 121; negative, 121; son, 81; ubiquity, 5

Campbell, Joseph, 73
Coleman, Elliott, 26
Color. *See* Individual colors
Color association. *See* Individual colors
Color, lack of, 15–16, 22
Color, naturalistic use of, 2, 12, 26, 30
Color patterns, 2, 4, 11, 21–22, 44, 59, 126, 165, 175–76; ambiguity, illustrative of, 23, 115; author's questions, 2; enigmatic, 165; functions, 46; opposition/complementarity, 5; unimportance, 1. *See also* Individual colors
Color references, 2, 4, 6, 7; concentration, 4, 6, 21–22, 26. *See also* Individual colors
Colors, bright, 6, 7, 10, 22; sexual desire, 7, 8; Tristan as invader, 114. *See also* Rainbow
Colors, discordant, 4, 6, 12, 21. *See also* Individual colors
Color schemas, 25–26, 165–68; explanation of charting, 168–75
Color, symbolism of, 2, 8, 9, 27. *See also* Individual colors
Color, traditional use of, 2, 4, 9, 13, 17; avoided, 9, 29

Dark: black, 11, 14, 23, 110; college, 12; doubt, 13; hell, 13; land, 12; sexual sin, 13, 14; waves, 12
Devlin, Kimberley, 61–62
DiBernard, Barbara, 175
Dickens, Charles, 7, 108
Dreams, 49, 52, 55, 56–57, 85, 100; ambiguity, 62, 121, 144; censors, 46, 98, 100, 108–9; censors, loosening of, 133, 174; conflicts,

61, 102, 125, 168, 169; displacement, 53, 124, 130; distortion, 53, 62; dreamer/reader, 116, 176; dreamer/reader vision of self, 116; dreamer, threat to, 135; dreamer's attitude toward woman, 119–20, 130, 168, 169; dreamer's fears, 144, 145, 173; dreamer's response, 133; guilt, 91, 145; *Interpretation of Dreams, The,* 52; manifest/latent content, 53; native/invader, 72; projection, 120, 137, 148; rainbow, 97–98, 158; reality, 98, 105, 110, 115, 118, 168, 176–77; self/other, 62; sexuality, 57, 98–99, 100–101, 125, 133, 148, 161; wish fulfillment, 100, 145; within dreams, 100

Dublin, Ireland, 12, 23, 24–25, 36, 46, 60, 94; colors, 60, 69, 76, 83; vs. Dublin, Georgia, 60, 88, 89, 122; personification, 66, 81

Dubliners: ambiguities, 3, 4, 5, 7, 10; color patterns, 46; color references, lowest number of, 4; color use as precursor to *Finnegans Wake,* 7; Dublin society influence, 24; epiphanies, 8; failure, 2; psychic pain, 3, 10; reader, role of, 10; sexual white, 8, 9, 19, 169; symbolism, 7, 9

Ellmann, Richard, 12, 25, 120, 134
Epiphanies, 8, 11, 20, 21, 175; revelations of psyche, 117; vehicles for hero, 8
Epstein, E. L., 61

Failure, 2, 4, 10; and fall, 55–56, 104, 123, 173
Finnegans Wake: alchemy, 175; author's intent, 54; author's methods, 47, 54, 58, 176; critical analysis, 47–49, 59, 73, 75; dove/raven, 93, 94, 95, 96, 103; druid/saint, 73–75, 105, 115, 168, 169; inaccessibility, 50; Liddell, Alice Pleasance, 123, 153; manifest content, 172; motif-controlled frames of reference, 172; title as microcosm, 50, 59
Finn mythology, 50, 82–83
Flags: British, 67–68; French, 67; German, 67; Irish, 64, 66, 67–68, 75, 112, 171; United States, 68
French, Marilyn, 39, 42, 43
Freud, Sigmund, 52–53, 100
Fuger, Wilhelm, 93–94

Gilbert, Stuart, 48
Glasheen, Adaline, 49, 54, 84, 86, 87, 88, 89, 96, 97, 103, 114, 125, 144, 156, 165
Gold, 37, 112–13; reader/narrator relationships, 42–43; sound, 42
Goldberg, S. L., 48
Goldman, Arnold, 47

Gold/silver: mature sexual relationships, 162
Goldsmith, Oliver, 120
Gordon, John, 77, 123, 151, 153, 157
Great Britain, 18; Imperialism/Irish Nationalism, 62, 64, 74, 104, 172
Green, 4, 125; blindness, 2, 62, 63, 64, 110; death, 63; female sexuality, 153; fertilization/female/growing/urination, 154, 155, 162, 172; incest, 155; Ireland, 28, 29; Ireland's Eye, 64; Irish Nationalism, 30, 62, 74, 75, 114, 172; mother/sea/drowning, 27–29, 162, 172; naivete, 63; neutral uses, 30; resurrection, 80; sadism, 30; traditional associations, rejection of, 30
Green/orange: native/invader, 60; temptress/Lily, 143–44; Ulster vs. Nationalists, 61, 64, 64
Green/red: political significance, 18–19, 65, 67, 74, 75
Grey: ambivalence, 16, 17; blindness, 2, 63, 110; church, 17; complexity of use, 16, 17; death, 4, 6, 38; fall of authors, 80; hell, 16; neutral uses, 17, 37; paralysis, 4, 6; rejected choices, 22; snow, 6
Groden, Michael, 47–48, 58

Hart, Clive, 1, 119, 172, 175–76
Heliotrope: critical attention, 150–51; female role dictated by convention, 151; Mime, 149, 150, 151, 152; sexual attraction, 149
Henke, Suzette, 28, 43, 119

Imagery. *See* Symbolism
Incest. *See* Oedipal issues
Ireland, 12, 14, 15, 18–19, 50, 63; emasculating mother, 28; history as metaphor for self/other conflict, 62; Nationalism, 30, 74, 75, 114, 169; Nationalism vs. British Imperialism, 62, 64, 67, 104; native/invader, 61, 67, 72, 73, 75–76, 90, 114; resurrection myth, 79; Ulster, 61, 64, 65, 66, 114

Joyce, James: composition methods, 47, 54, 58, 176; decline of exterior world/upsurge of artistic vision, 110; drinking problem, 111, 115; eye trouble, 107, 108, 110, 115, 174; frustration, 112; as writer, 107

Kain, Richard, 25
Kenner, Hugh, 12, 23, 54

Language, distortions of, 50, 51, 54, 59–60, 61, 63, 68, 69–70, 71, 82–83, 84, 86, 87, 89–90, 93–94, 95, 104–5, 107, 108, 109, 135, 171. *See also* Ambiguity

Levin, Harry, 21
Literary devices, 42, 58, 116
Litz, A. Walton, 9

Man. *See* Ambiguity; Sexuality
Metaphor, 1, 57, 62, 74, 117, 130, 175, 176
Mitchell, Breon, 10–11
Morse, J. Mitchell, 87
McCarthy, Patrick A., 49, 56, 57, 132, 149, 150, 159
McHugh, Roland, 49, 54, 95, 96, 103, 107, 140, 144, 145, 148, 157, 159, 160

Narrator/narrative, 10, 42–43, 48, 58, 107, 109–10, 111, 115, 137; intimacy with characters, 58; malevolence of, 43; techniques, 10, 74; as untrustworthy, 90, 102
Native/invader, 60–61, 66–67, 75, 76; ambiguities, 72; black/white, 72; druid/saint, 73–74; green/orange, 60–61; invader, triumph of, 76; metaphor for conflict of psyche, 76; rainbow, 72
Norris, Margot, 48, 49, 53, 55, 56, 119, 121, 122, 123

O'Connor, Frank, 21
Oedipal issues, 31, 56, 57, 99, 145, 154, 155–56, 175

Picture of Dorian Gray, The, 80, 91, 109, 110, 136
Poe, Edgar Allan, 96; dove/raven, 96
Portrait of the Artist as a Young Man, A: ambiguities, 10, 11, 17, 23; birth process, 12, 13, 14, 22–23; black/dark, 11–12; Church, authority of, 15–16; color, lack of, 15; color patterns, 46; Dublin society influence, 23; epiphanies, 8, 11, 20, 21, 175; hero, emotional growth of, 12, 14, 17; narrative technique, 10; narrator, 11; reader difficulties, 10–11, 24; rose, 17–18; sexual white, 19, 23, 169; stream of thought, 21, 29; villanelle, 10, 11, 13, 14, 16, 22, 45, 175; woman as artistic creation/sexual object, 19
Psyche: conflicts, 76, 91, 98, 169, 171; depths, threatening, 85; duality of being, 119; forces, uncontrolled, 76; integrative/disruptive tendencies, 98, 116; paradox of human nature, 117–18; revelations, 117; rainbow metaphor, 118; self destruction, 84; splinters, 61, 117; split against self, 117; split, very first, 119
Psychic pain, 3, 10
Putz, Manfred, 59

Rainbow, 66, 75; artistic vision, 112; death, 100; dream, 158; dream/reality, 98, 108; druid/saint conflict, 73–74; dualities, 97, 100, 105, 174; garments, seven, 96, 99, 112, 173–74; girls, seven, 96, 116, 152, 156–57; God's covenant with Noah, 60, 75, 90, 101, 158, 172, 174; human perception, limits of, 97; illusion, 97; importance of, 97; inebriation, 111; Lily, 143–44; man's fall, 60, 90, 173; patriarchy, 173; peace/piss/woman, 158–59; psychic conflict, 118; red end of, 87, 96; how referenced, 97; sexuality, 102, 104, 158, 173; temptresses, 157, 173; white, contrast with, 103; woman's challenge of man, 173; writer/reader, 97
Reader: artistic detachment, 25; associative patterns, 25, 54; awareness, conscious, 168; color patterns, 46; confusion with writer, 59; conventional contract with author, 10; detachment from narrator, 42; difficulties with language, 10, 48–49, 53–54, 171; distancing, 112; in dreams, 53, 116; dreamer, 55, 116, 176; as hero, 25; reader, posited, 59; reading/re-reading, 49–50, 58; reading/re-writing, 54, 58; rebellion from narrator, 43; relationship with narrator/personae, 58–59, 74, 176; role of, 10–11; self-examination, 59. *See also* Ambiguity
Red, 1, 6, 22; Adam, 85, 86, 89, 139–40, 170; art/sexual consummation, 22; birth, 22; Dublin, Georgia, 88; ecstasy, 22; female color, 138; history, discourse on, 85; life-tree, 87; male color, 91, 92, 116, 161; military, 140; sexuality, 39–40, 85–86, 87, 138, 139, 140, 141; villanelle, composition of, 21; virginity, 140
Religion, 37, 74, 91, 95, 101, 143, 171; Adam as father, 85; Adam/Eve, 119, 125; Adam/Eve, offspring, 124; authority, 15, 19; Catholic Nationalism, 75; fall from grace, 89, 123–24, 139; Genesis, 93, 95, 124, 172; God's covenant with Noah, 60, 75, 90, 95, 101, 158, 172, monotheism, 92; rejection, 20; tyranny, 37, 80, 113; Virgin, 7, 9, 21, 41, 127, 129, 144, 145
Riquelme, John Paul, 49, 51, 58–59
Robinson, Marian, 73
Rose: associations, traditional, 18; conflicting messages of sexual mores, 142; importance of, 17; sexuality, 142–43; woman, 43
Rose/green, 18, 29; artifice/nature, 19, 21–22; foreshadowing of red/green, 18

Scholes, Robert, 2–3, 22

Senn, Fritz, 77
Sexuality, 16, 22, 24, 31–32, 33, 34, 35, 41, 51, 56–57, 79, 86, 132, 133–34, 135; Adam's shame, 85, 86; ambiguity, 102; autoeroticism, 128; as characterization, 39; domination by woman, 132–33, 134, 135, 151–52; dove/raven, 160–61; dreams, 98, 148; man's attitude toward woman, 119; masturbation, 35, 91, 92, 136; metaphor for artistic creation, 57; mirror image, 117, 129, 142, 157, 160; polarization of sex roles, 24; politics, 60, 61; rainbow, 102–3, 104; tensions, 22, 144; white-horse motif, 82. *See also* Ambiguity; Dreams; Red; White; White/red
Smith, Thomas F., 5, 7
Solomon, Margaret, 49, 57, 150
Stream of thought, 21, 29, 37
Symbolism, 7, 9, 42, 47; dove/raven, 72, 93, 95–96, 123, 159–61, 171; Columbus, Christopher, 95–96; druid/saint conflict, 73–75, 105, 114–15, 168, 169; flags, 67–68, 100; keys, 24; persecution, 80; rainbow, 97, 102–3, 174; salmon, 88. *See also* Ambiguity; Dreams; Individual colors

Thomas, Brook, 25, 58
Tindall, William York, 19, 20, 73
Twain, Mark: example of human duality, 117

Ulysses: color associations/women, 31; color patterns, 46; color schemas, 25–26; Dublin society influence, 24–25, 36; green, 29–31, 53; grey, 37–38; reader, role of, 25; reader/writer relationship, 58; sea/drowning/mother, 27–28, 29; sexual white, 31–32, 33–35, 169; stream of thought, 37

Villanelle, 10, 11; artistic release, 13; colors, 22; composition, 14, 16, 21, 22; creation, 14, 175; landmark of maturation, 11; parody, 16; and woman, 22
Violet: rainbow, 96–97; Tristan, 114; Ulster Protestantism, 66; violate/violent, 60, 113, 114
Voyeurism, 31, 32, 92, 114. *See also* Sexuality

White: associations, negative, 9; associations, traditional, 9, 126; bodies, 21; conflicts, 169; contrast with Dublin, Ireland, 68–69, 76; contrast with rainbow, 103; England, 37; Isolde, 128, 136, 137; male sexual responses, certain, 135, 136; mankind, 116; neutral uses, 35; peace between green/orange, 75; religion, 35; 127, 129; sexual aspect of woman, 8–9, 19, 22–23, 41, 45, 126–27, 129, 131, 168; secret desires/frustrated desires/shame/guilt/ sexual entrapment, 9, 22, 31, 148; sex/woman/urination/wine, 111, 127, 129, 131, 132, 134, 162, 169; silver, 6; snow, 6; subversion of male authority, 132, 134, 135, 169; underwear, 8, 31–32, 33–34, 129, 131, 169; voyeurism, 31, 32, 33
White/black, 6, 8, 81, 108, 110, 111, 159; dove/raven, 93, 94, 95, 110, 160–61, 162, 171; Dublin, Ireland, 69–70; native/invader, 72; with red, 94, 113; splits in psyche, 171
White/blue: Virgin, 7, 9, 21, 41
White/gold: church tyranny, 37, 80, 100, 107, 108, 113, 137, 171; Virgin, 128, 137
White/green: commitment to intellectual imagery, 28; decay, 29; mother/drowning/sea, 28, 29
White/orange: Lily, 143
White, Patrick, 23
White/red, 16, 19; artistic creation, 19; celebration of life, 45; competition, 19; conflict, internal, 91; conflict/unity, 91; consummation of love, 45; Dublin, 46; father, 110; life/death, 91; male red/woman white, 146–47; male white/woman red, 147; mingle/counterpoint, 45–46; rainbow, 144; rose/lily, 142, 143, 144, 145, 170; sexual tensions, 22, 39–40, 44, 57, 60, 91–92, 142, 144, 147, 148–49, 170; unity of Christ, 91
Wilde, Oscar, 19, 55, 56, 83, 91, 92, 109, 136–37, 145
Woman. *See* Ambiguity; Sexuality
Wright, David G., 55

Yellow: bodies, 21; negative uses, 20